Aspects of enlightenment

"This is a fascinating, lucid and highly original book. It consists in a sustained sideways look at the dominant controversies in social theory. It shows how the antinomies of modernism and postmodernism, scientism and relativism are unsustainable. Social theory is redefined as a critical practice of enlightenment, conceived as an ethics of knowledge rather than dogmatic rationalism."
Paul Hirst, Birkbeck College, London

Aspects of enlightenment is a reconfiguration of the terrain of contemporary social theory. Attacking the centrality of notions of modernity and post-modernity in contemporary theory, Thomas Osborne argues that the proper subject matter of social theory is enlightenment. However, he departs from traditional accounts locating the vocation of social theory in the system of values established in the original Enlightenment by the French *philosophes* and others. Rather, he argues eloquently for the ethical status of enlightenment and for the place of the intellectual as the embodiment of particular kinds of critical ethos.

Outlining a social and critical theory geared to opening out specific problems in the practical "fieldwork" of enlightenment, Osborne illustrates his approach with case studies that consider the critical aspects and implications of scientific, therapeutic and aesthetic kinds of enlightenment.

This distinctive and sparkling study of the nature of the social sciences and their relationship to the question of enlightenment will be essential and pro-vocative reading for students and scholars of social and critical theory, philosophy, sociology and the human sciences.

Thomas Osborne is Lecturer in the Department of Sociology at the University of Bristol. His work in the fields of critical theory, epistemology and the history and sociology of medicine has appeared in *Economy and Society*, *The Journal of Historical Sociology*, *Social Studies of Science*, *Social Science and Medicine*, and *History of the Human Sciences*.

Aspects of enlightenment

Social theory and the ethics of truth

Thomas Osborne

University of Bristol

UCL PRESS
· UCL ·
PRESS
Taylor & Francis Group

First published in 1998 by UCL Press

UCL Press Limited
1 Gunpowder Square
London EC4A 3DE

The name of University College London (UCL) is a registered
trade mark used by UCL Press with the consent of the owner.

British Library Cataloguing-in-Publication Data
A CIP catalogue record for this book is available from the British Library

Library of Congress Cataloging-in-Publication Data are available

ISBNs: 1–85728–852–1 HB
        1–85728–853–X PB

Typeset in Garamond by Wilmaset Ltd., Birkenhead, Wirral, UK
Printed and bound by T. J. International Ltd, Padstow, UK

For J.M.O.

The world in which one thinks is not the same as the world in which one lives.

Gaston Bachelard

Contents

Preface   ix
Acknowledgements   xv
Introduction   Of *enlightenmentality*   1

1 Reason, truth and criticism   17
2 Aspects of scientific enlightenment   41
3 Aspects of therapeutic enlightenment   71
4 Aspects of aesthetic enlightenment   101
5 Questioning enlightenment: ethics of truth in Foucault and Weber   125
6 Agents of enlightenment: in praise of intellectuals   149
   Conclusion   Social theory, sociology and the ethics of criticism   177

Bibliography   195
Index   211

Preface

This book is about truth, criticism and ethics. It is concerned with the controversy over the consequences of various kinds of anti-foundationalism in social and critical theory, even affirming – albeit in a particular way – the *uses* of some restricted kinds of anti-foundationalism. It is concerned with the varied kinds of criticism that are available to the social sciences and social theory, and with the varied purposes and ends of such kinds of criticism. Above all, and to cut a long story short, it is concerned with the problem of *enlightenment*.

I wanted to write this book because of a certain dissatisfaction with some of the terms of debate in the social sciences and in contemporary social theory. It seemed to me, as I know to many others and in many different ways, that these fields were divided by a rather unproductive stand-off between competing positions – foundationalism and anti-foundationalism, realism and relativism, modernism and postmodernism, sensible (often German) rationalists and irresponsible (usually French) post-structuralists and so forth – which, while generating certain lucrative amounts of intellectual drama, tended nevertheless to make something of a mockery of each other. This book is by no means a studied or scholarly adjudication over these positions. Rather the notion of enlightenment, though hardly original, is intended neither as a synthesis of, nor exactly as an advance over, them but, more pragmatically, as a means of bypassing much of the substance of these debates altogether so as to get on to other things; so that we can begin to act again as "grown-ups" in these difficult matters of truth and criticism.

Perhaps the best way to think about the purposes of this book is as an *excursion* – the term is used advisedly – on some themes raised in Michel Foucault's late and famous essay, "What is enlightenment?". That is where Foucault insists that the idea of enlightenment should be understood as a general *ethos* or attitude rather than as a specific dogma (Foucault 1984a; cf. Foucault 1996). This book is, in effect, a rather personal elaboration of the consequences of such a view. Note that this makes of enlightenment a very general question; and one that is strictly speaking distinct from questions about *the* Enlightenment, that is about that period in intellectual history characterized by the great names of figures such as Rousseau, Voltaire or Montesquieu.

If some aspects of Foucault's thought about enlightenment are a stimulus to a certain amount of what follows, this book is emphatically not a "Foucauldian" work, whatever that would mean. In any case, it is nothing like a crib or a commentary on Foucault's texts. Foucault is not even mentioned that much. Happily, the only part of the book that actually addresses Foucault's work in a direct kind of way is Chapter 5, and his followers and critics alike may well be somewhat underwhelmed by what is said there, not least because the Foucault that makes an appearance is not perhaps the usual, erstwhile trendy one. The sort of Foucault that appeals to me is not, anyway, the Foucault that appears in the cribs; the subversive continental philosopher, the arcane prophet of transgression, the iconoclastic poststructuralist, the meta-theorist of power, the functionalist theorist of social control, or the gloomy prophet of the totally administered society. These sorts of Foucault can all safely be forgotten. The Foucault that motivates much of this book – more often than not behind the scenes – is a much more buttoned-up animal: an ethical thinker with a Kantian heritage, a good modernist rather than a faddish postmodernist, a rigorous and not so unconventional historical epistemologist concerned with the "immature" human sciences and, most unlikely of all, even something of an Anglo-Saxon empiricist *manqué*. This, then, is not the naughty, transgressive Foucault, but rather – as I once heard it described – Foucault with his clothes on. This book is a homage to that, still generally unknown or unimagined, Foucault.

Now, Foucault was a philosopher by vocation. Yet he was a philosopher who brought to bear a particular force of attention on the social and human sciences. This has led some people to conclude that Foucault was some kind of sociologist. As will become clear, I think this is a big mistake – or, if Foucault was a sociologist, he was a particularly bad one. Yet on the other hand, it is not exactly the "philosophical" Foucault that animates the following pages. Many books have been written about Foucault as a philosopher, but this – mercifully for those who have been well-trained in that discipline – is not one of those. Rather, the Foucault who appears, in so far as he does actually appear, does so above all in the guise of the critic of the social, human and other sciences, which is to say, not as someone who dismisses the possibility of such sciences as a matter of principle but someone for whom the status of such sciences was a constant source of reflection and questioning, even self-questioning. This is not to say that I think that these questions of the social and human sciences were Foucault's only concern; it is only that such are the predominant concerns of this book. And that is why readers will find fewer discussions of philosophy and philosophers in this book than discussions of questions relating to particular issues in social theory, and to the limits of certain kinds of sociological explanation.

Now, social theory is not, for the purposes of what follows, quite the same thing as sociology. Sociologists typically investigate something called society; but that is not necessarily what social theorists do, or should be doing. If the book is quite critical of various kinds of sociology, this is not because it aims to be one of those supercilious enterprises in "theory" that seeks to legislate them out of existence, but in that it seeks to isolate some of their explanatory limits in relation to particular problems. That is why most chapters include discussions of various limitations of certain sorts of sociological thought; of what I call "epochal" sociology, of the idea of a "science of society", of the idea of a radical or a critical sociology and so forth. The book does not condemn sociology; but in attempting to isolate some of its limits in various ways, it does seek to open out a space for social theory as an enterprise more or less distinct from sociology as such. This is not to dismiss sociology. For instance, I think that the effect of this separation is not least to rescue the idea of the "project": that is, the idea that sociology and the social sciences might actually be of some *use*, as opposed to being mere receptacles of an endless and pointless swirl of gratuitous "interpretations". It is not, then, that I wish to damn sociology – far from it – but rather to praise social theory.

This may well be social theory of a peculiar kind. Perhaps this book would be hard to describe as an orthodox exercise in social theory. This is partly because it may seem that social theory is not quite the right term for the discipline that I am addressing; the term "critical theory" would perhaps be preferable but I have not, in general, used it because of the specific connotations that it already has; partly because it often relates to quite specifically *literary* kinds of criticism and partly because it is more generally used to refer to a particular, justly celebrated, school of thinkers. So the term "social theory" will have to do, just so long as this "critical" element is understood to be implicit within it, even definitive of it. But perhaps this book is also unorthodox because it is not one of those wide-ranging diagnoses of the *Zeitgeist* or critical annihilations of all one's opponents that readers have come to expect from social theory books. In fact the book is rather critical of the hubris that lies behind certain kinds of social theory, and argues that the discipline – if it is to be a "discipline" as such – might do well to turn itself upon a central, restricted object of conceptualization. Now, there is no doubt that social theory might be envisaged in all kinds of terms, and as being about many things. This book argues that one of its central concepts might be – indeed, *is* – the concept of enlightenment. It is really an exercise in imagining a social theory that would be devoted to this question.

The kind of social theory that is imagined here is not devoted to big, macho theorizing of the continental – or pseudo-continental – variety. Nor even is the implication of the position on enlightenment that I outline here that social theory should be concerned with the development of positive "theories" about enlightenment. It is rather that, as I say in the conclusion, social theory might do well to consider itself to be a generically parasitic discipline. By that I do not mean that social theory, as so often these days, should be devoted to endless and depressing second-hand commentary ('Foucault

says this . . . Habermas says that . . . Haraway says this . . . Rorty says that . . .'),
but – and no doubt this constitutes its "social" aspect – that it should entail a
kind of ongoing fieldwork in our existing practices of enlightenment. This
kind of social theory would be parasitic, then, with regard to the kinds of enlightenment that already exist or aspire to exist. A commitment to such a parasitic spirit explains why, on the one hand, the central chapters of this book
(Chapters 2 to 4) are not commentaries in social theory but are devoted to the
assembly of some rather selective pictures of specific aspects of enlightenment,
and why, on the other, so much of this book is concerned with tendencies in
the actually existing social sciences – for not least of the functions of an "autonomous" social theory might be to reflect on the status of the claims of the
social sciences themselves to certain kinds of enlightenment. Although there
is little or no philosophy involved in this parasitic approach to things, it
might help to regard the way I go about the question of enlightenment here
as analogous to the approach to big topics like meaning, time or thought in
certain kinds of post-metaphysical philosophy; that is, not to attempt a theoretical excavation of the topic but to describe it when in use; to treat of enlightenment not like an engine idling but when it is doing work.

This approach is guided not least by the conviction that enlightenment is
something that, as it were, by definition cannot reach a final definition. If rationalist models of enlightenment will not do – as this book insists – this is
not necessarily to take the rather irrationalist view that all attempts at definition
are themselves bad. But it is to adopt a certain nominalism about enlightenment, a nominalism that, oddly enough, leads to a kind of realism, because
our only option becomes not to theorize about enlightenment but to attempt
to picture it at work. This is not, however, an entirely pointless exercise in
normative terms. It is, in fact, intended to provide some *relief* from some of
our characteristic anxieties over the question of enlightenment.

These kinds of anxiety could be given many names. Scepticism, relativism,
anti-foundationalism and postmodernism all spring to mind as good candidates. All point to a similar theme with regard to the question of enlightenment. They provoke the worry that truth is not perhaps what it was, hence
that all is not well in the house of criticism. There are two caricatures of a
position in relation to this kind of anxiety. The one is to embrace it with all
one's passion, and to avow a wholesale anything-goes postmodernism. The
other is to bolt down the hatches, denounce the renegades and insist on the
powers of reason and the rights of critique. Actually these are not wholly caricatures. In any case, this book, in refusing either option, takes a double stand
in relation to these questions.

First, in seeking to avoid the blackmail of being either for or against enlightenment, I adopt a *deflationary* perspective with regard to questions of truth
and criticism. By this I mean an approach that says that things are not necessarily as drastic as they may seem in contemporary "theory": an approach that
seeks to take the heat out of some of the extremes of controversy that beset

social theory and the social sciences, an approach that bids that we adjust our ideas to at least some of our existing practices. Just as certain non-aligned socialists used to have as their slogan that they owed allegiance to "neither Washington nor Moscow", so the motto of this book might be put crudely as "neither realist fideism nor postmodernism". This is not to say that the book is one of those programmatic endeavours which seeks to tell the uninitiated "how it should be done". On the contrary, one of its basic contentions is that we already have plenty of good practices in the social and human sciences, and that things are not quite as bad in theory – as distinct from the world itself, which because it is in many respects quite awful, has substantial need of the social sciences – as many seem to think; indeed, that we do not have to fear that the sky is about to fall on our heads at any or every moment. And with regard specifically to social theory, the purpose of this book is to contribute to a reconfiguration of a discipline that is in effect already there, not to succumb to the hubris of attempting to reinvent social theory from scratch, to provide a swingeing critique of everything that has gone before, or to re-evaluate all values.

Second, the book discusses the meaning of the attitude of a *critique* of enlightenment. I claim that the idea of such a critical attitude might be – indeed, *is* – quite central to social theory, and that such an idea needs to be distinguished from varieties of postmodern anti-foundationalism and should even be seen as an internal aspect of enlightenment itself. This book is very much concerned with this notion of a critical attitude to enlightenment. Perhaps what is most distinctive about this idea is that it is an *ethical* notion. That is, ethics in a very broad sense; recalling Foucault – ethics as *ethos* rather than morality. This book makes much of the idea of an ethics of truth, an ethics of enlightenment, an ethics of critique.

It could be said that the notion of ethics here is made to do rather a lot of things, perhaps too many. But the book is neither a contribution to ethical philosophy nor, in itself, an ethical work propounding a particular ethical or moral point of view. The usage of the notion of ethics is intended to be only suggestive of a general space of concerns; to insist on an ethical concern in matters of truth is to contrast such a concern with political or ideological or even epistemological concerns. It is also to stress the *difficulty* that is inherent in a commitment to different styles of telling the truth, or different styles of enlightenment; that such concerns are as much an "ordeal" as they are an application of pre-existing principles. Finally, and most important, the terminology of ethics is intended to signify something restricted and *deliberate*: that is, something that is not "ethical" in the sense that it guides all aspects of the conduct of our life but, on the contrary, something which might involve a deliberate break from everyday life; to submit to an ethic can mean a temporary retreat into a particular commitment, and deliberately and rather artificially even at the expense of other commitments. The idea of an attitude of ongoing enlightenment critique is ethical precisely in this latter sense.

Because of this ethical concern, readers will find that the book is quite oriented in places to questions of teaching and education. It does not offer a "theory" of education, but it does seek to discuss what kind of values or effects we might expect from the teaching of a discipline like social theory. This can make the discussion seem perhaps more programmatic than it is meant to be, almost at times as if it were a matter of something like moral questions. But the very last thing I mean by the idea of an ethical or "educational" concern is anything to do with morals or morality. This book does not offer a morality of anything, and certainly not of enlightenment itself. To be concerned with ethics is not the same thing at all as assuming for oneself some kind of moral authority; on the contrary, it is rather to throw that kind of attitude – including that kind of *political* attitude that is often called "ethical" today, for instance in various forms of dubious, intrinsically moralistic, communitarianism – firmly into question. And if this book is itself very much about the idea of an *ethos* that would seek, at its limit, to hold everything into question that might conceivably be held into question, this does not imply the boring, self-indulgent and ultimately pointless advocacy of a morality of endless questioning as such. As for teaching such a thing, that would scarcely be less irresponsible and immature than informing our interlocutors once and for all that, having found the right and final road, we had finally come upon and grasped, as if in our very hands, the truth itself.

Acknowledgements

Given the fact that the references in this book are meant to be minimally indicative rather than absolutely comprehensive, my first duty is to thank all those people whose work I have plundered for my own ends and to apologise to them if I have done so carelessly, or worse, if I have anywhere neglected to acknowledge the act of the plunder itself. Meanwhile, Graham Burchell, Colin Gordon, Ian Hacking, Ian Hunter and – more than anyone – Nikolas Rose have motivated this book in ways they do not know, and would probably not much like. The fact that I take the liberty of thanking them – without their consent, and even though none of them have seen this book – cannot unfortunately be used to imply any kind of endorsement of it on their part, or even necessarily the slightest interest in it. They are certainly not to blame for anything. More secure thanks – albeit for things that may not always have seemed of any direct relevance to this book – are due to Andrew Barry, Catharine Edwards, Alan Irwin, Judith Osborne, Aaron Ridley, Ralph Schroeder, George Davey Smith, Judith Squires, Lisa Tamlin, Charlie Turner and Irving Velody, as well as to my unforgettable friend Ivan Connor who, though he never saw or knew anything of this book, somehow found himself present in its pages. David Owen read through the whole thing and I am most grateful to him not least for the many specific ideas, concepts, formulations and references that he has given me. Thanks also to James Brown, to an anonymous reader at UCL Press, and to Caroline Wintersgill who commissioned the book and who – in spite of her misgivings that my title made it seem as if I were more a devotee of Andrew Lloyd Webber than of Max Weber – was the source of many essential modifications to its structure and argument. I also owe a debt to the kindness of colleagues at Bristol, and in particular to Steve Fenton who initiated a period of leave for me to write this book, thus enabling me to take more or less constant benefit from the invaluable intellectual inspiration of Samuel and Imogen.

Introduction

Of *enlightenmentality*

Blackmail – Negative enlightenment – Critique of enlightenment – Postmodernism – Realism and enlightenment – Aspects of enlightenment – Negative anthropology – Ethics of enlightenment

A spectre is haunting the social sciences: *enlightenment*. Everywhere the extent to which "we" are enlightened – whether such a "we" refers to "we" moderns (or postmoderns), "we" Westerners, "we" Europeans, or even "we" citizens of the world – is the focus for debate and controversy. There are some for whom the very idea of enlightenment is a sham, an excuse for the machinations of cultural experts and bureaucrats of all sorts, those who would even oblige us to be free. Others claim that enlightenment is our only hope in an age of violence, exploitation and despair; that merely to criticize enlightenment is to submit willingly to degeneracy. But whether we think of ourselves as being for or against enlightenment, what is certain is that the *concept* of enlightenment – the space of concerns that such a concept designates – is itself a key point of orientation for all those concerned with the status of the knowledges that we possess or pursue. This is so even if the *word* – enlightenment – is not often used. Rather, the conversation of enlightenment is taking place wherever people are concerned to debate or agonize over the links between truth and power, belief and ethics, knowledge and society, expertise and freedom, expression and redemption, and wherever they attempt, as all those who work in the social sciences must, to take a stand on such questions. In this sense at least, postmodern talk of being beyond enlightenment is certainly premature; we are all of us beholden to "enlightenmentality". As the philosopher, Kant, observed in his famous essay on the subject in 1784, we do not live so much in an enlightened age as in an age of enlightenment: that is, an age where enlightenment is a central cultural aspiration if not a demonstrable, existing reality (Kant 1970: 54).

This introduction seeks to situate the question of enlightenment in quite a rapid, indicative and impressionistic way, and then to sketch some of the main themes of the rest of the book. What is enlightenment? And why should it matter to the social sciences and to social theory in particular? In its broadest, most banal, sense, the notion refers to the application of reason to human affairs; enlightenment would be the process through which reason was to be applied to all aspects of human existence, above all in the name of freedom. The period of *the* Enlightenment – which usually means the eighteenth-century French Enlightenment – gave birth to the modern human and social sciences and their central ambition; to render freedom into rational form as an ordering principle in society (Kumar 1979; Hamilton 1996). The great thinkers of the Enlightenment all believed that reason as opposed to superstition or dogma was the one sure basis of a free and just society. The social sciences were centrally implicated in this project. Indeed we might say that the social sciences have a double interest in enlightenment, as subject and as object; on the one hand, in that they themselves are putative *agencies* of enlightenment, on the other in that, from the eighteenth century onwards, part of the *reality* of modern societies has been this will to enlightenment itself.

Blackmail

The social sciences have clearly found this double relation to be a difficult one. On the one hand, Auguste Comte's ideal of a sociology that would replace philosophy as the queen of the sciences has clearly not materialized. The very fact that sociology aspires to be an "-ology" of anything makes it rather laughable to a lot of people. In any case, the social sciences have not constituted themselves as the indispensable handmaiden of the enlightened society. On the other hand, those same disciplines have had some harsh things to say about the ideal of enlightenment itself. Indeed, many practitioners of the social sciences now appear to believe that the ideal of enlightenment has proved itself to be more of an iron-cage than a realm of freedom. Hence the struggles on the part of many thinkers – especially those associated with post-modernism – to escape from the logic of enlightenment itself, to denounce enlightenment and all its offspring. And hence the sense that today many in the human sciences find themselves to be stuck in the blackmail of a veritable *politics* of enlightenment. This is a politics in the strict sense of the term, one structured on the friend/enemy distinction that Carl Schmitt held to be at the heart of all politics; a resolute logic of being either for or against (Schmitt 1996). And hence, consequently, the anxiety of many in the social sciences and elsewhere who do not quite know where they should stand in relation to this politics.

Part of the inherent difficulty of such a politics is that the meaning of enlightenment itself does not seem to be entirely stable. People mean different things by it. Consider two such versions of enlightenment; the historical and the attitudinal.

There is the historical question of *the* Enlightenment. That is not the main subject of this book, and those who want scholarly treatments of Enlightenment thought should go no further and look elsewhere (Cassirer 1951; Gay 1966, 1972; Hampson 1968). It is not *entirely* irrelevant to our concerns, however. For instance, a popular question in social theory and the social sciences is the extent to which it can be said that the principles established during the eighteenth-century Enlightenment are living or dead today. Even here, it all depends on how the Enlightenment is defined; above all, whether we take what is really quite a narrow view of the matter, focusing on the work of Rousseau, Montesquieu and Voltaire and the French *philosophes* between 1715 and 1789, or a far wider view taking us beyond France and, in terms of periodization, back to Descartes (cf. Gay 1972; Porter & Teich 1981; Hulme & Jordanova 1990: 3). The wider our definition of the Enlightenment, the wider will be those core principles which will be selected as being definitive of it. On one such definition, the Enlightenment is just a family of intellectual ideas that emphasized the primacy of reason in the organization of social and political life. The thinkers of the Enlightenment shared a passion for the application of reason to all things, a love of science, a belief in and commitment to progress, the distrust of all superstition and the religious organization of life, and a veritable faith in the powers of freedom to improve the human condition and bring humanity ever closer to a realization of its essential nature.

We can regard enlightenment in this way. But there are also limitations to such a view. One is the fundamental limitation of equating – or trying to equate – the Enlightenment with a substantive or specific *dogma*. If we take an historical view of the Enlightenment and its legacy, we will find particular points of view taken on the part of the *philosophes* and others. But we would be hard pressed to locate a single, central doctrine of Enlightenment other than in rather negative terms. Reason itself can be a dogma; that of rationalism *per se*. But for the most part, and in spite of most subsequent commentaries on the matter, the thinkers of the Enlightenment were not advocates of the rationally ordered society; in fact, even the most "sociological" of them, such as Montesquieu or Adam Ferguson, cannot really be described as scientists of society at all – that had to wait for a later generation, indeed for Henri Saint-Simon and Comte himself. If, as postmodernists tell us, the dream of a rationally regulated society is now dead, then that is not a crisis of enlightenment as such but a crisis of a kind of sociological rationalism, which, in any case, has been in crisis since its inception. When enlightenment and when *the* Enlightenment is equated with sociological rationalism, or with rationalism of whatever kind, it is all too easy to dismiss it out of hand and find ourselves in the quagmire of denunciations of the social uses of reason in any form; stuck, that is, in a certain anti-enlightenment blackmail.

There are some – on both the Left and Right of the political spectrum – who, adopting this kind of logic, appear to believe that the recent collapse of communism and even of welfarism in the liberal societies of the West has signalled the end of the enlightenment project. This, for example, is the position of the political philosopher John Gray. He writes that the dream of an abstract theory of justice is now redundant because it adheres to what can now be seen as a spurious doctrine of universality, that people are potentially the same in all places, thus undermining all the essentials of cultural difference and diversity (Gray 1995; cf. Bauman 1992a). Such a viewpoint has an affinity with those doctrines that tell us that we are at the end of history, meaning that the great ideological battles of rival universalisms are now at an end and that all that remains are differing cultural conditions, habits and traditions (Fukuyama 1990, 1996; cf. Hirst 1989). For Gray and the other theorists of "endism", we are now beyond enlightenment, and effectively released from it; whereas to adhere to the principles of the Enlightenment is effectively to align ourselves, whether we like it or not, with the fateful forces of communism or totalitarianism.

But if there is a blackmail of anti-enlightenment there is also a blackmail of enlightenment itself. The great German philosopher, Jurgen Habermas, for instance, famously upbraided some of the French post-structuralists for their "young conservativism". They had turned their back on the Enlightenment in the name of relativism, irresponsibility and subservience to the *status quo* (Habermas 1985). For Habermas, it seems as if even to be quizzical of enlightenment immediately comes to run the risk of waking up in bed with the established order, and what could be the better mark of the renegade? To turn one's back on the Enlightenment was to turn one's back on progress, or on hope itself.

Negative enlightenment

Is there a way to escape these forms of blackmail? For Michel Foucault, enlightenment – this time, firmly with a lower case "e" – is best seen more as a kind of ethos or "attitude" than as a determinate series of historical doctrines. For one of its defining features is less a doctrinal core than a kind of negative principle; just the fact that enlightenment problematizes itself, that it is generically *self-conscious*, that it is liable to turn inward upon itself, to problematize its own fortunes (Foucault 1984a; Gordon 1986a; Hulme & Jordanova 1990: 1). That, anyway, is the feature of enlightenment that will be our focus of concern in this book. I propose to call this critical ethos of enlightenment in its extreme form, the principle of negative enlightenment; the principle that holds that to be enlightened may even entail that we do not know what enlightenment is. As Ernst Cassirer observed, "the permanent results of this philosophy do not lie in teaching which it develops and tries to formulate as its body of dogma" but rather just in the general attitude of being forever attentive to the need to "break through the rigid barriers of system" (Cassirer 1951: vi, ix). An analysis of enlightenment would be concerned to capture precisely this reflexive or negative character of enlightenment itself; to capture enlightenment, so to speak, as it regards its image of itself. As such, the analysis of enlightenment – even the *critique* of enlightenment – would be generically *on the side* of enlightenment in so far as it sought to conduct a permanent destabilization of enlightenment itself; to question enlightenment is an aspect of enlightenment and not necessarily an act of hostility towards it.

Critique of enlightenment

The correlate of the negative character of enlightenment, then, is a critical attitude to enlightenment. This book is fundamentally concerned with the character of such an attitude, with the kind of discipline that might be devoted to it, and equally with what differentiates it from other, perhaps less apparently peculiar, habits of criticism. At its most extreme the idea of a critique of enlightenment can entail the deliberate negation of enlightenment altogether. But not all forms of critique are necessarily this severe. In any case, it needs to be emphasized from the outset that, whatever its character, the idea of such a critique is in fact a difficult or, at least on occasion, a potentially eccentric affair. For in questioning the status of enlightenment, we do indeed run the risk either of damning it out of sight altogether or – perhaps worse – turning it into an excuse for postmodern triviality. Take as an instance of the former, Theodor Adorno and Max Horkheimer's celebrated work, *Dialectic of Enlightenment* (1986). For them, the legacy of enlightenment had been inverted and reason had become the tool of the domination of nature. Drawing as much upon Max Weber as upon Marx, they argued that enlightenment was itself the force that had led to the nightmares of fascism and the totally administered world. There are affinities here with later viewpoints such as those of the social theorist, Zygmunt Bauman, who argues that the Holocaust, far from being an aberration of Western civilization, was the coherent consequence of the very principles of our rational modernity in the West (Bauman 1986). Adorno and Horkheimer's own dialectical approach in fact insulated them somewhat from the more romanticized, not to say naïve, uses to which this argument has been put in the subsequent iron-cage versions of the thesis that have been quite popular in the social sciences and beyond. Similarly, it would be unfair to chalk up Peter Sloterdijk's *Critique of Cynical Reason* (1987) as a straightforward instance of post-modern trivia-mongering, although it is a brilliantly idiosyncratic diagnosis of such a move. Sloterdijk's target is the cynical "enlightened false consciousness" that has gripped the postmodern intelligentsia (well-off and miserable at the same time, as the blurb has it) in recent decades; a sensibility he would seek to replace with a dionysiac sense of laughter and *kynicism*.

Although it is not the strategy adopted in this book – which is not unfortunately the barrel of laughs that it might have been – the strategy of laughter might certainly be one way to transcend the varied blackmails of enlightenment. No doubt that would be only one of many ways, and – correlatively – I do not claim any stark *necessity* for the atittude that is outlined here. Not reading this book is unlikely to do anyone any harm; its purpose is only to bring some relief for those who feel the need from the blackmail of enlightenment and – most of all – from the logic of binarism that such blackmail presupposes. For such blackmail is always just a question of stark alternatives, of a logic of *either/ or*. It is essential to escape from this sort of binarism simply because *not* to escape it is to remain perpetually trapped in a cycle of what is best just called *immaturity*, a rather childish polemicism; in a perpetual state of firing blanks at our enemies without ever taking responsibility for the difficulty of cultivating a considered – as opposed to a kneejerk – attitude to the status of truth and the possibilities of criticism. Caught in such a logic of binarism, we define our position in relation to the projected position of the others. Hence the polemical character of the debates over enlightenment. We always position *ourselves* as the enlightened one; it is always the others that are unenlightened.

Postmodernism

This binary politics of enlightenment has been particularly in evidence in the case of the parallel debate in social theory over modernity and postmodernity. There is blackmail over modernity and postmodernity as well as over enlightenment. In fact the two debates are closely linked, and those who espouse postmodern epistemologies are often convicted of being opposed to enlightenment. But a certain amount of pointless heat has been generated by this controversy. As a sociological category, that is, as a descriptive term for an entire social formation, postmodernity is not very promising. Being opposed in binary form to modernity, the category necessarily overdramatizes social change and is, besides, more or less self-defeating in that it is not supposed to be a totalizing, sociological category at all. But taken in a narrower cultural sense, the category is at best harmless enough. Epistemologically it is certainly interesting. Jean-Francois Lyotard's notorious *Postmodern Condition* – which set the terms of the whole postmodernism debate – is really an imaginative book about the culture of knowledge in post-industrial societies which makes the case that the structures of the sciences have radically changed in recent times. But Lyotard's book does not function as a complete sociological description of any known society but, as its title states, a "report on knowledge", and it is best left that way (Lyotard 1984a).

Notwithstanding this rather qualified sympathy with Lyotard, this book is not a contribution to postmodern social theory. But nor is it the usual witchhunt against postmodernism (Eagleton 1996; Norris 1996). As with any witch-hunt, the purpose here is usually to bolster some outdated ideology rather than to extinguish one's enemies altogether. Indeed, one usually gets the sense in the vigorous diatribes against postmodernism that the polemicists of modernity need their postmodern counterparts fully as much as the seventeenth-century Church needed Galileo. In fact, a great deal of the very voluble resistance to postmodernism that one sees in social theory and the social sciences just takes the form of expediency; that is to argue that if we go along with the epistemological views of the postmodernists – whether right or wrong – we will fall into the self-defeating aporias of relativism and critical impotence. In short, for many, the fear appears to be that the sky will fall on our heads. But this is a misguided view to take. It is misguided epistemologically because although we can always point to the inadequacy of postmodern arguments, this does little to get away from the fact that *all* theories have internal problems of justification. Even rationalist theories, such as those of Emile Durkheim for instance, typically suffer from problems of circularity; that the conclusions and diagnoses are usually contained in the premises, while non-rationalist theories have difficulty connecting ought and is at all. The self-congratulatory jeers at postmodernism usually apply to those who jeer themselves.

Perhaps the most intractable problem, however, has to do with periodization. To read some of the professional anti-postmodernists, we sometimes feel as if until 1950 or thereabouts there were no imponderables at all in the house of epistemology. As if Sir Francis Bacon or C.S. Peirce, not to mention Montesquieu, Kant, Hegel, etc. had never existed. The fact is that if the sky were going to fall on our heads it would have done so a long time ago (cf. Toulmin 1990).

None of this is to say that things are easy in the world of theory. In fact it is just the opposite. It is rather to say that things are difficult and have always been so and that what is required is a critical ethos that is attuned to this very difficulty. But what makes things more difficult is if we choose to work with loose categories rather than concepts. I think that the modernity/postmodernity couple is just such a category. It masquerades as a realist sociological concept but in fact, as I shall argue in the next chapter, is not very promising as such. In discussions about modernity and postmodernity there are only rarely substantive discussions about the sociological aspects of such categories; rather what occurs is a proliferation of neologisms in seemingly empty space. Modernity and postmodernity are essentially idealist concepts and they do not work well at the level of society (cf. Giddens 1991a; Woodiwiss 1997). To take a sociologically realist view of modernity and postmodernity is arguably to come up with the realization that neither exist.

Realism and enlightenment

But enlightenment is another matter. The view that I put forward in this book is that instead of talking about modernity and postmodernity, social theorists would do better to restrict their discussions to questions of enlightenment. There really *is* such a thing as the question of enlightenment, even if it is a question that cannot promise – thank goodness – a finished solution. I think that we need to be realist about enlightenment. But to take such a realist attitude requires, oddly enough, a certain restricted idealism. That is because the reality of enlightenment is that it is an aspiration, an ideal, a spirit and it needs to be analysed in just such terms. I think that the debate over modernity/postmodernity is better translated out of its sociological idiom to become a debate about enlightenment. Crudely speaking, modernists like Habermas are saying that enlightenment is not dead; postmodernists like Bauman or Gray are saying that it is. Both, in a sense, inhabit a sociological idiom; both regard the status of enlightenment as reflecting a whole kind of society, be that modern or postmodern. But with all these thinkers we are still, in effect, in the provinces of blackmail. Enlightenment is presented to us as a kind of subjective preference or choice: albeit a choice on which we stand to be judged.

This brings me back to Foucault. As I said, he wanted to escape the logic of this blackmail of enlightenment altogether. Perhaps he failed to do so, but the attempt was important. He was not very much interested in the project of a "science of society"; indeed, as I indicate in Chapter 5, to think of Foucault in anything like sociological terms is really to misunderstand him. He was a philosopher but not perhaps in an orthodox sense; rather he was the doyen of a particular kind of genealogical thought, a critic of enlightenment (Gordon 1986; cf. Chapter 5 below). The idea of enlightenment, said Foucault, always runs the risk of becoming dogma. Once it has become dogma, it has ceased to be enlightenment for enlightenment – is best understood not as a determinate doctrine but as a kind of negative ethos, a sort of will to exit (*Ausgang*), or escape – or just to keep moving. Foucault too would resist the usual dichotomies between modernity and postmodernity; if modernity exists it is not a sociological or epochal concept.

> I wonder whether we may not envisage modernity rather as an attitude than as a period of history. And by "attitude" I mean a mode of relating to contemporary reality; a voluntary choice made by certain people; in the end a way of thinking and feeling; a way, too, of acting and behaving that at one and the same time marks a relation of belonging and presents itself as a task. A bit, no doubt, like what the Greeks called an ethos. And consequently, rather than seeking to distinguish the "modern era" from the "premodern" or the "postmodern", I think it would be more useful to find out how the attitude of modernity, ever since its formation, has found itself struggling with attitudes of "countermodernity". (Foucault 1984a: 39)

I think that Foucault's position can serve not least as a stimulus for distancing ourselves from the blackmail of enlightenment towards what might precisely be called – perhaps incongruously in the light of Foucault's own supposed philosophical affiliations – a realist view of enlightenment.

It is realist in the popular if not the strictly philosophical sense; it aims to be pragmatic, in-the-world, *mature* – social theory for "grown-ups", to paraphrase Stanley Cavell. Foucault's attitude saves us from having to take a position on those big sociological questions about modernity and post-modernity. It rescues us from the binarism and blackmail of enlightenment or anti-enlightenment. But it is realist too in the sense that it is to embrace the fact that, pragmatically-speaking, we *are* committed to enlightenment; that we do live in an age of enlightenment, an age in which enlightenment is at least *in question*, if not an enlightened age as such. There is, indeed, a sense in which even to engage in the debate over enlightenment is in fact to come down necessarily on the side of enlightenment itself. Otherwise, why would it be worth tackling our opponents through the public use of reason? The political theorist, John Gray, for instance, likes to think of himself as being post-enlightenment, but this is clearly not a wholly irrationalist or *anti*-enlightenment position simply because it cannot be one; he still clearly believes in justice and the good society; even it that society is "good" precisely in so far as it eschews the aspirations of perfectibility (Gray 1995: 30).

Now, something that is quite striking about these positions on the character of enlightenment is their *projective* character. The enlightenment debate is almost always couched in projective terms; what is stated is an ideal position intended to count as enlightenment. Here the basic discipline is philosophy or at least what is sometimes just called "theory". We are looking for foundations for our position, even and especially if, like the influential philosopher Richard Rorty, we have our doubts about the possibility of foundations in the first place; in which case we are looking for a kind of substitute for foundations (Rorty 1989). Most such foundational discussions are situated, then, at a general, theoretical level – very often they take the form of commentary. There is a healthy publishing market for such material, centred on informing the curious as to what kind of enlightenment they should or should not adopt (Dews 1987; Habermas 1987a; cf. Hoy & McCarthy 1994; Kelly 1994). This market is littered with good intentions, sophisticated analyses and non-starters, for instance what is rather misleadingly called the "Foucault–Habermas" debate.

In contrast to this sort of material, I suggest a more literally realist turn. I think that one of the consequences of Foucault's argument about enlightenment as "ethos" is that rather than a philosophical approach to enlightenment, it invites us to take something more like an empirical, medical or diagnostic one. Doctors diagnose by decomposing the elements of a condition, thus producing a profile of the disease – its characteristics, the possible forms of treatment, the prognosis. In order to be realist about enlightenment we do not need some abstract, foundational or anti-foundational theory of enlightenment but a diagnostics of enlightenment as it already exists. Rather than building a theory of enlightenment from the ground up, or providing endless commentary on the thoughts of others, social theory might do better to take a deliberately parasitic attitude, and look to the practices of enlightenment that we already have. Hence the particular, perhaps rather vulgar kind of realism I am advocating invokes a "worldly" attitude to enlightenment; a critique of impure reason (see Chapter 1 below).

Let me now give an indication of some of the orientations that such a worldly attitude might take, by previewing in what remains of this introduction some of the main themes of this book.

Aspects of enlightenment

If we are to be diagnostic about enlightenment, the concept needs to be broken down into some of its constituent parts. How do we dissect our enlightenmentality? As with all forms of dissection there may be many ways and so, at the risk of boring readers with excuses and special pleading, I now very briefly stress the limits of the particular strategies of dissection that are at stake here. If this book focuses in particular on three substantive aspects of enlightenment – those associated with science, therapeutics and art (Chapters 2 to 4) – this is not because these are to be regarded somehow as transcendental domains. It is rather that they represent particular kinds of *provocation* to the idea of an ongoing critique of enlightenment that might be so central to social theory. Other domains or practices could, obviously, have been chosen, but these aspectual domains are provocative because they are domains in which the intersection of questions of truth and criticism are especially problematic – difficult, ambiguous and hence exemplary. It may even be the case that these domains or their equivalents have been accorded transcendental status – for instance, in Kant's trinity of pure, practical and aesthetic reason – precisely because of this exemplary character which is really just of a conventional, historically conditioned sort.

So in focusing on the fields of science, therapeutic reason and art I do not mean to suggest that no other fields might be considered, or that the material I do address might not be cut up in different ways. I do not consider, as I might have done, aspects of enlightenment in the media industries, in management and business, in the sphere of politics, in bureaucratic fields or even, as would no doubt be possible, in religion. Another omission that people will notice is the question of gender; except that it is not really an omission at all precisely because we cannot imagine the question of gender as a mere aspect of enlightenment when really that question is an ongoing dimension of all such aspects. But if that question is scarcely considered even in terms of a general dimension of this sort, that is because – as the conclusion to this book seeks to indicate with regard to, among other things, some features of contemporary feminism – the question of gender, while being certainly *crucial* to all sorts of matters of enlightenment (as instanced by all the achievements of gender studies, women's studies and so forth), is not, dare I say it, all that *provocative* in relation to such matters.

This is emphatically not a dimissal of gender questions in general. Anything but. It is rather to say that if the critique of enlightenment is to take as its territory precisely those aspects of enlightenment that are most difficult, most insoluble, then the question of gender scarcely qualifies simply because to be *against* enlightenment in gender matters is not particularly "interesting" in any way but is simply to be *unenlightened*, which is to say, straightforwardly deplored. That is not to say that there is nothing of interest here for those who are interested in gender matters. In very general terms, it seems to me that a replacement of all those big, macho, epochal, build-everything-from-the-ground-up approaches that we see in the world of "Theory" (with a capital "t") in favour of critical approaches that are more mundane, parasitic and more messily within-the-world would not be without interest for those who notice and regret the fact that such "Theory" is almost exclusively the province of people who just happen to be men.

Even the areas I do manage to discuss are obviously problematic. Addressing the scientific spirit, as I do in Chapter 2, for instance, brings with it limitations that will be obvious. I focus on the natural sciences and the "central case" of the laboratory sciences; but this misses all sorts of scientific enterprises such as the biological or life sciences, or vital questions to do with the technological aspects of science. But my intention is not to produce anything approximating to a "general theory" of enlightenment; rather, the three aspects of enlightenment that I do consider are of particular interest in relation to the concerns of this book not least in so far as they are each domains which seek to evolve certain kinds of truth that are specific to themselves, domains to which social theory and the social sciences have been drawn whether by way of application or critique and which therefore serve well to throw the status of these disciplines themselves into question, and domains in which the theme of a critical attitude to enlightenment can be pictured at its most provocative, hence most salient.

My three aspects of enlightenment are, no doubt, provocative in different ways; science because it has traditionally been held up as the epitome of enlightenment, therapeutics because the therapies seek to aid humans themselves to enlightenment but with uncertain effects, and art because, no doubt, of its very ambiguity in relation to the idea of enlightenment, either as a reaction to or as a projected, if alternative, embodiment of that idea. The social sciences have been drawn to all three domains by way of critique; science has been subjected to the analyses of sociologists such as Bruno Latour, the therapies and the human sciences by Foucault himself and by those influenced by him such as Nikolas Rose, and art by theorists such as Pierre Bourdieu and others. In each case, issues of criticism are especially problematic, partly because those who subject these areas to critique often appear to be prone to a degree of uncertainty concerning the status of their own critical positions, and partly because each area of enlightenment is itself already a critique of some or other aspect of the world. But the point about my discussions of these kinds of enlightenment is not to close these problems of critique once and for all, nor to provide "theories" of each of these domains, but rather to sketch some restricted aspects of the kinds of critical dilemmas that are typically encountered within them and, if anything, to show why such dilemmas might be seen as *ordinary* consequences of their own internal logics. My aim is at once to complicate our understanding of some of the varied meanings of enlightenment and – perhaps more importantly – to deflate some of the interpretations of the consequences that such complexity might be said to bring.

Now, quite often, it is just *science* that is held up to be the embodiment of enlightenment as such (see Chapter 2). This is true even of anti-enlightenment critics of science. Such a perspective on science often entails a rationalist view of enlightenment. I want to insist that to take a realist view of enlightenment is not to take a rationalist view of it. Science is not the all-determining form of all reason; both the philosophy and the sociology of science have perhaps been rather prone to making the mistake of designating it as such. But science is neither a methodology nor just a sociological institution; rather it is most "real" as an aspiration of enlightenment. That is to say, science is real in this sense only at the level of the *spirit* or the *ethos* of science. What is required is a realism of that spirit or ethos. Such a realism will lead, if anything, in the opposite direction from that of an anti-science perspective. There may be such a thing as a culture of science; but we do not live in a "scientific culture", that is, a culture entirely determined by science. That very idea is to submit to a category mistake. I argue that scientific enlightenment is a limited rather than a universal thing; and that science has no intrinsic or inevitable moral implications of its own, even though the very idea of science has ethical preconditions, and that the deployment of anti-foundational arguments – such as those of Bruno Latour – can serve to praise science rather than to damn it.

Science is not the only apparatus of enlightenment, although it often seems to serve as the implicit measure of them all. To focus exclusively on science is to run the risk of fetishizing certain aspects of Western reason. The West becomes syonymous with Science (as, for example, in the work of Ernest Gellner, Francis Fukuyama and, on some readings, Max Weber). Certainly, from that perspective, other forms of reason lose their specificity or lend themselves to designation merely as pseudo-sciences. The therapeutic disciplines have often been labelled as such; and, in many cases, many do no doubt fall short of the standards that would be required of "scientific" forms of discourse (see Chapter 3). Foucault put this down to the fact that the disciplines, as he called them, had not gained autonomy from their origins in the politico-juridical model of the Inquisition whereas the empirical sciences had managed to escape these origins (Foucault 1979: 226–7). This at least suggests that the therapeutic disciplines need to be analysed in their own right, and not as by-products of scientific rationalization. However, my verdict will not necessarily parallel Foucault's complaint as to the "petty, malicious minutiae of the disciplines and their investigations". It is not that the Enlightenment discovered the Liberties *and* invented the disciplines; but rather that the disciplines are themselves an aspect of enlightenment, albeit one pertaining to a different logic to that of science. We need to avoid the naïve kind of approach that subjects all the disciplines to the formulae of science and thus so easily to anti-enlightenment prejudice.

Clearly, to insist on a non-rationalist theory of enlightenment reason is likewise to make room for analyses of forms of impure reason that are at some distance from the great models of science and philosophy. Since the early nineteenth century, and largely in reaction to tendencies inherent within the Enlightenment, the world of art has accorded itself the status of a peculiar kind of enlightenment (see Chapter 4). Romantics like Freidrich Schiller drew on the aesthetic paradigm to reconcile the twin pillars of subjectivism and objectivism; and, in our own times, Habermas has defended the legacy of enlightenment by recourse to the old idea of a redemption through art, while Foucault – in more anti-romantic vein – wrote of an aesthetics of existence, a principle of aesthetic creativity that was beyond moral codes and norms of knowledge (Habermas 1985: 12; Foucault 1989). I think that whereas we need a non-rationalist understanding of scientific enlightenment, the domain of art benefits from a dose of rationalism. Of course, art can be a model of anti-enlightenment, the positing of a domain of truth and reconciliation beyond that of reason as such; but, equally, aesthetic reason might be seen as a field of a certain rational *logic* of the aesthetic, a logic that – so long as it avoids the prejudice of aesthetic*ism* – might be enacted as a model, however limited, of enlightenment in domains beyond the artworld itself .

Much of my discussion of practices of enlightened reason is directed against the sociologism of approaches that regard the telos of forms of reason solely in the light of the social characteristics of those who purvey reason: the experts, the intellectuals or whoever. Yet any realist approach to enlightenment has to consider what could be called the question of enlightenment as a vocation; that is, the question as to *who* is speaking when we speak in the name of enlightenment. The eighteenth-century Enlightenment was, not least, an intellectual phenomenon. It was inconceivable without the emergence of a new, loose-knit corps of authorities who saw themselves speaking in the name of a universal reason that owed no – or few – proprietal dues to Church, patron or State. Indeed, the status of the intellectual is intrinsically tied to this meaning of enlightenment; the intellectual is the figure who is delegated or who delegates themselves to speak in the name of enlightenment, and to dramatize the continuing conscience of it (Chapter 6). But I argue that the question of enlightenment as a vocation is not a sociological question exactly. It is not a question of attributing a social function to a particular kind of intellectual voice but of indicating the extent to which the intellectual voice is the function only of a stylization of enlightenment principles. Hence to be realist about the intellectual voice is not to produce a structural sociology of the intellectual field and still less to produce a rationalist theory of intellectual power and its dissemination, but to analyse the varied agency of reason as it is embodied and individuated, by particular kinds of intellectual persona. In the end, it is even to defend the very idea of the intellectual.

Negative anthropology

This, then, is perhaps a peculiar sort of realism. But in the name of what does it speak? It is certainly not the critical realism that has been quite popular in social theory over recent years (Outhwaite 1987). This holds that the function of realism is to criticize reality from a particular perspective – usually that of a wholly just, classless society. That is all very well, even if such views always seem to contain an implicitly utopian moment. In fact, I argue that to take a realist approach to enlightenment also entails a utopian moment, albeit of an obviously different sort from that of critical realism (Chapter 1). This should not be surprising for it is often said that utopianism is the correlate of realism. The realist analyses the world as it is and then projects another, different world as an alternative; or, at least, that "other" world is the baseline for our purchase on the present state of reality. But what is the nature of that utopianism here? In a nutshell, I think it should be described as being counter-factual, "anthropological" and ethical rather than sociological.

I argue that the subject matter of a critical analytics of enlightenment – and of social theory – should not be with the structure of society so much as with the changeability of human capacities; it is anthropological rather than socio-logical in the sense that its concern would be more with the theme of human nature than with a science of society as such (Chapter 1).

If this critical attitude to enlightenment is anthropological in its concern with human nature, this entails – at least at its limit – what can be called a *negative* anthropology (cf. Honneth and Joas 1988: 8, quoting Kamper 1973: 26). Such an anthropology starts from the limit-assumption, the regulative ideal, that humans might be wholly given over to culture, to self-definition from the ground up; that their nature might even consist in having no nature. This assumption, though based on realist premises, is ethical rather than realistic. It is not *realistic* because humans are given over to traditions, to habit, to settled ways of living, to genetic determinations, and are shaped by their biology, their gender, by conventions, by their environment – all this before they can become cultural beings in imposing their own values, freely chosen or not, on themselves and the world. But it is ethical in so far as one of the value-orientations of a cultural science will be precisely with a problem-atization of humans *in so far as* they are cultural beings of this sort. In other words, it is a perspective that would, in effect, *will* humans to become cultural beings. It would seek to speak in the name of the cultural aspect of humans; and that is why the fully "negative" version of a critique of enlightenment – as, for example, in the genealogies of Foucault – might sometimes cultivate a certain unreality of perspective for deliberate, ethical ends. But the task of such a perspective of negative enlightenment, in a normative sense, might be to bring reality itself somewhat closer to what is demanded by such an ethic.

Ethics of enlightenment

When I say that part of the peculiarity of the idea of an ongoing critique of enlightenment is that it is ethical in character, I do not mean that this critical attitude should be thought of as pertaining to a whole way of life, but that it properly takes the form of a deliberate and restricted exercise that we perform on ourselves in rather determinate circumstances. This makes it quite distinct from some varieties of postmodernism. The critic of enlightenment in this sense might be compared with the "ironist", as described by the philosopher, Richard Rorty, who takes what might initially look to be a similarly contingent view of the world. For Rorty, ironism entails the embracing of a principle of contingency with regard to all things – culture, language, truth, the self. To be enlightened is, in effect, to acknowledge contingency. The difference from the perspective that is outlined in this book is that Rorty clearly regards ironism as a *general* rather than a deliberately restricted outlook on life, something like an ironist form of subjectivity, a morality, a complete epistemology or an ironist "worldview". The sceptical attitude of the sort of critique of enlightenment that this book is concerned with is not, as I see it, quite like that (Rorty 1989; see Chapter 1); its utopian moment does nothing to debunk the actual findings of the sciences or disciplines themselves; indeed, even though it imagines things as being completely otherwise, it can seem to leave them, in some aspects, more or less completely intact.

Indeed, I think that one of the pay-offs of such a negative view of enlightenment would be precisely that it retains a certain distance from postmodern or "ironic" understandings of truth. I say that such a view is ethical, as we have seen, in the limited sense that it entails a restricted value-orientation – that associated, at its limit, with negative anthropology – that it pushes to an extreme with a certain deliberation. As such, it is much more like an exercise than a determinate, nomological "doctrine". It is something that we do for *strategic* reasons; to invoke reminders that we are cultural beings and that, being so, we need to keep the search for a way out constantly on our mind. The negativity of a critical attitude to enlightenment does not, on this view, *prove* that humans are pure culture. Rather it imagines them to be so, and enjoins humans to push such an imagination to the limit in the interests precisely of a renewal of cultural imagination. But in so far as it is an exercise, then just as after any exercise, we have to dust ourselves down or change our clothes and get back – if hopefully with renewed powers of judgement – to the business of living. In the interests just of everyday security we cannot imagine ourselves – as do the postmodernists, even as a matter of morality – to be in the flux of culture through all the duties of the day, as if there were no such thing as knowledge or things that were good. In this sense, we might be forgiven for describing the idea of a critique of enlightenment in terms of moral education; but it would not educate the whole person but only deliberately place in question certain aspects of our cultural make-up. Cultural criticism of this sort is not itself a whole way of life – we do not enter a monastery to do a negative critique of enlightenment. However, we might enter a classroom or a lecture-hall (see Chapter 6; cf. MacIntyre 1990: 218).

We can no doubt find instances of a critical attitude to enlightenment – and of negative enlightenment – quite happily at work in philosophy, literary criticism, history, sociology, art, even in the physical sciences. There is no exclusive disciplinary privilege accorded to such an attitude, and it is very rare even for any discipline or work to be *exclusively* a contribution to it. There are – partial – exceptions. In the conclusion to this book I argue that social theory might be the discipline to take this critical attitude as a particular concern. As for individual thinkers, Weber and Foucault come to mind (Chapter 5). Both devoted their attentions quite specifically to the elaboration of something like a science of culture that was also a critique of enlightenment and which, in Foucault's case, appears to take on the guise of a full-scale negative attitude to the question of enlightenment. But these figures should not be seen as "founders" or "master-thinkers" of this kind of work. It is rather that aspects of a critique of enlightenment can be discovered, and illustrated, in their works; and that each exemplifies, for all their very fundamental differences, a certain possible orientation to such a discipline, a form of exemplification that is itself exemplified by the fact that they cannot be pinned down and reduced to any singular or determinate form of discourse, that each have had many self-proclaimed followers and disciples but no singular school, it being seemingly impossible to "follow" either without doing a certain amount of more or less regrettable kind of violence to their work.

Finally, I want to reiterate that the negativity entailed in the very idea of a critique of enlightenment does not mean that we have to adopt a "negative" view of enlightenment in the sense of being resolutely post- or anti-enlightenment. On the contrary, it is rather that enlightenment is itself embodied by a certain negativity towards itself. This negativism takes us in the direction of a concern with the genealogy of practices of enlightenment in particular contexts. For if the purpose of enlightenment is to realize freedom, part of that role has to be with the limits of our current realizations of freedom. It is this aspect of this book that makes it more – or rather less – than a work in abstract "theory", but rather a contribution to a sort of *fieldwork* in the spirit of enlightenment in some of its worldly aspects.

Chapter 1

Reason, truth and criticism

The limits of rationalization – The knowledge-society thesis – Truth and enlightenment – Truth-as-authority – Governing in the name of truth – Truth and anti-foundationalism – Utopianism – Asceticism and strategy

The introduction made the point that there already is an implicit and thriving conversation about the status of enlightenment going on among social theorists, philosophers and critics of various kinds. I think that it helps if this conversation is best understood *as* being about the status of enlightenment rather than, as some of its participants hold, the state and destiny of whole societies. There is obviously a certain scepticism with regard to certain kinds of sociology that is implicit in my argument. Lest this seem like a scepticism with regard to all forms of sociology or social science, readers should turn to the concluding chapter of this book where they will see that the opposite is the case. Rather, my doubts are directed primarily at what can be called *epochal* varieties of sociology or social theory.

Epochal social theories are those which seek to encapsulate the *Zeitgeist* in some kind of overarching societal designation; that we live in a postmodern society, a modern society, an information society, a rationalized society, a risk society and so on. They are particularly prevalent in that domain of studies known as social theory. Such epochal sociologies and theories tend to work against the spirit of a critical attitude to enlightenment because they tend to set up their coordinates in advance, leaving no "way out" from their terms of reference. This point needs to be made precisely in so far as critiques of enlightenment – those of Weber or Foucault, for example – are often taken to be such epochal sociologies themselves. That is why in this chapter I devote a certain amount of attention to discussing some of the limits of two kinds of epochalism that sail particularly close to the theme of enlightenment and are apt to be confused with it; these are the themes of rationalization and what I shall call the knowledge-society thesis. These two themes appear to be very common just as pictures that operate in people's heads; so it is important to discuss them if we are to get our own picture of enlightenment clear. After that, I turn to the more positive task of developing a sketch of what the kind of critical attitude to enlightenment that I envisage might look like, a task which involves a discussion of the concept of truth and some further reflections on "anthropology" and ethics.

The limits of rationalization

Epochal diagnoses of modernity have a tendency to privilege the particular characteristics of Western kinds of *reason* at the centre of their explanatory frameworks. Here, reason is given a sociological force. Often this emphasis is implicit as, for example, in the ever-popular thesis of secularization – or analagous concepts such as detraditionalization or deinstitutionalization – which tend very easily to regard various kinds of rationalization process as corrosive of collective "ethicality" and belief. In other words, thinking about modernity as a specific problem tends very easily to lead to thinking about modernity in terms of the betrayal of enlightenment coupled with the progressive rationalization of life, and the eclipse of ethics, freedom and choice.

There are triumphalist versions of the rationalization thesis. One thinks, for example, of Ernest Gellner's accounts in *Legitimation of Belief*, or *Reason and Culture* (Gellner 1974, 1992a). Here the specificity of the West is accorded to certain distinctive facets of cognitive style – rationalism, mechanism, empiricism. But more usually rationalization is held to be a malign or at least an ambivalent affair. Here the central figure in the canon has been that of the greatest of all social theorists, Max Weber. Perhaps it is the very disparateness of Weber's works that has led commentators to search for central themes in his oeuvre. Rationalization for a long time certainly fitted the bill. Weber's message seemed to many to be that the world had become disenchanted in the face of the progress of modern science, technology and bureaucracy; taken together, the famous "iron-cage" (Weber 1992b: 181, where the reference is, incidentally, to asceticism and "external goods" rather than rationalization as such). For the Weberians, rationalization in this context meant something like the capacity to control the world through procedures of calculation, although the extent to which a definition can ever be found is itself in dispute (Schluchter 1979: 14; cf. Brubaker 1984). Suffice to say that rationalization is an inherently critical concept in that, as it describes a process, the concept generally presupposes the existence of a dialectic between subjectivity and rationalization itself, with rationalization tending to be seen as corrosive of subjectivity. This definition leads, then, to certain characteristic limitations which set up in advance what can and cannot be done with a concept like rationalization.

The first of these limitations is the dichotomy that the rationalization thesis tends implicitly to posit between subjectivity and rationality itself (Hindess 1987). We assume a pre-given subjectivity that is subject to rationalization processes, as it were, from outside. Now, it is ironic that in fact Weber cannot really be said to have worked, himself, quite within the terms of such a dichotomy (cf. Turner 1992). This is not least because Weber himself did not simply correlate rationalization with modernity alone. Rather, rationalization for him was something that originated, first, within religions themselves; indeed, its protoypes were the world-views of the so-called world religions, and even charisma was, in its own sense, a rationalizing force. In other words, this already suggests that Weber himself did not work with a distinction between rationality and subjectivity, nor with any straightforward understanding of a paradigmatic Western process of rationalization; something borne out by the fact that one of his more recent commentators on this subject has thought best to distinguish between scientific-technical rationalism, metaphysical-ethical rationalism and practical rationalism (Schluchter 1979: 14–15). The point is that, from Weber's point of view, the concept of rationalization was less a description of the world than a tool of research, or a principle for measuring ideal types against reality. What was distinctive about the West was not so much the process of rationalization itself but the *kind* of rationalization that it had experienced; namely, one pertaining to what Weber termed a "universal point of view" (Weber 1992a: 13).

Now, aside from the question of the subject-reason dichotomy, a further problem with the rationalization thesis relates to the question of periodization. The thesis implicitly promotes what might be called "supplementary-dualist" theories of the world. A dualism is posited between an era of pre-rationalization or non-rationalization and the era of rationalization itself. But then a problem of the supplement arises. For it is scarcely ever possible to sustain a periodization indefinitely. So what comes after the period of rationalization? Post-rationalization? The undermining of rationalization? These problems of dichotomization are the same as those which beset sociological theories of modernity themselves; all are alike in that they over-dramatize the characteristics of social change, and reduce such change to one or two fundamental elements. The corollary of this kind of image of thought is that we find ourselves in the trilemma of either a blanket denunciation of modernity, a blanket endorsement of it, or – perhaps most dubious of all, because pertaining to a certain subtlety – the fudged option of an exposure of the ambivalence that structures the heart of modernity.

The problem, rather, resides with the very idea of rationalization as the guiding feature of a positive sociology of modernity; the view that modernity can be somehow reduced to a question of rationalization in the abstract. So long as the concept of modernity is understood in *epochal* terms, that is, attached to a periodization rather than an ethos or an attitude, then we will encounter problems at the level of critique. That is because such epochal periodizations lend themselves intrinsically to a logic of dichotomization that establishes the available terms of critique in advance, either for or against. Thinking of the modernity of reason in terms of the attitude of enlightenment helps us to escape from the logic of this dichotomy. But instead of reducing modernity to enlightenment, it might be preferable to enquire, in a more limited way, only into the modernity *of* enlightenment – which is to say, the extent to which reason is "modern".

Such an enquiry would not aspire to be a "science of society" but it might still make use of sociology, even if predominantly by way of a critique of various assumptions that are prevalent in that discipline when it comes to the analysis of practices of reason.

The knowledge-society thesis

Any minimal sociology of modern enlightenment would, it seems, have to hold that the ideal of enlightenment is tied to the progress of our systems of knowledge. A society in the throes of an age of enlightenment is surely an age of knowledge; a *knowledge-society* perhaps. We can think of enlightenment in other terms, which do not necessarily offer recourse to the authority of knowledge in any conventional sense of that term. For instance, enlightenment can take a mystical form; as in various schoolings in enlightenment practised in the Eastern religions. Or enlightenment can take an ethical form; as in the practices of the self in the Ancient World discussed by Foucault or Pierre Hadot. Or enlightenment can take what might be called a dialogic form; that is, enlightenment can be understood as an open-ended practice undertaken in the context of *learning*. I shall have some more to say about such dialogical models of enlightenment a little later on, and especially at the end of Chapter 6 and in the conclusion. Suffice to say, for now, that the idea of enlightenment as being tied specifically to the pursuit of objective knowledge is relatively novel if we are rash enough to take the entirety of human history as our horizon; it dates from some time prior to the golden age of *the* Enlightenment itself – perhaps a sociologist of knowledge might want to pick 1620 as the date of its formal inauguration: the publication of Bacon's *Novum Organon*.

But I want to contend that there are problems with conceiving of the specific characteristics of modernity in terms of the production and diffusion of knowledge; and having sketched some of these, I shall argue that the notion of systems of *truth* might open up the way to a better – because more restricted – terminology. This will not surprise readers of Foucault. He often wrote of the history of truth or games of truth. Typically this vocabulary is held to have been adopted in the interests of post-structuralist iconoclasm or mischeviousness, for how can one have a *history* of *truth*? I think, however, that there are good reasons for talking about enlightenment in terms of truth rather than in the language of knowledge.

One reason is just that the language of knowledge is, rather like the language of rationalization, too flexible to be of much use. Take, for instance, the issue of the periodization of the knowledge-society. I think we can distinguish the way in which this theme is put to work in economic sociology from the way in which it is deployed by epochally inclined sociologists of modernity. Economic sociologists might trace the emergence of a knowledge component in production to the early twentieth century. For that early management guru, F.W. Taylor, working for Ford entailed a rigorous *knowledge* of what working for Ford entailed: measuring the productive capabilities of workers under differing forms of organization and control – to "prove that the best management is a true science, resting upon clearly defined laws, rules and principles, as a foundation" (Taylor 1967: 7). Increasingly even the immanent problems of the Fordist organizsation of production lead to further intensification of the contribution of knowledge within production (Aglietta 1987: 124–5; Lipietz 1987: 35). Henceforth, the productive processes of capitalism were to be regulated by an expanding corps of engineers while the management of capitalism was to fall to an increasingly autonomous class of specialized managers, charged with directing the process of capital accumulation on essentially rational grounds (Abercrombie and Urry 1983: 167–8, 170–5). A further set of developments occurred in the economic organization of advanced capitalist societies with the break-up of Fordist regimes of production and the inauguration of something like a post-Fordist or "disorganized" regime of accumulation. Production came to be split into ever smaller, ever more specialized units; but there is also a strong sense in which the quality of the leading-edge of productive capacity had changed – from the massified, productive industries of Fordism to the scaled-down, communicational "Sunrise" companies of post-Fordism.

I think that problems arise, however, when such developments are translated out of the quite specific idiom of economic sociology and into the terms of a wholesale epochalism. That is the strategy of much of the sociology of modernity. So, for some, post-Fordist developments have marked the end of industrialism itself, and we have now entered something of the order of a post-industrial world; a world that appears to be more or less determined by systems of knowledge (Bell 1973; Touraine 1974). Even the idea of a post-modern society is, in its most famous formulation, only the analogue at the level of knowledge of the post-industrial society that was inaugurated sometime towards the end of the 1950s; and notions of the information society are certainly not dissimilar (Lyotard 1984a: 3; Lyon 1986). The American social theorist, Daniel Bell, argued, for example, that the information society rested on a "knowledge theory of value" such that knowledge itself took the form of a kind of capital with productive capacities in its own right (Bell 1980; Forester 1985; Webster 1995).

Thus we arrive at the knowledge-society thesis *in extremis*; that our societies in the West are not capitalist societies, or industrial societies or consumer societies but *knowledge-societies* as such (Stehr 1995; cf. Machlup 1962, 1981). Although this idea obviously takes a variety of forms, its *sine qua non* is the idea of a society that was organized above all around production but now tends towards relations of information, communication and cognition

(Poster 1990). It is at this point, I think, that a certain scepticism is justified. For, once the category of knowledge has been translated from an instrument for diagnosing the specificity of changes in production to being definitive of an entire kind of society, a certain elasticity of interpretation is likely to take over our critical faculties.

For are not all societies in some sense or other knowledge-societies? Is not the knowledge-society rather like the bourgeoisie in some vulgar versions of historical materialism: *always* rising, and explanatory of just about anything and everything? For instance, one of the foremost sociologists of modernity, Zygmunt Bauman, would, no doubt, refer the knowledge-society – not a term he uses himself, though it is implicit in what he says – back to the eighteenth century. For the sociologist of modernity, a society characterized by knowledge appears to be the same thing as an enlightened society. In any case, for Bauman, the spirits of enlightenment and modernity are, to all intents and purposes, the same thing. Or rather, the spirit of enlightenment appears as the "superstructure" of modernity. Bauman radicalizes Foucault's notion of power/knowledge relations, turning it into a theory of society as such. Here it is the Enlightenment itself that gives us Bentham's Panopticon, that paranoiac, carceral space where all watch themselves because all believe that they are watched:

> The institutions which the grand design of Bentham's "Panopticon" symbolically represented were the first to apply on a massive scale, as a "normal" technology of power in society, an asymmetry of surveillance. It put the majority, the objects of power, permanently in the position of "the watched", without a right, or a realistic hope, ever to reciprocate or to change places with their surveillors (Bauman 1987: 47; cf. Foucault 1979).

In short, enlightened reason is at the very origin of what Bauman calls the "power/knowledge" syndrome of modernity. And for Bauman, this spirit of modernity is beset by a horror of indeterminacy and ambiguity, a horror that leads it to build an iron-cage around its practices, hence tending towards the nightmare of a totally administered world. At all costs, the stranger – the one who is outside, ambiguous – must be eliminated. In Bauman's claustrophic vision of modernity, we move in the space of a few pages from Francis Bacon, Kant, Descartes and Locke through to the social control policies of Frederick the Great through to a discussion of the extermination policies of the Nazis (Bauman 1991: 26–8). For Bauman, we are now irrevocably beyond modernity; but we are certainly not *beyond* the knowledge-society thesis. If anything, there is now more than ever a demand for knowledge and expertise, for in Bauman's vision of today's postmodern cognitive diaspora, "communication across traditions becomes the major problem of our time" calling for an array of specialists in all the varied conversations of mankind; "specialists in translation between cultural conditions", specialists who will have "a most central place among the experts contemporary life may require" (Bauman 1987: 143).

Such epochalist views do not all take the pessimistic cast of Bauman's own analysis. Again, Ernest Gellner's influential work might be a case in point. Gellner points to what he sees as a paradox of the modern age in the West wherein knowledge becomes both democratized or autonomized and yet generalized. The ubiquity of knowledge – in educating persons for loyalty to culture and the State – leads to a marked decline in the division of labour as regards knowledge.

> When knowledge is the slave of social considerations, it defines a special class; when it serves its own ends only, it no longer does so. There is of course a profound logic in this paradox; genuine knowledge is egalitarian in that it allows no privileged sources, testers, messengers of Truth. It tolerates no privileged and circumscribed data. The autonomy of knowledge is a leveller. (Gellner 1988: 123).

For Gellner, now we have not only specialists in cognition but a "single conceptual community in cognition" which leaves behind a kind of "cultural buttermilk", indeed *culture per se* (ibid: 205–6).

The example of Gellner's work is illuminating particularly in relation to a paradox that – aside from the difficulties of periodizing the knowledge-society – seems to be a necessary aspect of thinking about the effects of systems of knowledge in a sociological and epochal way. For, in this sort of position, the more that knowledge is augmented as a social resource, somehow the more difficult it is to specify precisely what *is* specific about knowledge *per se*; that is, the more it is disseminated, the more it is integrated with the fabric of social life, with culture, the less like *knowledge* it is. Hence the remarkable elasticity – and indeterminacy – of the key term in the knowledge-society thesis. Indeed, in Gellner's modernity, cognition eventually shades into culture (while, for other theorists, it slides into symbolic communication or just representation, or information). In short, the role of knowledge seems to oscillate from being a specialized resource to being a generic facet of all cultural activity – and back again. This all means that knowledge is essentially indeterminate as an *explanandum*; we cannot base an epochal theory of modernity on the thesis of a growth in the social utility of knowledge.

Now, I do not want to say that all the variants on the narrative of the knowledge-society are *ipso facto* false, but rather that each is essentially indeterminate as an interpretation from the perspective of an overall science of society. The debates over the knowledge-society, postmodernization, the information society: all these, I suggest, are not amenable to any form of closure at the level of empirical data alone. They are for the most part gestural categories. Aside from the elasticity that such accounts encounter by way of periodization and their indeterminacy with regard to their principles of explanation, this may be not least for what might be termed an anthropological reason. It is simply that humans are, among other things, *thinking* beings; that is, beings endowed with capacities for cognition or intellect. Thinking, to echo Mannheim, is simply an existential aspect of being human (Mannheim 1936: 268; cf. Gramsci 1971: 9; Godelier 1986). This affects the logic of all arguments that are committed to some version of the knowledge-society thesis. For, given this baseline of knowledge in all things human, it is always difficult to specify and give weight to the *singularity* of the particular changes that are under discussion; for in an anthropological sense, all human societies are knowledge-societies of a sort.

Such versions of the knowledge-society thesis tend to be epochal about society. They tend to be realist too. They say that certain kinds of society relate to knowledge, expertise or science in particular ways and they also seek to explore what is uniquely *modern* about this relation. In place of such sociol-epochal realism, I want to substitute a much more restricted, less ambitious, perspective: a realism about enlightenment. For sociological modernity and the ideal of enlightenment are different things. In order to operationalize this difference I suggest that – at least within the confines of a social theory oriented to the question of enlightenment – we substitute an explanatory focus on relations of truth as opposed to one centred on knowledge.

Truth and enlightenment

Our everyday grammar in talking about these matters usually leads us to think of knowledge in terms of a conceptual "capture" of an "object of knowledge" by a "subject of knowledge". Such a conception has come under attack from numerous forms of sociological and other kinds of thought. One response has been from the hermeneutic tradition which sees the vocation of the human sciences in the interpretation of human action. Such interpretation would hardly conform to a subject–object model of knowledge. Indeed, we can always respond to the proponent of the subject–object model with a question: Where does the subject come from? And we can always argue, with the phenomenologists and others, that the very subject–object relation presupposes prior forms of relating to the world that form a kind of everyday background to what we can – and cannot – know. Another, and currently more fashionable, trend has occurred in what used to be called the sociology of knowledge. Today it is very common in the social sciences to hear people saying that all knowledge is a "construct". It is often difficult to know exactly what this means, but one thing is more or less certain: that social constructionism scarcely disturbs the subject–object model of knowledge; it is only that here the subject does not "capture" the object but produces it, fabricates it, constructs it – which assuredly amounts in logical terms to much the same thing as capturing it. Constructionism always runs the risk of being just a variant on subjectivism.

But when it comes to specifying our dreams of enlightenment I suggest we talk not about knowledge – however it is constructed – but about truth. *Knowledge*, it might be granted, is the product of a subject perceiving an object; thus we have knowledge of the external world. But not all forms of telling the *truth* are exhausted by this question of knowledge in bearing such a straightforward subject–object relation. I think that the concept of truth, unlike that of knowledge, suggests an ethical component to the labour of thought; it is that ethical moment that a critical attitude to enlightenment would attempt to capture and describe. There are different kinds of truths: the truth we seek of ourselves and the well-springs of our conduct, the particular truths that are the objective of aesthetic work, as well as scientific truth or the forms of critical truth that animate the humanities. All these presuppose different ethical orientations to the questions in hand; different ways of telling the truth, and different functions for truth itself.

It is worth noting, in parenthesis as it were, that to speak of different rationalities of truth in this way is not necessarily to impose some mystical hierarchy on things. This has been all too tempting for those who have wanted to import some element of subjectivism into the question of truth. Even J.S. Mill, to take one celebrated example, observed that truth was *more* than mere knowledge in that to know the truth one had to know oneself: "The most important phenomena of human nature cannot even be conceived, except by a mind which has actively studied itself." For Mill, the excavation of the truth was an ethical matter, involving something like a relation to self (Mill 1980: 332). Similarly, Martin Heidegger, at least in his later philosophical writings, went in for a rather unattractive, romantic or mystical, not to say – arguably – anti-scientific claim that there may be a deeper, more "meditative" kind of truth that is worth more than propositional thought or truth of a calculative kind (cf. Heidegger 1966: 46).

In contrast to this kind of emphasis, our perspective on enlightenment need not be committed to any particular *philosophical* view of truth. It would only be to say that all forms of truth rely on an ethics; what might be called, if only in an abstract way, deontologies of truth-telling. I want to insist at the outset that this ethical perspective on truth does not in any way commit us to a relativism – or, still less, a subjectivism – about the truth; although it is to acknowledge that there may be many ways of telling the truth. Games of truth-telling are not necessarily relative to anything other than themselves; moreover, such games make possible what can be recognized as being true or false (cf. Hacking 1982; Hacking 1983b). The effects of such a view are in fact much less iconoclastic than we might be led to think, if only because games of truth are fairly rare; it is not that there is a multiplicity of different truths but rather that truth is difficult, hard to come by, and ultimately ethical, derivative of human involvement in the world. Nor is to say as much to adopt an argument equivalent to that taken up today by contemporary postmodern or post-pragmatic philosophers such as Richard Rorty. For Rorty, truth is above all a question of language and metaphor; and progress in the truth consists of finding only "increasingly useful metaphors" (Rorty 1989: 9). Down this road lie indeed all the usual perils of subjectivism and relativism because, according to such conceptions, truth can be just about anything at all, sliding down the logic of a rather pointless and undiscriminating conventionalism.

A critical attitude to enlightenment that focused on this question of truth might perhaps be pragmatic in orientation, but in a different way from the kind of pragmatism espoused by Rorty. It would be concerned not with, say, a linguistic view of truth but with an ethical conception of the possibility of truth. By the ethics of truth I do not mean the *morality* of truth – the good and bad ways of telling the truth – but the different ways in which telling the truth is related to "ethical work"; that is, the work we perform upon ourselves in order to turn ourselves into the subject of our actions. Take, as an illustration, science as an ethic of truth. What I am saying is not that in order to do science we have to orientate ourselves ethically to our work. Plenty of scientists, no doubt, do what they do through habit, instinct, raw intelligence or laborious training and do not "work upon themselves" in any obvious way. But that is not my point. It is rather that a scientist, in order to recognize him or herself *as* a scientist, someone who embodies, so to speak, the vocation of "scientificity" – and in order to be recognized as such – will have to embrace such scientificity as more than just a particular behavioural kind of activity but as a particular *calling* that entails a particular model of the make-up of scientific personality. What would be at stake, then, would be something akin to the self-image of science as a particular kind of ethical orientation. Such ethical pictures are not just ideology, although there *are*, no doubt, plenty of ideologies in science. Rather, they can be regarded as being internal to the very normativity of what science is as an activity, and as such they do have a practical status; they are the means by which science recognizes itself and is recognized.

Such an "ethical" view on truth does not mean that it is impossible, without being subversively reflexive, to attempt to speak the truth for oneself; but it does mean that truth is a difficult enterprise. To take an ethical view on truth is clearly not to allow the idea of truth effectively to dissolve altogether but, on the contrary, to stress that truth is both an obligation and a labour (cf. Malpas 1996). All *styles* of truth depend on styles of ethical work in this restricted sense of the term. Even Descartes – to take the classic example of a rationalist model of truth – performed such a work on himself. For what else is the famous method of doubt? Certainly not an attempt at the definitive founding of all knowledge, but more like an ethical attempt to bring about self-conviction (Gaukroger 1995: 321). And what else are Descartes' *Meditations* but ethical exercises in a certain style of submission to the truth? – or an account, as Descartes' most recent biographer puts it, "of a spiritual journey in which the truth is only to be discovered by a purging, followed by a kind of rebirth" (ibid: 336; cf. Blumenberg 1983: 183).

This begs the question as to why we need to defer to the truth at all, and this is where a minimal sociology might indeed be required. What is, after all, so great about truth? Our minimal sociology needs to explain the fact that truth has taken on a legitimatory function in our age of enlightenment. In so far as ours is an enlightened age – and only in so far as such – the final arbiter of judgement *à propos* conduct more often than not tends to be *the truth itself*. In judging forms of action, in judging the past, in assessing ourselves and our conduct, it tends to be the truth to which we turn. This specificity of the function of truth should perhaps be more surprising to us than it tends to be. It is a function that might itself be said to be ethical in so far as the notion of an *objective* truth that stands outside the immediate interests of humans has employed the methods of "detachment", or what Charles Taylor calls "disengaged identity" is the product of a kind of subjective or rather ascetic work – that is, it is a cultural *achievement* (Taylor 1985a: 5–7). In short, if we want to say *both* that there is such a thing as objective truth *and* that truth is something that we find in human discourse, then we have to see truth-telling as something like a success story in ethics.

Truth-as-authority

What is significant in the context of this achievement is less the age-old idea of the "love of truth" than the idea that truth itself should be a form of authority in its own right. This achievement somewhat predates the era of *the* Enlightenment. In order to clarify the nature of this achievement we might, in this context, distinguish between authority-as-truth and truth-as-authority. The historian Hans Blumenberg has described the "Platonic" ideal of truth which prevailed in the Middle Ages, holding that what is "true" about the truth here is its relevance to particular kinds of authorities.

> The early Christian authors lay claim to the truth that can be found in the ancient philosophers ... in order not only to integrate it into their system as something that has now become available to everyone – as what we would call "objective" truth – but also to return it to truth in a stricter sense of the term by re-establishing its genetic influence. (Blumenberg 1983: 72)

Contrast this problematic of authority-as-truth with that inaugurated (or, anyway, represented) by the writings of Sir Francis Bacon in the seventeenth century. Bacon's significance lay in saying that truth is *not* merely the offspring of authority, but of time itself. Now, mention of Bacon's name might lead us to associate this – "modern" – idea of truth more or less exclusively with the rationality of inductive science. However, in fact what Bacon was more likely to be thinking of was not just experimental science but what he called "civil history" – or, we might say, secular history – which, for him, was a discipline in the best sense in that it presents least of the author's own point of view but is closely related to reality in that it requires a rigorous working over of materials. For Bacon, civil history is the true terrain of experience; science invents reality, poetry imagines it, and civil history works on it, coupling events to causes and concerning "everything which relates to the state of learning" (Bacon 1870: 300–1; Wormald 1993: 74). As Blumenberg observes, this conception of truth is endemically open-ended: "False trust in the world – that is the dominant concern in Bacon's momentous exclusion of the teleological view of nature" (1983: 384). Yet it is simultaneously connected to a great sense of trust in the eventual appearance of the truth:

> the image of contemporary voyages of discovery dominates Bacon's thought. No assumption of an unknown goal guides the ship's voyage; rather the compass enables one to hold to a path on which, in the field of the unknown, new land will eventually appear. (ibid: 389)

The inductive, open-ended model of the truth leaves us, nonetheless, in no doubt of the ultimate appearance of the truth; truth is an objective kind of thing, one that is *capable* of making an appearance.

The fact that this "objective" ideal of truth should open on to something like the possibility of its own *universality* should not blind us to its original contingency. It may be that the modern West has made truth the index of all things; but, for all that, we have to hold fast, to the contingency – the achievement – of such an idea of truth. Weber gave this notion of universality exactly the right paradoxical edge: "A product of modern European civilization, studying any problem of universal history, is bound to ask himself to what combination of circumstances the fact should be attributed that in Western civilization only, cultural phenomena have appeared which (as we like to think) lie in a line of development having *universal* significance and value" (Weber 1992a: 13).

Note that this rather minimal perspective on truth does not presume to the status of a *philosophical* line on things, even if all this talk of truth has made the critique of enlightenment appear the godchild of a particular philosopher: Nietzsche. For it was Nietzsche who most famously drew our attention to the "will to truth" that animated modern Western societies. It is true that Nietzsche's perspective opens up a space for questioning the self-evidence of the truth as the primary requirement of judgement, and to that end his thought is eminently useful. Nietzsche makes the point in *The Gay Science* and elsewhere that the concern for truth itself relies on a prior moral commitment, namely – as he puts it – in the perception of the duty not to deceive, even myself (Nietzsche 1974: 283). In that sense, truth itself rests on what is really a prior metaphysical belief; "a faith must always be there first of all, so that science can acquire from it a direction, a meaning, a limit, a method, a *right* to exist" (Nietzsche 1969: 152). But Nietzsche's view was for all its iconoclastic pretensions, still a philosophical one. He located the modern version of the will to truth as stemming from the ascetic, and world-denying, propensities of Christianity. In that sense, at least, Nietzsche was suspicious of the truth and his is a *critique* of our concern for the truth ultimately in the name of a higher – more profound, if more profane – kind of truth. "The will to truth requires a critique – let us thus define our own task – the value of truth must at once be *experimentally called into question*" (ibid: 153; cf. Owen 1998).

Now, a critical attitude to enlightenment need not, in fact, be so philosophically ambitious as this, although it might be. But we are not necessarily dealing here with anything so ineluctably revelatory as a critique of the truth – unless we simply use the notion of critique in the widest, Kantian sense. Suffice to say that in so far as it is philosopically pertinent at all, the very notion of a critique of enlightenment might owe at least as much to Kant as to Nietzsche. But the importance of the original *question* of truth rests, in any case, on more mundane foundations; even if it is not conventionally sociological, this question is practical or at least "worldly" rather than metaphysical, abstract or logical.

That is one reason why the attitude of a critique of enlightenment might be referred more to the discipline of social theory than to that of philosophy. It is not that we require a philosophical critique of the very idea of truth, but an analytics of aspects of our enlightenment. But what might this look like? I think that analyses of what Foucault called "arts of government" might, among other things, be useful here; that is, in the widest sense of the meaning of Foucault's neologism, "governmentality" – the rationalities and types of mentality that are attached to the direction and shaping of conduct. Such studies can at least serve to show why it is an aspect of certain Western societies to regard themselves as being rather appreciative towards the truth.

Governing in the name of truth

Let me now very quickly rehearse some aspects of this work on governmentality, which is to be valued in this context not least for its distance from any sociologism of perspective. In an age of enlightenment, truth is closely related to the varied ways in which humans seek to *govern* – that is, in a very general sense, to *shape* – their own and others conduct. Control over humans is not exercised simply on the basis of sovereignty or coercion but through appeals to the truth; the modern, Western version of the art of government being, as Foucault once put it, oriented to "government in the name of truth" (Gordon 1991: 8). What, briefly, are the characteristics of this modern governmentalization of truth?

On the one hand, government and the shaping of conduct became predicated on something like a true science of the terrain that is to be governed. To govern, one had to *know*. Modern and early-modern – liberal, neo-liberal, welfarist – techniques of government sought to be dependent on a knowledge of the characteristics of populations (Foucault 1991a). Crudely speaking, this kind of will to know can be contrasted with pre-modern characteristics of government. Whereas Machiavelli had sought to advise the Prince how to retain control of a territory, modern government – especially that pertaining to a broadly liberal or democratic form – presupposed a knowledge of the regularities and circumstances of population: its vital capacities, opinions, political propensities and so forth. Government, in that sense, sought to be *in the true*. Perhaps the first form of "governmentality", in this sense, in the modern West can be associated with the German science of *polizeiwissenschaft*. The point about "police" was that it entailed a secular form of government, embracing the entirety of the state understood as a population (Kneymeyer 1980). By the early nineteenth century, this notion of population had itself undergone transformation towards a broadly *liberal* understanding of population. Foucault documented the transition in some countries from a model of government based on sovereignty and the family to that based on the immanent regularities of population, consisting of "a range of intrinsic, aggregate effects, phenomena that are irreducible to those of the family, such as epidemics, endemic levels of mortality, ascending spirals of labour and wealth" and so forth (Foucault 1991a: 99). Put schematically: to govern in a "liberal" way – and in the hightly restricted sense we need to give to the notion of liberalism here, which is not the sense that is usual in political philosophy – one had to subject the terrain over which one governed to apparatuses of truth, and the knowledge that this supplied would likewise supply the ends of government – the security, welfare and tranquillity of population.

In talking of these kinds of transformation, we are not talking about change at the level of societies as such. To talk of modern arts of government is not the same as talking, in epochal terms, about the characteristics of whole societies. The *mentality* in "governmentality" is important. What is at stake are quite restricted rationalities or mentalities for the governing of conduct, not the structural principles of whole societies; there is a difference between, on the one hand, talking about the transformation from a form of governmentality based on reason of State to one based on something like "liberalism" and, on the other, talking about a transition from a police State to a liberal society. It is equally important to note that this conception of governmentality takes us a world away from epochal pictures of modernity that are centred on ideas about a more or less malign surveillance or social control of the population – for instance, as depicted in Bauman's rather claustrophobic presentations of modern "gardening" rationality (that form of regulation which orders, classifies and controls rather than leaving be), an epitome of what can be called iron-cage theories of modernity (Bauman 1987). On the contrary, at least in those countries which aspired to a liberal art of governing in Foucault's specific sense and where political economy was the central science of government, security entailed not a vigorous, interventionist principle of social control but something more like a concern to affirm "the necessarily opaque, dense autonomous character of the processes of population" combined with a preoccupation with "the vulnerability of these same processes, with the need to enframe them in 'mechanisms of security'" (Gordon 1991: 20; cf. Hacking 1990).

On the other hand, this requirement of the truth for good government possessed a further aspect in the classic liberal presentation of freedom of opinion. Here truth was not just a means of government but an aspect – even, for some, a measure – of good, enlightened government. It was not just that there had to be a knowledge of the processes of population but that such processes worked best when most linked up with "freedom"; and, correlatively, that only through freedom could their truth be manifested. In other words, truth became a function, in effect, of enlightenment. This idea is central, to take just one classic case, in Mill's *On Liberty* where freedom of opinion is explicitly posited as the precondition for the manifestation of truth, which in turn is a precondition for good government. This is a kind of equilibrium theory of truth; tranquillity is possible only on the basis of a free run of the truth:

> Truth, in the great practical concerns of life, is so much a question of the re-conciling and combining of opposites, that very few have minds sufficiently capacious and impartial to make the adjustment with an approach to correctness, and it has to be made by the rough process of a struggle betwen combatants fighting under hostile banners. (Mill 1992: 47)

Government here was not, to be sure, opposed to a public sphere which would somehow be a countervailing power to government; rather the existence of a public sphere was itself regarded as a healthy aspect of good government. Now, no one in their right mind would read off the sociological reality of modernity from texts such as *On Liberty*; but such evidence does point at least towards some of the underlying aspirations of what good government might be. What Mill exemplifies is a position which takes the link between government and the pursuit of the truth as being something like an imperative consideration of modern, broadly "liberal" Western societies.

So the advent of a certain government in the name of truth is not meant to account for the surface symptoms of some underlying sociological principle. In a sense, all societies are societies of truth in that the role of knowledge and thought will play a part in their organization. But saying that modern Western societies are oriented in particular ways to the question of truth is not to say that these societies are definitively enlightened or that they have discovered *the* road to the truth, nor – as with epochal categories such as the risk society, the information society, postmodern society and so on – that the guiding principles of such societies are *reducible* to the question of truth. It is to say, rather, that these societies have turned the concern for truth above all into a quizzical, even sceptical, concern; that such societies are animated, among a great many other things, by a veritable "politics" of truth. According to the logic of such a politics, truth is up for grabs *as a question*; in fact, we might say that what determines the concern for truth in our societies is that we do not know what that concern involves. This commitment to the truth is itself what leads to uncertainty as to the nature of truth; it may even be that our commitment to truth leads to a certain tendency to anti-foundationalism with regard to it. That may just be the consequence of the notion of truth-as-authority which is at the basis of the very meaning of enlightenment. The modern concern for truth has such a problematizing character as an internal aspect.

Truth and anti-foundationalism

Let me consider the ethics of this situation a little further. Perhaps recognition of this intrinsically problematic status of truth has only been possible on the basis of a particular transformation that has occurred in our *current* relations to the truth. We are frequently told today that knowledge has gone local, anti-foundational, context-dependent, relative. Many different strands of argument are involved here. In part, as in the work of anthropologically minded scholars such as Clifford Geertz or Bruno Latour, this anti-foundational turn is a question of opening up some previously closed black boxes or master-concepts that had hindered the ethnographic investigation of thought (Geertz 1983; Latour 1987). There are other quite familiar forces at work too; the political aspiration to subvert science on the part of Paul Feyerabend, discontent with the philosophical tradition on the part of Jacques Derrida and so on. Anti-foundationalism is not, however, a single doctrine but may be animated by all sorts of things, none of which necessarily add up, as many opponents of these ideas seem to think, into a single idiom of irresponsibility, infantilism or infamy. Yet the emphasis on truth that animates a critical attitude to enlightenment is intended just as much to hold us aloof from these exciting, anti-foundationalist notions as it is from pseudo-Weberian iron-cage theories of modernity according to which Western experience is but a tale told of rationalization signifying only domination. The critique of enlightenment does not necessarily speak in the name of a facile plurality of truths any more than it speaks of the end of truth altogether (cf. Malpas 1996: 161). No doubt it is better to hold as a picture of what has occurred not the advent of a new kind of society – postmodernity or whatever – but only a shift in the concerns of the politics of truth. In this context, it would not be the existence of such a politics that is new, only the shape that such a politics has begun to take. We are not at the end of the truth today, but only at the intersection of a series of changing ways of relating to the truth.

If truth has not disappeared, may be it is the case that we have seen the emergence of new pictures of what the truth might be said to be. Now, this is seen by some as being a very dangerous situation. It seems to open out the floodgates to an "anything-goes" epistemology, where all chances of responsibility are lost. Perhaps there are indeed dangers of this and it has to be acknowledged that those who bemoan the loss of responsibility in matters of truth do see themselves as carrying out their duty to the truth; they are fully as involved in our modern concern for truth as are their opponents. But the response need not be to dig deeper into one's bunker and claim some kind of special relation to truth. Such a fideist attitude to the truth will not really do. For example – to take one quite influential voice – the critic Christopher Norris demands, in effect, that the real is the rational is the true and berates anybody else who will not submit to this ideal (Norris 1996; cf. Barry 1993). I think this is really a very unenlightened model of truth: one which mirrors quite well the frivolity of some of the postmodern and irrationalistically anti-foundational attitudes that Norris seeks to condemn. Norris finds himself in the strange position – for someone who would like to be designated a friend of reason – of advocating what looks alarmingly like a blind *faith* in the truth, and his critique is less a reasoned exposé than a sort of epistemological *fatwa* on all those who will not submit.

Such intolerance should not, surely, be characteristic of the critique of enlightenment, or of attitudes to enlightenment at all. Professional anti-postmodernists like Norris resemble those persons described by Mill who "make Truth just one superstition the more" (Mill 1992: 35). For Norris, truth really does seem to be out there in the world, even though he is reluctant to say exactly what it is. But, still, I think that the problem is not really with this realism itself, but with the moralism that lies behind this position. Norris' outlook needs to be contrasted with those philosophical realists such as John Searle who give a *content* to their faith in the truth; in this case, in an account of the structuring of social reality, by basing all truth on a fundamental ontology derived from the specifics of evolutionary biology and the atomic theory of matter (Searle 1995: 5–7). Searle here, by giving us his account of what his fundamental ontology actually amounts to in terms of its content, is acting in good faith precisely by not engaging in a form of fideism. Searle is either right or wrong; and what he says is empirically up for grabs. On the other hand, I think we need to be wary of people like Norris – and there are many. They assert the sanctity of the truth as a faith without trying to convince us of the content of any particular truth, other than – seemingly – truths which simply have a moral content. For critics like Norris it is all just a matter of the treason of the clercs, and the villains are damned out of hand. He is like Julian Benda, that arch scourge of the treachery of intellectuals, arguing for the "Platonic-universalist metaphysics of binding, eternal values" but on grounds not of actual knowledge but of expediency: that is, in terms not of truth or falsity but of the regrettable effects that so-called irrationalists get into when they question the truth (Gellner 1990: 21; cf. Gellner 1992a: 129–32). As Gellner insists in his nice discussion of the ethics of this matter, we can act in good faith, as with Nietzsche, even in attempting to get rid of the truth, and in bad faith – as with many of the anti-postmodernists – by protesting too much in the name of the truth. As Gellner puts it: "The strident denunciation of the treason of the clerics, which pretends that our situation is far clearer and unambiguous than it in fact is, is itself a form of the betrayal of the truth" (Gellner 1990: 26). In other words, truth is difficult. Truth requires care as well as work. Now, what form would be taken by such a notion of care when applied in the context of a critical attitude to enlightenment?

At the beginning of this chapter I said that we would have to investigate the particular meaning that needed to be given to the idea of a critical attitude to enlightenment. What, above all, is "critical" about such a notion? That is what I now proceed to do in what remains of this first chapter. I say that the kind of enlightenment that a critical analytics of enlightenment would itself aim at – even one that took a fully "negative" form – would be utopian in an "anthropological" sense and, also in a certain sense, "ascetic" and strategic.

Utopianism

If I say that the attitude of a critique of enlightenment is properly the concern of social theory, then this is not only because that discipline has quite often been specifically animated by the problem of enlightenment but also because it shares, even tends to dramatize, a peculiar characteristic that can be associated with all the social sciences, and especially sociology (see further, the Conclusion below). It is a very common experience in teaching such disciplines that students undergo learning in terms of a sort of "experience". No doubt it would be unfair to say of properly "scientific" disciplines like physics or chemistry that, in pedagogic terms, they entail simply a transfer of knowledge. But the point is that sociology is never *just* about such a kind of transfer. It is an inherently experiential discipline; which is to say, it is involved in producing an experience or set of affects for those who study it. Typically this experiential effect consists in a denaturalization of a person's experience. Sociology exists to provoke in us the possibility of our contingency or, at least, our changeability; to cause us to ask of ourselves the extent to which things might not have been as they have been. In doing so, it can use the procedures of science, or something like that, but in so far as it invokes a particular kind of experience of contingency, then it is itself more an ethical than a scientific discipline.

For many people – critical or radical sociologists, for example – contingency would hardly be the issue. They would say that the function of social theory or empirical sociology is with *critique* which would mean the criticism of an existing form of society in the name of another kind of society, for instance one of a socialist kind. Indeed, one can imagine it being said by some that any cognitive scepticism concerning the object of analysis analysed by works of social theory betrays the original grounds of the discipline which was tied to the idea of the creation of a "social" or *socialist* society. But in fact even such an aspiration is an ethical rather than a strictly "scientific" one; and this ethical character is by no means necessarily to the discredit of empirical sociology. As well as being ethical in orientation, such sociology is likewise utopian. Again, this is not meant to denigrate critical sociology. Zygmunt Bauman once described socialism in terms of what he called an "active Utopia" (Bauman 1976). Far from being something that existed out of time and beyond possibility, utopia, for Bauman, is a way of gaining a certain leverage upon present-day actuality. Utopianism, he says, is like technical invention; both abandon the vehicle of current experience in the name of another experience (ibid: 12; cf. Velody 1981: 134). In so far as the fates of critical sociology and socialism seem to be more or less bound up with each other, we might say that the socialist society functions as a kind of active utopia for sociology. Critical sociology would then be a critique of the present in the name of the good society. It would be more a question of ethics than some of its practitoners might like to think.

But, still, I say that a critical attitude to enlightenment takes this sort of attitude to an extreme; it radicalizes, and makes something of a spectacle of, a pedagogic – or rather, dialogic – principle that is basic to all the critical social sciences. That too might be squared with a kind of active counter-factual utopianism of its own. But, as I outlined in the Introduction, a critique of enlightenment would be utopian, rather, from an *anthropological* point of view; that is to say, reflecting on the current state of our nature rather than our society; a discipline of human nature and human capacities rather than a positive science of society.

This is to use the term "anthropology" in its now largely discredited sense. The old discipline of "philosophical anthropology" analysed the limits of the plasticity of "man"; it was a discipline concerned with, so to speak, the nature of human nature (Honneth & Joas 1988). There are grounds for attempting to reimagine a more enlightened version of that discipline. Immanuel Kant labelled his philosophical kind of anthropology an anthropology from a "pragmatic point of view". This pragmatic conception was to be distinguished from anthropology of a physiological sort which was concerned with "what Nature makes of man". Pragmatic anthropology, on the other hand, would be concerned with "what man makes, can, or should make of himself as a freely acting being" (Kant 1978: 3). Perhaps we should not be taking too many liberties were we to gloss pragmatic anthropology in more general terms as that branch of anthropology concerned with "enlightened man". That may not be quite right from Kant's own point of view. For him, freedom, as Charles Taylor has written, was "a property of, and hence a demand on, all men, indeed on all rational agents, whether human or not. And his conception is linked to a metaphysical theory of what man is"

(Taylor 1985b: 326). In that sense, Kant's anthropology may be pragmatic but it is also philosophical, metaphysical, theoretical. But if we start from a position that has it that we do not actually know what "man" is; that one of the features of human nature, indeed of human freedom, is that we cannot know what "man" is, then this might be a pragmatic anthropology but it might also be, if in a peculiar way, an anthropology tied to an active utopia. This active utopia would consist of a dream of freedom that would have it that human nature has an infinite capacity to invent new forms of freedom for itself; a utopia of our capacities rather than of our society – in short, an ethical rather than a sociological picture of utopia.

Asceticism and strategy

The sociological tradition itself *might* be drawn on here, though not in its critical realist or positive guises, but only in the sense that one interpretation might have it that the sociological tradition – and especially the distinct tradition of social theory – might already be seen as being centred on human capacities – as being anthropological and ethical – in this way. Take, for instance, the example of Max Weber.

Probably the most famous work in what today goes by the name of "classical" social theory is Weber's *The Protestant Ethic and the Spirit of Capitalism* (Weber 1992b). Weber was much more a social theorist than he was an empirical sociologist, even if he was that too. For Weber's work is best seen not in terms of a science of society, but rather in terms of a science of culture (Turner 1992; Chapter 5). The *Protestant Ethic* proposes that ascetic Protestantism was the main prototype of the spirit of capitalism. It is less an argument, in fact, about the causes of capitalism than about modern orientations to the everyday world of actuality, to one's vocation in life, and its concerns are more with cultural rationality than with social organization. Hence the concern with asceticism indicated in the title. This is usually interpreted to mean asceticism in the Christian sense, that is, the renunciation of pleasure, and that is indeed part of Weber's intention; but a wider aspect of it is the concern with *askesis* in rather a more general sense. The Christian perception of asceticism – as something negative and world-denying – is, we might say, limited and local. Glossed by the French intellectual historian, Pierre Hadot, the Christian view of asceticism is of abstinence, but in ancient philosophy it corresponded to something like "spiritual exercises"; "inner activities of the thought and will" (cf. Foucault 1986: 9, 27; Hadot 1995: 128). *Askesis* in this rather wider sense means not the interdictions that we place upon oneself but the work that one does to turn oneself into an ethical subject capable of shaping one's own nature.

Weber's interest was no doubt with both asceticism and *askesis* in this wide sense. For him, cultural critique had to mirror what was given to us by necessity in the world: ascetic, vocational culture. To that extent, Weber was a realist, the practitioner of what he called a "science of reality". One had to work with the territory that one was given, and face up to the fact with clarity and dignity. For Weber, this means that social science is itself a form of asceticism, perhaps even in the sense fully of self-denial: "We shall set to work and meet the 'demands of the day', in human relations as well as in our vocation" (Weber 1991a: 156). For Weber, there is no going back to the pre-modern era of enchantment, and Weber's work is certainly nothing like an attempt to reverse the effects of the disenchantment of the world. Rather, the only honest way to live, for him, was to submit to one's *daemon*; in the context of "Science as a Vocation", to commit oneself to the arid terrain of science with full conviction and without illusions. But cultural science, as Weber thought of it, was also ascetic in the wider sense – the sense, that is, of *askesis*. Weber's goal was not merely to induce a sense of despair or self-denial but also to transform the relations we have with our understanding of ourselves; it was itself a kind of ascetic work on the truth of ourselves and an attempt to find the conditions for breaking free from the current truths that hold us back. That, no doubt, is why, in "Science as a Vocation", Weber talks in such passionate terms about clarity. To have clarity is to be able to act without illusions. Clarity does not just concern the relation of means to ends, but the meaning of our convictions themselves: "Thus, if we are competent in our pursuit ... we can force the individual, or at least we can help him, to give himself an *account of the ultimate meaning of his own conduct*" (ibid: 152; Chapter 5, below). This means that we have to comprehend this critical style fully as much in terms of an ethical as a positive or conventionally "scientific" form of intellectual intervention.

Let me sketch this critical idea of *askesis* and its relevance to the idea of a critical atittude to enlightenment through further reference to Hadot's work on ancient ethics and philosophy. Hadot draws out a number of features common to spiritual exercises in the Ancient world. He insists, for instance, that philosophy was not initially conceived as a theoretical discourse but as a way of working on the will through the exercise of thought. Only from the seventeenth century did philosophy take on the mantle of an authoritative theoretical discourse, developing the premise that truth was the result of "a process of elaboration, carried out by a reason grounded in itself" (Hadot 1995: 76). Hadot also insists that the exercise that animated the vocation of philosophy was "spiritual" in that it involved the transformation of the individual on to a new course of life (indeed, in effect, a form of conversion), yet also essentially *calmative* in effect, being in that sense a sort of "therapeutic of the passions" (ibid: 83, 138, 275). Taking Stoic thought as his paradigm, Hadot argues that the task of philosophy was to develop exercises that would enable subjects to become reconciled with the natural limits of their freedom, and to connect themselves up with the "cosmological" dimensions of existence (ibid: 275, 285). Finally, Hadot hints that in the contemporary period, philosophy may be in the process of rediscovering some of its roots in the form of spiritual exercises; and he is clearly thinking, above all, of Wittgenstein's therapeutic philosophy, that is to say a philosophy concerned with "assembling reminders" for particular purposes rather than with building metaphysical theories (ibid: 280, 285; cf. Wittgenstein 1994: 267).

What is useful about Hadot's discussion for the purposes of my own concerns here is that, while eschewing irrationalism, it actually provides us with a view of a style of critical thought that is at some remove from what we conventionally think of as rational philosophy. In spite of the fact that Hadot's is really a project directed at philosophy itself, it may be useful as much for the extent to which it frees us from philosophy as with the extent to which it enjoins us to return to a different kind of philosophy. What counts here is Hadot's vision of a thought that is primarily pedagogic rather than theoretical, transformative rather than representational, and ethical rather than ideological. In short, it offers up a view of thought precisely as a kind of ethical *askesis*. But Hadot's description may also serve in a negative way: that is, to put a certain distance between the kinds of philosophy that interest him and the broad picture that I am trying to outline of a critical attitude to enlightenment that might be of some use to social theory.

Hadot likes the term "spiritual exercise" because it has connotations of totality; both in the sense that it entails a work on the subject's "entire psychism" and in that the object of the exercise is to transcend subjectivity, to replace oneself, as Hadot puts it, "in the perspective of the Whole" (Hadot 1995: 82). But an enlightening asceticism need not have quite such exalted pretensions as this. It need not be about effecting a kind of total experience of "conversion" in the subject; one can work on oneself in a piecemeal fashion without expecting a uniformally directional transformation, nor need one necessarily connect up ascesis to "cosmological" pretensions even if, as Hadot insists, this was indeed the perspective of thinkers such as the Stoics (ibid: 207). *Askesis* can be open-ended and pragmatic; seeking, so to speak, effects that are also affects, without determining in advance of what order these will necessarily be. That, anyway, is how we might envisage the style of critique proper to a critical attitude to enlightenment.

This brings us to consideration of another concern that was central to the kinds of spiritual exercise described by Hadot and which might be pertinent to us. For Hadot, such exercises were designed, above all, to calm the passions, to reconcile oneself with the world. Hadot emphasizes a high level of continuity pertaining on this issue between the traditions of Antique philosophy and early Christian traditions:

Apatheia plays an essential role, not only in theoretical constructions such as Evagrian metaphysics, but also in monastic spirituality. There, its value is closely linked to that of peace of mind and absence of worry; *amerimnia* or *tranquillitas*. Dorotheus of Gaza does not hesitate to declare that peace of mind is so important that one must, if necessary, drop what one has undertaken if one's peace of mind is endangered. Peace of mind – *tranquillitas animi* – had, moreover, always been a central value within the philosophical tradition. (Hadot 1995: 138)

Our critical attitude to enlightenment might actually aspire to have the *opposite* effect as this; not, so to speak, to calm us down, to reconcile us with things as they are but to make things rather difficult, to open us up to the possibility of transformation, to unsettle us (cf. Burchell 1993). This effect might seem more disabling than enabling but that too is a positive thing in terms of *affect*; and such difficulties would certainly figure among the pedagogic aims of such a form of criticism – to make it more difficult to think, to subvert the easy ways of thought that come to us as if by nature alone; in short, to make us better capable of judgement.

This is not quite the same thing as saying that what is required in criticism are "anaesthetic" effects: that is, the effect of deliberate disablement that leads to the working out of problems on the ground (Foucault 1991b: 84). I think that it might be preferable to think more in terms of inducing *countervailing powers* in persons. Indeed, that is the whole point of ascetic exercises:

And since habit is a powerful influence, when we are accustomed ourselves to employ desire and aversion only upon those externals, we must get a contrary habit to counteract this habit, and where the very slippery nature of sense-impressions is in play, there we must set our training as a countervailing force ... I am inclined to pleasure: I will betake myself to the opposite side of the rolling ship, and that beyond measure, in order to train myself. I am inclined to avoid hard work: I will strain and exercise my sense-impressions to this end, so that my aversion for everything of this kind shall cease. (Epictetus 1928: 83)

The point about countervailing powers is that they are *strategic*. One does not just criticize anything and everything but only those kinds of problematic that *require* the exercise of countervailing powers. In short, we direct our attentions precisely at those cultural forms that are given to us *as if* they came direct from nature or necessity (cf. Burchell 1993).

In sum, the critical attitude to the question of enlightenment that I am sketching here might not have aspirations of a universal science but only as a very particular form of strategic or ethical discourse. Other forms of criticism carry on just as before; they do not necessarily require the sneering disestablishment that postmodernists demand. The aim, as I see it, is not to succumb to the hubris of attempting to found some universal – or even indispensable – model or "theory" of critique but to direct ourselves only to particular kinds of enterprise: those that seem most desirable, most self-evident, most clearly an aspect of what it means to be enlightened yet which simultaneously throw up ambiguities and difficulties with regard to the very idea of such a thing as enlightenment; those aspects of enlightenment that are, in other words, most *provocative* precisely of the kind of restricted, slightly eccentric, critical attitude to enlightenment that I have been sketching out. And if *science* is such an important example of just such an aspect of enlightenment, it is because it is so often regarded, implicitly or not, as the "central case" or model of enlightenment itself; thus to engage with the issue of the "scientificity" of science is to put ourselves straightaway into the midst of the very question of enlightenment.

Chapter 2

Aspects of scientific enlightenment

Science and anti-science – Science and society – Enlightenment and social science – Scientific enlightenment – Laboratory sciences – Fallibilism and historicity – A disclaimer – Latourian anti-foundationalism – Science and ethics – Anti-simplicism – Ways of escape

Ours appears to be both a scientific and an anti-scientific age. We are surrounded by evidence of what the sociologist Bruno Latour calls "science already made" – cars, space rockets, televisions, central heating, computers, light bulbs, cancer treatments and all the expert and technological paraphernalia of the modern world. But does this mean that ours is an age that is actually "enlightened" by the natural sciences? Many people would say not. Scientists themselves apply for grants to further "public understanding" of their activities, young people blow up laboratories in protest at animal experiments, sociologists write tracts about the limits of science and the waning of the public's faith in scientists, and the majority of the US population appear to believe that they have been abducted by flying saucers. The social sciences, in particular, have tended to take a rather vexed view of science. The trends towards relativism, anti-foundationalism and postmodernism that have characterized the social study of science in the past few decades appear to make of natural science either just another language game, or an enterprise that is more or less fraudulent in its exaggerated claims for itself. From such a perspective, the very idea of scientific enlightenment can come itself to seem a fraud, and to make little sense.

I think, however, that it would be a mistake for social theory and the social sciences to leave things this way. We all walk around with pictures of science in our heads. The question of the status of science – of what is "scientific" about this thing we agree to call in our everyday grammar, even if we are cynics, by the name of science – will not go away as easily as those who want to dismantle the unities of the scientific enterprise would appear to think. In this chapter I defend the idea of scientific enlightenment – or, at least, I defend the idea of such an idea. To do so requires, however, more or less exclusive attention not to "science already made" but to the idea of what Latour calls "science in the making", to what it takes to produce this strange thing known as science. On this view, that the motley jumble of activities that we call science is less an institution or a finite, definable set of activities – or still less the outcome of a rationalist methodology – than, if it is anything coherent at all, a particular stylized orientation to an ethics of truth. In arguing that there is an ethics of truth that we can associate with the natural sciences, I find what might seem to be an unlikely ally in Bruno Latour himself and those other relativist analysts of science who have investigated science in the making. In particular, I argue that their anti-foundationalism leads in the opposite direction from the anti-scientific prejudice that has so often dogged the social sciences. In this chapter I shall discuss the work of Latour, and – prior to that – of some of his French predecessors (and antagonists) – Gaston Bachelard and Georges Canguilhem – in a certain amount of detail.

In using this work, I do not come up with anything so exciting as a general theory of science, but only seek to indicate that our enlightenment about science does not consist in preaching the eternal merits of science nor in a critique of the instrumentalist character of scientific reason but, on the contrary, in a constant attention to the kinds of truth that science makes available. Scientific enlightenment, on this view, would consist from the outset in a *critique* of itself; hence there is an irony at the heart of the argument of this chapter which is that the social sciences understand science best and are at their most sympathetic to science when they are least afraid to take nothing for granted with regard to it. Finally, at the end of the proceedings of this chapter, I make some general comments about the "ethical" implications of this view of science.

Science and anti-science

But I begin with some models of the connection between science and enlightenment. My comments are aimed at an important preliminary task: at detaching us from the temptation of rationalist understandings of scientific enlightenment, all of which have a tendency to lead, I think, to an anti-science perspective on the part of the social sciences.

We can usefully begin by considering some of the aspects of *the* Enlightenment itself. This was not so much an age *of* natural science as an age characterized by admiration for the achievements of natural science, or to reduce these to a name – Isaac Newton. What was at stake here was the question of natural science as a model for enlightenment more generally. So for the Marquis de Condorcet, the very ideal of enlightenment was subservient to the paradigm of the natural sciences, and at each step, as he put it, such sciences held out to enlightened men the model to be followed (Baker 1975: 85). But what model of science is the appropriate one here? There are two rather different ways to think about this. First, there is what could be called the extensive model, or *science as enlightenment*; here the paradigm of all enlightenment is based on the model of the natural sciences. Newton, *esprit géometrique*, rational method; these might be the shibboleths of this sort of enlightenment. Certainly Jean d'Alembert and Condorcet himself were representatives of a scientific spirit of the Enlightenment, centred on theoretical physics, and among the proponents of which we might include the names of Clairaut, Maupertius, Borelli and Lagrange. What is interesting about such thinkers, however, is the extent to which they were actually in a minority in pressing for the merits of a rationalist, deductive model of science that was, in some ways, opposed to the more experimental spirit of Newton's own work (Gay 1966: 127; Hankins 1970). For the most part, Enlightenment thinkers eschewed what Hankins calls the model of a "rather arrogant rationalism" in favour of a more open spirit of humanism. In any case, the *Encyclopédie* was hardly overwhelmingly devoted to the promotion of natural science, and notable paragons of enlightenment – Jean-Jacques Rousseau, Voltaire – preferred to emphasize the spirit of humanism and *philosophie* rather than the values of natural science. Perhaps, then, Condorcet's faith in science put him in a minority.

But, equally, may be not. For there is a different – one might say, more intensive – way to link the model of science to that of enlightenment; that is, according to the model of what may just be called *scientific enlightenment*. Here science is regarded as an *aspect* of enlightenment rather than its exclusive model; to emphasize not that all enlightenment takes a scientific form but that there are enlightening lessons to be learned from the specific example of science; which, in turn, means getting straight what such a model might be. Evidence that this model might not best be cast on rationalist lines might come, surprisingly enough, from consideration of the influential figure of Condorcet himself. For Condorcet, it seems, enlightenment consisted not so much in the hegemony of science but in the establishment of something like the proper *ethos* of science. Instead of the "spirit of system", science embodied a "systematic spirit". This meant not a universal rationalization of everything but rather an epistemological *modesty* of approach – observing, calculating, remaining sensitive to the necessary limits of human knowledge – for "man succeeds best in discovering truths of nature when he first recognizes the limits of his own knowledge" (Baker 1975: 90). According to such a model, science was distinctive for being descriptive rather than systematic, a potent human instrument, relative perhaps to man, but not a universal calculus for plumbing the "Ocean of Being". Above all, science was an emblem of a particular model of progress; not a rationalist model wherein progress consisted simply of applying the findings of science on the basis of a kind of *coup d'état*, but a humanistic model according to which slow and partial progress came as evidence of the otherwise opaque and limited successes of science – where science was progressive in so far as it embodied a spirit of humility (ibid: 93–4). Such was the model of enlightenment that might be discovered as inherent to the actual logic of scientific rationality itself; it was the very *modesty* of the natural sciences, their limited nature, that, as Condorcet maintained in his *Esquisse d'un tableau historique des progrès de l'esprit humain*, marked them out as the model to be followed (ibid: 94, 189).

I think this puts a different perspective on the commonly held view, especially within an older tradition of critical theory, that the hubris of enlightenment is somehow consequent on the hubris of science. Perhaps, on the contrary, the essence of the model of natural science might be that it should act as a brake on the hubris of enlightenment; and by distancing themselves from a rationalist model of science, the social sciences, so it could be argued, might be able to avoid some of the tempting but disabling perspectives consequent on considering science according to the paradigm of what often amounts to just the prejudice of *anti-science*.

The quite prevalent anti-enlightenment perspective on science derives from a simple source; the idea that science has disseminated beyond its legitimate confines and has resulted, in Weber's terms, in the "conquest of life by science" (Schroeder 1995). Those sociologists and others who have taken an epochal attitude to their times have been particularly taken with such an idea. For some thinkers, the fact of a "scientific civilization" is a cause for celebration; for many, including most in the humanities, it is generative of something like alarm. Western modernity comes to be seen in terms of scientific organization and rational bureaucracy; the dream that human societies can be organized according to scientific principles. To hold such a view is to hold that a rational model of science has been translated, no doubt through the mediation of the social sciences, into the world of human relations. There are two different components to this perspective: one is a particular view of the dominance of science over society (that is, science as *modernity*), the other, an anti-enlightenment reading of the social sciences themselves.

Science and society

It is actually quite difficult to assess the status of science from an orthodox sociological point of view, especially one committed to an epochal perspective. Certainly it is much more difficult than people tend to think. Orthodox sociologists – as opposed to some of their more iconoclastic successors in the sociology of knowledge, who shall be considered later – have taken an interest in science because it has seemed to them that there just happens to be an awful lot of science around. Such perspectives often take the view that science is determinant of the character of modernity itself; that the nature of modern societies can be read off from the nature of science. But I want to say that such views are romantic in that they inevitably tend to overdramatize the effects of science, and likewise often tend towards the prejudice of anti-science.

Does science colonize society? In fact, understood in such senses, science would have to be seen as a very recent development and we would have to date our "modernity" somewhere around the postwar boom. "Big science", says Derek de Solla Price, writing in the early 1960s, is a very recent phenomenon, perhaps with some 90 per cent of all the scientists that have ever lived currently still alive; and scientific publications growing as never before, at an exponential rate (Price 1963). But, even then, is science really all that significant from an orthodox sociological point of view? When we look at the evidence, it can seem that the "spread" of scientific activities is not all that great. In 1989 the OECD reported that there were around 1.66 million researchers in R&D working in OECD countries, amounting to some 0.5 per cent of total employment – which hardly seems like an overwhelming preponderance of scientists and technical experts; with R&D accounting for only an average of some 2.3 per cent of GDP in these countries (OECD 1989: 9). On the other hand, we might argue that what counts are, above all, certain particular spheres of scientific *impact*; say, on industry, on health care technologies and on warfare and defence (cf. Latour 1987: 162–73). But even such an approach will not, arguably, tell us all that much. For, again, developments in these spheres came fairly late in the day. The scientization of industrial processes occurred, still in a fairly limited way, in the latter part of the nineteenth century: Thomas Edison opened the world's first industrial laboratory in 1876. Even then, these developments were more or less confined to countries where there was a large-scale concentration of industry, notably Germany and the USA after 1880. By 1927, there were around 1000 industrial research laboratories in the USA, which is a little or a lot depending on your point of view (Inkster 1991: 113). And the scientization of warfare and health are different stories again, with plots that develop even later; in health, only on a large scale with the development of socialized forms of medical service, and in war, only in the latter half of the twentieth century.

In short, science may be sociologically important, but such importance post-dates the onset of the age of enlightenment by quite some way. We shall not get much insight into the character of scientific enlightenment from epochal kinds of sociology. But since we all know that science *is* significant, not least as a model of knowledge, we need to think in terms that are less akin to the aspirations of such orthodox, epochalist sciences of society. This involves taking a certain amount of care when it comes to ascribing the impact of such apparently independent variables as "science" on such apparently dependent variables such as "society". To be realist about scientific enlightenment is not automatically to adopt a sociologically realist theory of a scientific modernity. What counts may not be so much the empirical "reach" of science in modernity (however we are to define that), but the whole question of the status of science as a form of enlightenment. This would mean that the object of a critique of enlightenment in the context of natural science should not necessarily be the actual behaviour of scientists or the real, institutional dimensions of science but something more akin to the *spirit* of science. Being realist about this spirit – which long predates the narrower, sociological significance of science as such – is not the same thing as being sociologically realist about science.

Enlightenment and social science

As for the social sciences, I have already referred to Zygmunt Bauman's thesis that Western modernity is characterized by a "power/knowledge" syndrome or a disciplinary power that has spread its tentacles throughout the social body and the State. On this kind of perspective, science would be synonymous with rational calculation, and transferring the spirit of natural science to the social sciences entails translating that spirit of calculation from the one to the others, such that the social sciences effectively become just so many branches of a more overarching managerial or administrative regime. No doubt there is a *rationalist* model of enlightenment that needs to be rejected which would hold that we can solve problems of human conduct with administration and expertise. Forms of political rationalism which would reduce politics to administration have long been the target of (mostly conservative) forms of critique. But, more often than not, such critiques misrecognize their object. Above all, they make too easy a link between forms of knowledge and forms of administration, assuming that forms of administrative rationalism require a source within the sphere of "pure knowledge" itself. In fact, the relation is probably better seen in terms of the effects of administrative rationality on the social sciences rather than *vice versa*. But even then such effects are never total. The model of a singular, monolithic administrative rationality dominating society is rather a lazy myth, one designed to shortcut the tiresome difficulties entailed in substantive criticism. I think that to hold to such a model is to hold to a particular image of enlightenment in the social sciences, one which holds enlightenment to consist in the obligations of progress imposed by the practical applications of such sciences themselves. This model of enlightenment has only ever existed as ideology. There are, no doubt, elements of it in Comte, Saint-Simon and if not Marx then perhaps certain kinds of Marxism, but these really represent *romantic* visions of social science. Such romantic visions inevitably tend to invoke the reaction of an equally romantic form of *anti-science* which would hold that all the endeavours of the social sciences are redundant or conspiratorial. Scientific enlightenment should consist not least in escaping the blackmail of this dichotomy.

As Baker shows in his marvellous study of Condorcet's work, there was another enlightenment notion of social science which was really quite different from the later romantic model. This was a model based not on hubris but, as with natural science, on epistemological *modesty*. Natural science was relevant to social science because it was relative to the concerns and interests of man;

it was locally utilitarian, experiential, deliberately restricted. That was no doubt the original meaning of the idea that the proper study for man *is* man; not that all science should manipulate man, but that all knowledge is already always humanistic: that is, related to human ends. This gave a certain legitimacy to the uncertain projects of the social sciences, and brought them into a certain limited continuity with the natural sciences. What united all sciences was not a rationalist model but a Humean, probabilistic one, based on the calculus of belief (Baker 1975: 190–1). A certain logic of perfectability could be perceived here; as Baker says, "without the instinctive habit of probable belief, civil society would not continue; and only with its rationalization in a mathematical science of conduct can civil society be perfected" (ibid: 191). But this is less conducive to a logic of human engineering – Bauman or Gellner's "gardening" mentality – than might initially appear to be the case; not so much because such mathematization was to prove to be an idle dream, but because the project was tempered with the recognition that the corollary of a science based on the probability of beliefs must be a respect for such beliefs and for the reality and hence the integrity of public opinion. Science could not therefore just act like a juggernaut of rationalism. That would be against the very interests and logic of science. Naturally, we may see here a certain degree of tension between an élitism that is intrinsic to scientific activity and expertise, and democratic liberalism, as Baker has it. But such tension is something that we have to live with and accommodate as an aspect of an enlightened *ethos* rather than to overcome on one side or the other. Enlightenment, even scientific enlightenment, is quite a difficult, worldly business.

Scientific enlightenment

So if, as these remarks certainly suggest, it is misleading to take a rationalist view of scientific enlightenment, what view should be taken? I suggest that a critique of enlightenment undertaken in the context of natural science would neither seek to legislate *for* a particular kind of natural science, nor undertake a critique of science in the name of anti-scientific prejudice. It would rather investigate the extent to which natural science is itself a question of an ethos, and the extent to which this ethical character is significant for questions of enlightenment more generally.

Here I am obviously using the term ethics in quite a particular sense; not really in any technical way but simply to invoke the fact that science is the product not simply of a rational response to the natural world but of certain kinds of human commitment. I think that two aspects of the ethos of this spirit can be designated immediately: science as projection and science as detachment.

First, the idea of projection. The scientific spirit is governed by an ideal of convergence. This does not mean that some idea of a convergence of all truths into one truth is a distinctive feature of science, rather that it is implicit in science that there exists some kind of truth on which science itself will converge. The attitude of convergence means that science is an enterprise that is oriented towards the future. Indeed, as we shall see further below, it is difficult not to associate the scientific enterprise with the principle of fallibilism that holds that the truth is always up for correction; that science is an ongoing search for truth – a *project*, without closure, existing beyond the immediate activities of its proponents (Williams 1985: 136; cf. Peirce 1992: 52). The great French philosopher of science, Gaston Bachelard, observed that:

> scientific truth is a prediction or, better still, a predication. By announcing the scientific truth we call for a meeting of minds; together we convey both an idea and an experience, we link thought to experience in an act of verification: *The scientific world is therefore that which we verify.* Above the *subject* and beyond the *object*, modern science is based on the *project*. In scientific thought the subject's meditation upon the object always takes the form of a project. (Bachelard 1984: 11–12)

Second, there is what Bernard Williams calls in his controversial account of science, the "absolute conception of the world"; a conception that the world is independent of our own immediate perspective as a person (Williams 1985: 139). But, *pace* Williams, this is not a "conception" of the world so much as an ethical attitude towards it; ethical in the sense that such an attitude involves an evaluative rather than just a normative or rationalistic orientation towards the world. It does not make sense to regard science as being in opposition to ethics (ibid: 135). In any case, it is not as if science has no ethical component; rather for science to work as science, certain broad ethical orientations are in order even if these are subsequently to fall away or to become redundant through dull compulsion or habit.

Laboratory sciences

Such definitions are not really enough to isolate the ethos of scientific enlightenment. They relate to what might be termed ethics of cognition; certain ways of stylizing the functions of knowledge. But we can possess such cognitive ethics without actually having science as such. A further feature of the scientific ethos has to do with what, after Ian Hacking, we can call its interventionist character (Hacking 1983a). He might have taken this perspective from Max Weber. As Weber pointed out, the conceptual basis of science was available long before the advent of modern science itself. The Greeks, he said, discovered the concept: "In Greece for the first time, appeared a handy means by which one could put the logical screws upon somebody so that he could not come out without admitting either that he knew nothing or that this and nothing else was truth, the *eternal* truth that never would vanish as the doings of the blind men vanish" (Weber 1991a: 141). But modern science is dependent on something else: namely, the idea of the rational experiment as a principle of research. The experiment is as its etymology suggests, and as Weber observed, not a rationalist conception of how to acquire knowledge but something that suggests an ethical component, the deliberate and stylized staging of an "experience".

The ethos of the experiment is dependent not just on a set of ideas as to what science is but on a particular kind of setting: the laboratory. What is it about the laboratory that ties it so closely to our central pictures of scientific activity? It is both a workshop, a place where things are produced, but also a sequestrated space. Laboratories are not of this world. They are places in which particular elements of the world can be isolated and held stable. Laboratories spawn their own characteristic technologies of knowledge: the so-called "laboratory sciences". Such sciences, comments Hacking, "use apparatus in isolation to interfere with the course of that aspect of nature that is under study, the end in view being an increase in knowledge, understanding, and control of a general or generalizable sort" (Hacking 1992a: 33). Laboratories are not, then, simply places where things called experiments take place, but places where – ideally – new relations are made visible, new events are made possible and new phenomena are produced. Laboratory sciences "study phenomena that seldom or never occur in a pure state before people have brought them under surveillance ... the phenomena under study are created in the laboratory" (ibid: 33; cf. Hacking 1983a: 220–32). So the experiments and activities that are supposed to take place in laboratories are not to be seen on the rationalist model of a fitting of theories to the facts or *vice versa*; they are rather productive of new experiences, and laboratories are not places of objectivity so much as places of *work* (Lynch 1984). In that sense, in the laboratory scientific results are produced that could not exist outside the laboratory because it is a controlled – or disciplined – environment, a space in which various, carefully specified, associations are accomplished and observed. But it is precisely this aspect of laboratory life that makes the laboratory powerful because what it is able to do is, in Hacking's words, to "remake little bits of our environment so that they reproduce phenomena first generated in a pure state in the laboratory" (Hacking 1992a: 59). Even the rational determinism so often expected of science would be, then, but the effect of these particular characteristics of the laboratory sciences. In being thus not of this world, laboratories make determinism a possibility even in an otherwise messy and indeterminate world because, since the laboratory space is one in which there is a "restriction on the allowable range of experimentation", they allow for a delimitation and localization of their objects of concern (cf. Bachelard 1984: 107).

Experimentalism is, then, as much the product of certain practical or ethical commitments as it is of a universally "rational" approach to knowledge.

Hence the exceptional value of a work which seeks to show some of the values of the scientific attitude at the time of its modern emergence: that is, as an ethic of experimentalism prior to the elaboration of any overall "theory" of it. Shapin and Schaffer's now classic *Leviathan and the Air-Pump* (1985) (cf. Latour 1993a: 16; cf. Shapin 1994) provides us with a memorable genealogy of experimentalism as a particular kind of ethic which is constitutive of our very idea of scientific activity; their motto a comment by the Ludwig Wittgenstein of *On Certainty* (1969): "If the true is what is grounded, then the ground is not the *true*, nor yet the false." Experimentalism is the ground; it is not self-evident but had to be invented as an ethos, and then legitimated as a practice. Hence Shapin and Schaffer show that the virtues of experiment, far from being self-evident, had to be the object of a struggle within competing "modes of assent" for different kinds of truth. On the one hand, the experiment, as advocated by the seventeenth-century "gentleman-scientist", Robert Boyle, was a way of disciplining the senses. Truth required discipline, and the senses were a tool of discipline: "In this respect, the discipline enforced by devices such as the microscope or the air-pump were analagous to the discipline imposed upon the senses by reason. The senses alone were inadequate to constitute proper knowledge, but the senses disciplined were far more fit to the task" (Shapin and Schaffer 1985: 37). On the other hand, this experimentalism was more a matter of a form of life or an ethic of reason than a matter of theory or ideas or ideology.

In fact, Shapin and Schaffer insist that Boyle had no "experimental philosophy" as such; Boyle lived the life of the experimenter. He was an ethical exemplar of experiment; "by showing others through his own example what it was to work and to talk as an experimental philosopher" (ibid: 49). This is to say that Boyle is something like a "conceptual persona"; he embodies a kind of attitude towards knowledge that is meant to be exemplary for others and which encapsulates a complete ethic of cognition (cf. Deleuze and Guattari 1991). What does Boyle exemplify? He is the epitome of a certain style of a devotion to truth, one who gives all the details, who writes in a deliberately ascetic style, who concedes all to the powers of vision and witnessing, who rigidly separates observation and interpretation, who adopts a moral tone of "reporting" what he sees in a modest way, and one who is prepared to confess freely to error when necessary (ibid: 60–6). The experimental life implies a whole infrastructure or horizon of organization which sustains it. So, for instance, the scientific society is to be the place of experiment, a space in which the individual restrains his passions and engages in the peaceable freedom of rational dispute with others in a "union of eyes and hands" (ibid: 78). Meanwhile, Boyle's opponent, Thomas Hobbes, recognized the ethical implications of the experimental style of conduct precisely in rejecting it as an analogue of the pastoralism of the Church; whereas, for Boyle, Hooke and others, the experimental ethos was precisely of value as a way of attaining consent in a peaceable way.

Fallibilism and historicity

The model of scientific truth – or to be more precise, the forms of truth conventionally associated with the "central case" of the experimental, laboratory sciences – has origins, then, that are as much ethical or practical as rational. Shapin and Schaffer do not write about ethics, but prefer the term "form of life". I talk of ethics instead because it seems to me that to talk of an experimental form of life can seem as if we are referring to a whole worldview or morality rather than a particular, restricted chain of interpretative and cultural habits. Even so, even if it does avoid some of the conventionalism that might be associated with the notion of a form of life, does not such an ethical view imply the abandonment of any meaningful notion of scientific truth altogether?

Certainly, for postmodernists and others the idea that truth could be conceived on anything other than a rationalist – "modernist" – model might be evidence that truth itself is a redundant concept; and either we accept this or adopt a fundamentalism with regard to scientific truth (cf. Lawson & Appignanesi 1989). But, in truth, we are not faced with a choice between realist fundamentalism and relativistic subjectivism. Science is not, as postmodern philosophers like Richard Rorty and others would have it, just another language-game or style of conversation, nor does science merely "construct" its objects; it offers – above all in the image of laboratory science – a practical embodiment of a certain set of styles of telling the truth. There *are* right answers in physical causality, not least because the limits of what can be encountered can be so delimited in the laboratory with such exactitude; the laboratory is a place where nature is, so to speak, primed to take its revenge on any wrong-headed approach (cf. Heidegger 1977: 118; Dreyfus 1991: 263–5). It is as if nature has to be set up or fashioned in order to be appropriated by knowledge and put to the test; it is not that nature does not pre-exist knowledge nor that it is "constructed" but, rather, that we have to construct a stage on which nature can be allowed to perform – that is, where it can be seen by certain eyes, manipulated by certain hands, allowed to appear in a controlled and recognizable way – such an idea of performance necessarily entailing the capacity on nature's part to prove that one is on the wrong track, that one has got nature wrong. Obviously this stance is some way away from the more uncompromising brands of realism or anti-realism. It is to say that science is dependent on the fabrication of a particular way of looking at the world of objects, and the different sciences are not relative to anything beyond scientific truth itself.

The natural sciences do not just disclose any kind of truth. Rather they cultivate what should be regarded as a deliberately peculiar attitude to the truth. Epistemological fundamentalists would hold that scientific truth is the most philosophically impermeable kind of truth of all. In fact, to do justice to science, we would have to say that something like the very opposite of this is the case. To analyse science from the perspective of a critical attitude to enlightenment is to distance ourselves as far as possible from the idea that to "deconstruct" a form of knowledge is to dismantle it or disprove it. Rather, it is to show how truth is produced, not to say that truth can be just about anything. Such a critical attitude is not a question of deconstructing objectivity, but analysing it in its historicity. Indeed, such a deconstructive spirit is an aspect of scientific enlightenment itself, not just an aspect of hostile critiques of science. As Hacking puts it in a nice apothegm: "Objectivity is not the less massive, impenetrable, resistant, because it is the product of our history" (Hacking 1992b: 155).

Such a viewpoint clearly depends on the conviction that it is part of the essence of scientific enlightenment – as opposed to the mere "findings" of "science already made" – that science is never finished. The mode of existence of science confirms that there can be no such thing as a final scientific truth even though what makes science psychologically possible is the belief in the imminent revelation of the truth; at the end of each day the scientist must repeat what is really an article of faith: "Tomorrow I shall know the truth" (Bachelard 1984: 171).

This idea, that we can never really speak of a finished scientific truth, is not the progeny of some misguided postmodernist or anti-foundationalist fad, but is more conveniently associated with the well-known notion of fallibilism (Peirce 1992; Hookway 1995: 49). Some philosophers have attempted to turn this doctrine into a general ethical orientation towards the world. It is certainly of the essence of *scientific* enlightenment. But more than that, it is only with the "hard" sciences that questions of truth become complex enough to make fallibilism – which in itself is a peculiar doctrine – a sensible, that is, desirable attitude. In fact, the notion of a hard science is really a misnomer; perhaps we should speak instead of epistemologically complex ones. It is always possible to split philosophical hairs in relation to everyday sentences of an ordinary kind, for instance as to whether this table or this typewriter is or is not in front of me. But these are not particularly interesting issues of truth when compared to the styles of truth proper to scientific activity. This is one of many engaging themes in Ian Hacking's work on science. For him, truth only becomes really interesting when – as is the case with the complex sciences – it is creative of its own difficulties with regard to truth. This too is his point when he observes that the representations of physics are "entirely different from simple, non-representational assertions about, for instance, the location of my typewriter. There is a truth of the matter about the typewriter. In physics there is no final truth of the matter, only a barrage of more or less instructive representations ... Absence of final truth in physics should be the very opposite of disturbing" (Hacking 1983a: 145; cf. Hacking 1992b: 134–5). Complex issues of truth, of realism or anti-realism, only become particularly interesting in the context of phenomena like the electron: that is, where issues of representation are inherently more complex than we are likely to find in "boring observation sentences" about tables or typewriters (Hacking 1983a: 272–3).

This, in turn, obviously makes the *history* of science a peculiarly interesting endeavour, as well as an interestingly peculiar one. For in fact, science simply does not have a history in any normal sense of that term (Canguilhem 1968; Introduction). That is because science – "science in the making" – exists precisely to repudiate its history – "science already made"; to place its present in discontinuity from its past. It is this very sense of critical correction that needs to be associated with the truth in science. As Georges Canguilhem – an historian of science unfortunately better known for his respect for Foucault than for his own work – put it with rather deceptive simplicity: scientific truth is not inscribed within objects or intellect, rather it is inscribed within the ongoing practices of correction that make up scientific activity, such that truth is, as he put it, "simply what science speaks" (Canguilhem 1988: 11). Science is simply an institution for producing scientific kinds of truth – which is to say, endless kinds of error. Indeed, the history of science is strictly speaking only the history of past error. Science makes itself and remakes itself, constantly renewing its own foundations. The very essence of scientific enlightenment lies in its own repudiation of itself – science possessing a structure consisting of "its awareness of its historical errors" (Bachelard 1984: 172).

Science is, then, a peculiar kind of enterprise in that its very existence appears to be predicated on its desire to undo itself. That anyway – regardless of rationalism, rationalization, progress or any other such ideology commonly associated with science – is the essence of scientific *enlightenment*, or in other words, of "progress" in science. We are so certain about the truths of science, yet science exists to go beyond its own findings; science – at least in spirit – does nothing but endlessly criticize and correct its errors. It is a form of truth predicated on the contingency of truth and the universality of error. Indeed, science breeds indeterminism as much as it breeds determinism. And if today it is not uncommon to celebrate the "postmodernization" of the sciences, this is just a recent generalization of a basic feature of the scientific spirit (Lyotard 1984a: 53–60; cf. Crawford 1993: 254). For some it is amazingly recent. Science, said Prigogine and Stengers in 1984, is only now rediscovering time. The age of determinism, mechanism and reversibility is now at an end; we now live in a world of becoming rather than being, of chance and fluctuation rather than determinism (Prigogine and Stengers 1984). But the roots of these changes are rather older. They certainly predate postmodernism. The roots of what is better termed modernist science no doubt go back to the early part of the twentieth century, if not before – with the work of Einstein on relativity theory, and especially with the advent of quantum mechanics. Einstein had some celebrated worries over some of the consequences of what was then the new scientific spirit, writing to Max Born that there could be no such thing as a "dice-playing God" (see Born 1949). For Born, however, the effect of the new physics was a revision of the very principles of scientific method themselves. It was not just God that played dice, but science too. Science itself could only be uncertain, approximating to truth, because science itself only existed in time: "No observation or experiment, however extended, can give more than a finite number of repetitions; and the statement of a law – B depends on A – always transcends experience"; concluding that "There is no unique image of our world of experience" (ibid: 6, 208).

The fact that such an ethos of indeterminacy is not some latter-day post-modern frivolity can be further illustrated through the otherwise improbable example of the social sciences in the nineteenth century. Research into the history of statistics – the "driest of subjects" – indicates, in any case, that such indeterminism has a longer genealogy than we might otherwise think. Hacking draws attention to a paradox – one that is also, as Lyotard has pointed out, central to the so-called postmodern, cybernetically oriented sciences of today – to the effect that the greater the indetermination, the greater the possibilities for "control". That is the nub of it; control and indeterminacy are not opposites but go together. Nineteenth-century ideas about how to control "deviant" populations of criminals, madmen, prostitutes and others through enumeration and classification are really precursors to twentieth-century notions about chance and information: "By the end of the century chance had attained the respectability of a Victorian valet, ready to be the loyal servant of the natural, biological and social sciences" (Hacking 1990: 2).

Science exists to revolutionize itself, to show that all science is error, to undercut its own truths. Such may not be the consciousness of scientists themselves; but such is the consciousness of science when understood as an aspect of enlightenment. Indeed science might be described – were the idea not an apparent absurdity – as being by definition "postmodern". Even for someone like Shapin and Schaffer's hero, Robert Boyle, the very essence of scientific activity consisted in breaking up our received ideas about phenomena and their causation; natural science as deconstruction. For Boyle, natural philosophy, in order to progress, had even to abandon what must have seemed to most to be its central postulate – the very idea of *nature*. Boyle sought to dissuade the cultivators of science:

> from employing often, and without great need, in their philosophical discourses and writings, a term, (I mean nature) which, by reason of its great ambiguity, and the little or no care, which those, that use it, are wont to take, to distinguish its different acceptions, occasions both a great deal of darkness and confusedness in what men say and write about things corporeal; and a multitude of controversies, wherein really men do but wrangle about words, while they think they dispute of things; and perhaps would not differ at all, if they had the skill or luck to express themselves clearly. (Boyle 1772: 246–7)

My point about the way that social theory and the social sciences should regard the natural sciences is simple. It is that any "critique" of science has to take account of the fact that science is already a form of critique. What the history of science is a history *of* is the ongoing critical correction of concepts, and science is not really a method or a single worldview – let alone a single kind of *activity* – but a family of styles of such critical correction. This means, at least for historical epistemologists like Canguilhem and his mentor, Bachelard, that the sciences have to adopt a rather peculiar approach to their own history. The historian of science has to adopt a rigorous perspectivism, working from what is "known" to be truth in the present and working backwards, tracing the filiations of truth recursively. This, however, is not the confidence of a final knowledge: on the contrary. As Canguilhem continues:

> There is a clear difference between retrospective critical evaluation of the scientific past in the light of a present state of knowledge (certain, precisely because it is scientific, to be surpassed or rectified in the future) and systematic, quasi-automatic application to the past of some standard model of scientific theory. The latter is more in the nature of an epistemological inquisition than a historical enquiry. (Canguilhem 1988: 12; cf. Canguilhem 1968: 9–23)

What emerges is not exactly a history of truth, but a history of something like "veridicality", of being *in the true*.

To say that there is a critical ethos at the heart of scientific activity is not to say that all scientists are intrinsically historians of science in that they should know the history of science in order to go about doing science; but rather that such a critical orientation is an aspect of the very idea of a commitment to science. And this does mean that the history of scientific concepts should not be seen as somehow a scholastic annex to the proper business of science. On the contrary: such history is itself an aspect of the conceptual conscience of science; in other words, the possibility of epistemological history is an internal aspect of scientific enlightenment.

Pursuit of such history is one way in which science settles its accounts with itself: that is, by writing down its own memory. And if the results are so often contentious, this is because the conceptual history of science is necessarily *not* a factual history of "what has happened in science", of "science already made". It is possible to write a certain kind of history of science in that way. We can write a life of Maxwell in terms of the ideas that Maxwell had in relation to his scientific activity. But this would not be exactly to place Maxwell within the history of science; for that would require judgement in terms of the something like the *directionality* of Maxwell's ideas in relation to the past and future development of science itself. The history of science is given directionality by the truth-values of current science. In short, the history of science to be a history of science, as opposed to a history of anything else, would have to have an epistemological dimension which in some senses means that it would have to part from the usual norms of historical writing. "The historian of the sciences must take ideas as facts. The epistemologist must take facts as ideas, inserting them into a system of thoughts" (Canguilhem 1968: 177). In other words, the "memory" of science is a "recursive" one. Histories of science, in order to be histories of science rather than histories of anything else, have to be "recurrent histories" (ibid: 181–3). Such histories are themselves expressive of something like an ethics of scientific truth. Not ethics in the sense of whether or not it is good to tell the truth, but the ethics of one's relation to truth; the ethics of bringing oneself and one's times into a closer relation with the truth by scrupulously investigating its limits and conditions of possibility. Such histories express an ethic in that – far from being expressive of an abandonment of truth – they are an aspect of a commitment or a duty to the peculiarity of scientific kinds of truth.

A disclaimer

Is not this so far a rather breathless vindication of science? And are we not aware that scientific enlightenment has not always been master in its own house? The proponents of a more anti-scientific perspective are no doubt getting restless. Perhaps they would be justified in suggesting precisely that more critical attitudes need to be counterposed to this notion of scientific enlightenment; that instead of the glorification of the critical character of science, there should be exploration of the collusions of science with the machinations of power, not just in cases such as the development of weaponries and "defense" but in areas of expertise such as the administration of food hygiene or the regulation of industrial hazards (Irwin 1995: 9–36).

All this might be pertinent. Hence all the more reason to distinguish between the idea of a critique of scientific enlightenment which would be concerned with science in so far as it is science in the making and a critical sociology of science concerned with the social and institutional effects of science already made. The real is not necessarily coterminous with the actual. Being realist about enlightenment does not excuse us of our responsibilities in being realist about the activities and results of science – or science already made – only that such critical realism is itself always the product of choices that are ultimately ethical. But in any case, by scientific enlightenment I mean to designate a kind of spirit internal to scientific activity, not to endorse the view, held by prominent scientists themselves, that the public needs to be "educated" in an understanding of science (cf. ibid: 12–13). In fact, nothing could be further from the spirit of a critique of scientific enlightenment. Such a critique is indeed a form of education, though not at all in the name of the rather patronizing, self-congratulatory phraseology of "public understanding". Indeed, the kind of "enlightenment" that is required might even come from a different but perhaps still rather peculiar – on the face of it, quite unlikely – source.

In recent decades, the sociology of science has been in a ferment. Ethnographically oriented investigators have entered the world of the scientific laboratory and have come back with some fairly exotic – occasionally gruesome – accounts of the goings-on there. Sociologists had long argued that there might be a social aspect to contexts of justification in science; in short, that particular kinds of society only got the kinds of science appropriate to them. But the notion that there could also be a social context to discovery itself was more or less new, and spawned some innovative detailed studies (e.g. Shapin 1979; Mackenzie 1981; Shapin 1982). The next step was the realization that the sociologists were not being symmetrical enough. They had abandoned the asymmetry involved in explaining only falsity and not truth on the basis of social facts, but had been unable to relinquish their attachment to another asymmetry, namely that which posited society as a more important source of causation than nature itself (Latour 1992). This was the inauguration of the Latourian moment.

Latourian anti-foundationalism

I want to make use of Latour's work not least because I think that its true value lies somewhere other than where it is often held to lie. The implication of Latour's work is not to lead us into an anti-scientific perspective, nor to force us to embrace a naïvely relativistic epistemological worldview. Rather his work is best seen not as a critique of science nor even as a social-scientific representation of science but as a critique of scientific enlightenment; an exercise that does at least as much to sow the seeds of our judgement in relation to an enterprise like science than it does more exactly to represent the world of actually existing science as such.

Latour's basic premise is that we should not think of science and society as stable things, or of society and science somehow as heterogeneous entities acting on one another. Rather, sociologists of science should attend to the ongoing fabrications of the very distinction between science and society. Perhaps what we call science and society are just alike the product of negotiation. Hence, in explaining science, no causal priority is given to any single entity or dimension. And hence, the import of the notion of the so-called *actor-network*; the task of the social investigator being to follow the patient building up of various networks that bind people, objects, resources and so forth into a relatively durable combination of forces (Callon & Latour 1981; Callon 1986; Latour 1987; Latour 1996).

For example, in his study of Louis Pasteur, Latour eschews breathless description of Pasteur's great discoveries and instead describes the fabrication of various networks of entities including laboratories, sheep, farmers, anthrax and so forth, thus giving back to the scientists "the crowd of heterogeneous allies which make up their troops and of which they are merely the much-decorated high command whose function is always uncertain ... [showing that] these disreputable allies (hygienists, drains, Agar gels, chickens, farms, insects of all kinds) were an integral part of so-called scientific objects" (Latour 1988a: 147). In this account, no single dimension of reality has priority. For Latour, it makes no sense to replace a realism about nature with a realism about society; rather, both sorts of realism have to go in the name of a sort of ethnographic *irrealism*. "We live in a Society we did not make, individually or collectively, and in a Nature which is not of our fabrication. But Nature 'out there' and Society 'up there' are no longer ontologically different. We do not make Society, anymore than we do Nature, and their opposition is no longer necessary" (Latour 1992: 281; Latour 1988a: 148; cf. for irrealism, Hacking 1988).

Above all, no *particular* kind of actor should be prioritized. That is the basis of Latour's particular brand of anti-foundationalism. For instance, Pasteur works in some experiments with lactic acid yeast. Latour says:

> Who is doing the action in the new medium of culture? *Pasteur*, since he sprinkles, and boils, and filters, and sees. *The lactic acid yeast*, since it grows fast, uses up its food, gains in power ... and enters into competition with other similar beings growing like plants in the same plot of land. If I ignore Pasteur's work, I fall into the pitfalls of realism ... if we ignore the lactic acid ... we fall into the other pit, as bottomless as the first, of *social* constructivism. (Latour 1993b: 143–4)

The task of the sociologist of science is, as Latour sees it, to follow our designated actors and actants, without assumption or presumption. We might think that such a viewpoint would lead to an anti-scientific perspective. And not surprisingly many have taken offence at the findings of Latourianism. Some have found fault with it because it provides no grounds for a hostile critique of science (Fuller 1992). For others, the Latourian turn is precisely just another excuse for subverting the moral values of realism and truth in the name of a conspiracy-theory of science. For some critics, it is enough to dismiss this work as relativism or irresponsibility (Gross & Levitt 1994: 57–62; cf. Norris 1996) – or even, albeit rather bizzarely, as synonymous with something that appears to some to be obviously reprehensible, namely Marxism (Harré 1983: 166).

Perhaps we might be forgiven for thinking that the aim of the Latourian outlook was to dismantle science. Consider certain characteristic emphases of Latour's problematic. In Latour's work, science and power become more or less synonymous; and rather than associating the laboratory simply with the production of scientific truth, he associates it with the production of power, and calls it a "centre of calculation" or a power centre (Latour 1987: 235). So, for instance, Pasteur was able, with the help of a rather complex set of negotiations, effectively to turn the farm into a kind of simulacrum of his own laboratory. In attempting to combat anthrax, Pasteur knew, says Latour, that he could not bring the farm to his laboratory, so he has to extend the circumstances of the laboratory to the farms. Pasteur and his collaborators:

know that in a dirty farm thronged by hundreds of onlookers they will be unable to repeat exactly the situation that had been so favourable to them ... They have to strike a compromise with the organisers of a field test, to transform enough features of the farm in laboratory-like conditions – so that the same balance of forces can be maintained – but taking enough risk – so that the test is realistic enough to count as a trial done outside. (ibid: 249; Latour 1988a: 89)

In short, the laboratory becomes a site for a peculiar kind of discipline; one that is designed to isolate forces and turn them into hard, strictly *local* – albeit if, given the right networks, logistically transferrable – facts, and to define and keep out the soggy world of "social" and other kinds of weakly-defined resources.

A similar kind of assault is enacted on the idea of a scientific "fact". The truth of science, for the apologists of science, seems always to lie just in the facts. The new sociologists of science would not deny that there are such things as scientific facts but would certainly argue that they are the products of scientific activity; they do not exist "out there" in nature (Latour and Woolgar 1979). Or again, the scientific research paper, that pillar of objectivity and cool analysis is, for these writers, as much a piece of rhetoric as anything else. For Latour, the scientific paper is hardly an objective statement but includes all sorts of means of persuasion to convince the reader. There is the citation of a cascade of outside authorities; there is the stacking of "levels of induction" (do not derive your evidence from lumps of flesh but from mammal counter-current structure in the kidney); there is the projection of the desirable image of the authors and the attempt to control the moves of possible objectors through strategies of "captation" (Latour 1987: 30–59). The aim of the scientific paper is typically to give the illusion of an immediate representation of reality, to convince the reader of the immediate presence or availability, and hence the coimplication and reinforcement, of all the resources that are being used in the structure of the argument. And hence, above all, the emphasis in all these writings on various techniques of representation – the table, the graph, visual inscriptions of all sorts – as a means of giving a high level of immediate presence and stability, and hence authority, to as many aspects of information all at once (Latour 1987: 46–7; Lynch and Woolgar 1988; also Latour 1986). In short, the scientific article is a means of disciplining as many resources as possible into a single space in order to convince – or discipline in the direction of the author's point of view – as many potential allies and to forestall as many potential objectors as possible.

But in spite of these emphases, it would be a grave mistake to imagine that Latour, for all his relativism about facts and the findings of science, is representative of an anti-scientific view. Take the example of the scientific fact. As Latour and his colleagues are very well aware, sceptical approaches to factuality are not the novel invention of an irresponsible postmodernism. In *The Genesis and Development of a Scientific Fact*, first published in 1935, the venearologist Ludwig Fleck wrote that "there is probably no such thing as complete error or complete truth. Sooner or later a modification of the law of conservation of energy will prove necessary, and then we will perhaps be obliged to fall back upon an abandoned 'error'" (Fleck 1979: 20). All properly scientific truths, all facts, are conditional; moreover all have definite circumstances of production that are inseparable from the characteristics of the thought collectives that produced them. Fleck, a practising venearologist who certainly knew what he was talking about, was something like an irrealist when it comes to facts (cf. Hacking 1988: 281–2). It is not that all facts, are equally untrue but that to be true, to become true, facts require an environment (a general discourse of "proto-ideas') in which they make sense; a series of insights, accidents and experiments, all conditioned by a general thought style; and a carrying "thought collective" of scientific authorities. None of this is to sink into the subjectivism that says that all facts are equally true or untrue depending on your point of view; it is rather to urge that it is possible to investigate the *how* of factuality without giving up on notions of truth altogether.

So, in spite of appearances to the contrary, I think that we can deduce neither an anti-scientific critique of science from this work, nor for that matter any solution to venerable epistemological problems like those of realism and relativism. In fact the achivement of Latourianism is not really in relation to epistemological problems at all. The constructionist language should not deceive us on this account. To be sure, we learn that science is *constructed*, that it is in part a matter of *rhetoric*, that is as much about *power* as it is about truth – or, more exactly, that truth itself is largely a question of the logistics of power. But this constructionist language does not in itself mean very much. The whole debate over so-called constructionism that seems to have excited so many people is really a non-starter. In the early days of the usage of this term, it seemed to carry a rather subversive, even Marxist, ring to it (Wright and Treacher 1982). On this view, knowledge is like motor cars or ships: it has to be *constructed*, which was presumably intended to have the happy effect of making the intellectuals responsible for the construction appear to be dangerous proletarians. Here at least the term was doing some specific work. But, once neutralized – that is, once one has gone anti-foundational and have ceased to talk of constructions of a particular sort – it really means very little other than that truth is not out there in the world but is what is spoken by persons, hence produced through discourses, techniques, controversies.

As for the question of realism, Latour is making a very apposite point when he says that one of the main effects of the new sociologies of science is – or should be – to get back to the things themselves: "Let us get back to the world, still unknown and despised. If you sneer at this claim and say 'this is going back to realism', yes it is. A little relativism takes one away from realism; a lot brings one back" (Latour 1988b: 173). In fact, Latour has done well to avoid the whole question of realism; that is one of the very merits of his terminological revolution. For that question – interesting as we have seen it to be – is certainly insoluble on a general theoretical level: that is, at the level of discussions of *representation*; for one side will always say that the representation is real, the other that it is not, and since they agree on the fact that science is in some manner or other a system of representation, they will assuredly always disagree on the issue of realism (Hacking 1983a: 145).

So all in all, the Latourian problematic has not changed the received image of science very much in epistemological terms. Some familiar demarcations have remained in place and science still appears as a single enterprise. Any sociologist will tell you that science is not "better" than magic or superstition, religion or anything else. But still, in Latour's work, the differences are smuggled back in what is quite a traditional way; science is more "successful", it commands more "resources", it operates with tighter networks, or just according to "differences of scale" (Latour 1988b: 163–4; Latour 1992: 289). Even the old demarcation between natural science and the social sciences also remains intact. So far as Latour is concerned, the natural and social sciences essentially employ the same methods: namely, something like the logistical fabrication of networks. But what results from this is the replacement of an ontological divide with a logistical one – for the huge divide remains; the natural sciences certainly have much greater logistical capacities and this results in the very different status of each. We should not be deceived by the rather offhand language on this point. For example, Latour says that the social sciences merely have a different degree of resources from the natural sciences; but this terminology conceals the enormous *scale* of that difference of resources. Where there was a divide, now there is only distance; but the (huge) *difference* remains, a difference that, being thus so great in quantitative terms, might just as well be described in terms of quality (Latour 1988b: 163–4; cf. Latour 1992: 289).

So is this to say that the Latourian problematic has achieved nothing but a redescription of scientific practices (cf. Collins & Yearley 1992: 315)? Not at all. In fact, Latourianism might be seen as the epitome, albeit a deliberately eccentric epitome, of a critique of scientific enlightenment because it allows science to speak against the very forms of *romanticism* that it is apt to generate about itself. Indeed, I think that the eccentricity of Latourianism has a strategic relation to such romanticism; it is directed against it in the spirit of a countervailing power.

By the romantic interpretation of science, I mean those kinds of interpretation that hold that scientific enlightenment is the province of brilliant minds, utilizing rigorous, exact and basically sensible methods, and working towards a finished truth. Such an interpretation accords with what Gaston Bachelard called the nocturnal posturings of many scientists themselves; it is the tone of venerable scientific memoirs, solemn-minded research reports and sternly worded textbooks. The true spirit of science, on the other hand, implies a rather different view; one which corresponds more to the diurnal reality of scientific activity.

In place of brilliant minds, the Latourian story of the scientific spirit is rather one of obscurity and anonymity. This is often seen as an element of the anti-science perspective of Latourianism, but it might equally recall Georges Canguilhem's gloss of Bachelard's view of science: "How, then, do we recognize that a statement is scientific? By the fact that scientific truth never springs fully blown from the head of its creator" (Canguilhem 1988: 11). There is a complete absence of even an inkling of psychologism in Latour's own work. Humans are, it is true, seen as being basically creative but their creativity is assumed to exist at a sort of uninterestingly aggregate level; it is creativity itself, rather than its human carriers, that Latourianism celebrates. What counts are just the resources available to individuals, and the "great man" beloved of the romantic hagiographies of science is, says Latour in a well-known formulation, just a little man looking at a jolly good map. Instead of sensible methods, the spirit of science embodies an attitude that is more akin to the wheeler-dealings of power. Science is but war by other means and Pasteur is a general, a Napoleon in civies, with troops, strategies, resources and enemies. Far from being a form of empty cynicism, this is an approach which does in fact demonstrate much more respect for the truly creative dimension of scientific activity than does most philosophy of science with its emphasis on methodology. We are reminded of the philosopher Paul Feyerabend's judgement on Galileo; that after Feyerabend's hyper-relativist treatment he was much more interesting and creative, and much less the "constipated searcher after truth" that he had been when the victim of the hagiographers (Feyerabend 1974).

I think that Latourian relativistic anti-foundationalism is in fact even, in a way, a "realist" response to the nature of the scientific spirit in so far as it captures, even mirrors, the fallibilism of approach that is integral to that spirit itself. For if we need to make ourselves relativists, sceptics and so forth with regard to natural science then this is itself down not least to the influence of a scientific culture which itself constantly deconstructs and remakes reality. Even some scientists are happy to acknowledge the "unnatural nature" of science (Wolpert 1993). It is a great mistake to see such relativism as just a misguided way of representing science. The relativism of the Latourian moment is not so much epistemological as ethical; a dramatization by other means of the scientific spirit itself. Far from being a sloppy, anything-goes attitude to the subject matter in hand, relativism in its recent forms is more like a particularly rigorous asceticism. It is a self-conscious, ascetic work; an attempt to sheer away all foundations; to see clearly in a single light, without giving absolute advantage to any single candidate to truth. The anthropological roots of the practices in the sociology of science are pertinent; the attempt to observe freely without obstacle with a pure – perhaps even enlightened – gaze. The motto of such enlightenment might be that one can assume nothing; and what could be a better motto for the scientific spirit itself?

One can point to the slippery-slope that leads from epistemic relativism to moral relativism and hence to all kinds of diabolical politics. If one assumes that relativism is a kind of permanent doctrine or epistemology, then such a negative view would be understandable. But I think it is better to see the relativistic attitude less as a doctrine about the world than as a kind of restricted, ethical perspective. The mind-set and activities of scientists themselves are another matter. For there are such things as more or less settled truths in science, those truths which Latour himself, for instance, glosses in his terminology of the "black box", those domains, often inscribed in the very apparatuses that scientists use, which constitute the unsaid ground of science. Scientists may black box things in the form of experimental apparatuses and technical equipment or in the form of past findings that are more or less taken for granted. But no one can ever say definitively that something in science is finally true, that no modification or elaboration will ever be required, that one day we will not have to return to some of those black boxes and look inside. It is that perception that Latourianism dramatizes to an extreme, not in the name of an anti-scientific perspective but in the name – in effect – of scientific enlightenment itself. It is that which makes Latour not just a run-of-the-mill sociologist of science but a social theorist – of quite general import – with something to say in relation to the very character of our obligations to enlightenment.

There might be a postmodern way to read Latour. Perhaps he would read himself in such a way. He purports to hold that "we have never been modern" let alone postmodern, but then even Jean-Francois Lyotard, proponent of a postmodern perspective himself, supposes that postmodernity is something that happens in some senses prior to modernity (Lyotard 1984a, postscript; cf. Lyotard 1992; Latour 1993a). But if a Latourian postmodernism would entail the reduction of his work to a radical epistemology, holding that Latour has taught us that the very idea of scientific truth is redundant, this would be in fact to romanticize the Latourian message itself, and to turn it into a sort of morality, a determinate way to live. Instead, I propose a reading that is oriented to what might be described as the ascetic character of Latour's concerns.

We can say there is a kind of lesson to be gleaned from the Latourian moment, but it is a peculiar one. The Latourian idea – and by extension other kinds of relativism and anti-foundationalism with regard to science – is a kind of latter-day cognitive asceticism; it is a sort of experiment that we do to ourselves, a deliberate stretching and exercise of the judgement. *Teaching* Latourianism is conducive to a certain kind of experience; the complete symmetry of approach causes the ground to fall away from beneath our feet if just for a while. While we are – or should not be – "converted" to Latourianism as if it were itself a belief-system, a morality or an ideology instead of a form of discourse, one of its ethical effects is certainly a feeling of being rather deeply unsettled. This Latourian kind of affect can itself be regarded as an aspect of an enlightenment of a particular kind. Latour makes science at once a quotidian activity, practised by perfectly normal people, but he also makes it seem like a rather eccentric exercise in human judgement. Perhaps the moral lesson of his work lies, then, with its celebration of something like the imagination that is required for judgement – that imagination and judgement occupy the same domain – coupled with an ethos of scepticism with regard to the truth; the surmise that in order to know the nature of truth we periodically have to free ourselves from it altogether. Latourianism is an ascetics of such a practice of judgement.

But let me restate that this is best seen as a restricted kind of outlook and not something that would amount to anything so grandiose as an epistemology, a morality or a philosophy of life. This is the sense in which Latourianism is really *strategic*. It might be considered as a deliberate exercise that we perform; the stripping away of all prejudice in the domain of knowledge, the complete resistance to the romanticisms of psychology. Such an exercise is strategic in that it is only pertinent in relation to a particular tendency: namely, the romanticisms and psychologisms of science itself or, if we prefer, of science already made. But we cannot *live* Latourianism as if it were a moral worldview consequent on an epistemology; for, at the end of the day – or rather at the beginning of it – we have to live in the world rather than away from it. Latourianism is thus a sort of staged demonstration of a certain kind of scientific enlightenment; but such enlightenment does not consist in taking such a worldview all the time any more than an individual scientist can be expected to hold that nothing that they ever say is "true" or that there is no such thing as scientific "discovery", only endless correction in science. It is an ethic but it is not a morality.

All this is to say that what looks like an extreme relativist epistemology can itself be read in what in my particular usage I am calling ethical as opposed to epistemological terms. In a sense, relativism might be considered to be epistemologically true; from the perspective of the cosmos, nothing exists for ever, everything is relative to its time and nothing can be taken for granted. Worlds, things, species all come and go. So far so good; but such a perspective might make for a very bad form of "absolutist" relativism. Latourianism is limited as an epistemology by the fact that it ignores, the "relative" aspects of relativism. It reduces everything to a single time in which everything is equally relative. But that is to engage in an ethical exercise, not a real representation of the world. For entities exist in different times; a species is relative to its time in a different way from either a scallop, an electron, a scientist or a social class. Latour's terminology of "black boxes" and such like does a good job of concealing this differential historicity of things; nothing is stable but some things are black-boxed and hence become part of the infrastructure. But this is itself to black-box the very idea of a black box, which is also to black-box the very idea of the history of science (as opposed to a history of scientific logistics, or of power). Hence there is a cost to Latour's relativist ethic, which is his refusal to contemplate that science might be analysed – as Bachelard and Canguilhem held – at the level of its concepts, which is to say at the level of its *own* internal historicity. There is a truth in this relativism, and it is far from being a truth hostile to the spirit of science; but, precisely because it is ethical rather than epistemological, this truth is never itself able to become, so to speak, the object of analysis.

There is a further limitation that besets this radically anti-psychologistic strategy of relativism, and this time it may not be such a productive one. The Latourian problematic, perhaps precisely because of its hostility to psychologism, has trouble in perceiving the kinds of ethical relation that are required to do science in the first place. Its radical anti-humanism leads it to ignore the fact that – to put things too bluntly – science itself is an ethical choice made in the world by certain people called scientists. What happens, then, were we to ignore this anti-ethical tendency in Latour and ask this prior question as to the nature of the ethical motivations of science? It should be said that my comments on this score are rather speculative, if not to say also old-fashioned.

Science and ethics

Sociologists supposedly made rather a hash of thinking about scientific judgement in terms of the ethos of science. The Latourian problematic is certainly an attempt to get beyond such apparently naïve approaches. But perhaps there are costs to its vigorous anti-psychologism too. Robert Merton's four institutional imperatives of science – the attitudes of universalism, communalism, disinterestedness, and organized scepticism – may not be visible to the participant observer of science precisely because they are unproblematic assumptions of what science actually is; they are perhaps meant to form part of the background assumptions of scientific activity (Merton 1968). In fact the ethical aspect of scientific enlightenment really exists not at the level of the consciousness of scientists – for there is no such thing as a "pure" scientist – but more as an aspect of the logic of science itself, not as a particular institution but as a particular kind of orientation towards truth. This is what could be called "personality" in science. As in Weber's designation of that term, this does not refer to a psychological make-up but to an ideal which embodies not just the general aspects but also the contradictions and tensions of a particular life-order or sphere of existence. Weber's notion of political personality, for instance, did not designate an aggregate psychological make-up of the modern-day politician but rather the profile of somebody able to face the contradictions of living up to the demands of politics.

A full account of the making-up of scientific personality is well beyond my scope here; in any case, my point is not to give this notion any determinate form so much as to emphasize the more general point that even the most hardline anti-foundationalism, far from allowing us to bypass the question of ethics, might actually lead us back towards it. Suffice to say the model of the gentleman-experimenter associated with Boyle hardly remained unchanged (cf. Schaffer 1988). To an extent the image of the scientist and that of the experimenter became separated from each other. The nineteenth-century ethos of science came to be dominated by an ethos of precision, which no doubt seems a narrower model than that of the gentleman-scientist of the sort described by Shapin and Schaffer. The Scientist became a measurer, a man of exactitude (Wise 1995). But such an ethos can, in fact, be regarded as only an extension of the model of the experimenter, for an ethic of precision can only be an aspiration in the context of a scientific culture that has given itself reasons for measurement and motivations for precision. Measurement for its own sake can become a kind of fetish within science, but that is not to say that its very rationale is such; rather the precision of measurement serves to focus experimental work and precision was an aspect of experiment (Hacking 1983a: 243–5; cf. Kuhn 1979: 178–224).

Instead of pursuing such questions in the detail they deserve, I shall settle with making a few comments concerning Michael Polanyi's interesting and general treatment of this problem, under the heading of the "moral element" in science (Polanyi 1946). Polanyi's discussion is interesting because it says something specifically about the ethical basis of scientific reason. Sociologists and other critics of science have tended to think of science as having negative ethical consequences, as leading to the disenchantment of the world and so forth. Not so for Polanyi. Science is characterized, Polanyi thought, above all by a certain stylization of *conscience*. It is itself a schooling in conscience. But attainment of such conscience requires a reconciliation of contrary elements. The scientist, to judge phenomena *as* a scientist, has to reconcile the cognitive virtues of speculation with the rigorous, trained rules of precision and method; it is the scientist's scientific conscience that enables him to balance these two elements (ibid: 27). It is a conscience that operates speculatively in relation to the methodological faculty and methodologically in relation to the speculative faculty. Thus for Polanyi science is not a rationalistic enterprise but involves rules of "art" rather than strict, formulaic rules of method; and these rules of art are developed through tradition, largely through the exemplary conduct of our teachers – for, as we know, even measurement is something that has to be learned in a practical way – and through inculcation into the practical techniques of research (ibid: 44). To cultivate such a conscience would amount to what it means to have an enlightened personality in science, even if it can be acknowledged that few if any scientists live up to this ideal; it is rather that the ideal is projected as a possibility by the logic of scientificity itself.

Is such an idealistic conception of scientific personality of any use to those social sciences which make it their business to concern themselves with science? Polanyi's account is of interest not least in that it points up the way to how we might think of the scientific ethos in terms of a more general consciousness of freedom, which is to say enlightenment. For Polanyi, science is simultaneously a form of commitment (the "gift of one's own person" to the-scientific ideal) but also fundamentally a form of enlightenment in itself; a way of practising freedom in the domain of cognition. There can be no absolute freedom, for that would just amount to the anarchy of pure speculation. In fact, Polanyi thinks of the scientist as someone who is "obliged to be free"; someone who has learned to fashion freedom in the form of a certain style of discipline (ibid: 50–1). Scientists are "free" in so far as they are prepared to think the implausible in the interests of truth. This is obviously not a pure or abstract freedom; to be given a positive form such freedom has to be learned in particular contexts, in relation to particular problems and tempered with the conscience of rigour and methodological and speculative restraint. Science discloses to us that freedom and discipline are not opposites; which, in turn, implies that if we wish to draw up a picture of different forms of freedom, we have to look at the actual disciplines in which different kinds of freedom are exercised. That is what a critique of enlightenment, rather than drawing up so many abstract models or "theories" of freedom, should be all about.

Polanyi actually derives a fairly well-worn idea from this notion of an obligation to freedom. It is that there is an elective affinity between science and democracy; that the central principle of science is free discussion and ultimately liberal democracy itself (ibid: 53–4). This overstates the matter. Polanyi especially does so when he claims that only liberal societies have a commitment to the spiritual values that promote freedom. There is no reason why scientific advance should be incompatible with political totalitarianism or State control so long as there are local forms of pluralism *within* science. In the nineteenth century the Germans interfered with science no end; but they established within scientific culture the grounds for free discussion. This is what T.H. Huxley saw, when he observed that in Germany, the universities were open to the talents; that in Germany, of all places, we might find the paradigm of a liberal education (Huxley 1925: 107). In other words, what counts is not necessarily good government in general, but good governance in the realm of truth itself.

Anti-simplicism

And it depends what you mean by freedom. Polanyi's rather Kantian association of freedom with a certain sense of obligation and discipline seems, however, exactly right. For him, the scientist is someone who is trained in a certain freedom at the level of judgement. The scientist is someone who seeks, while being committed to exactitude, to step at all costs into the unknown. In that sense, the training for scientific culture is indeed a kind of moral education, for it is a training in judgement itself. "Science and art are not so different as they appear. The laws in the realm of truth and beauty are laid down by the masters, who wrote eternal works" (Born 1949: 7). Science is an art of judgement taught largely through exemplary means.

This thought can actually be used to bring us back to our discussion of Latourianism as the incarnation of anti-foundationalism with regard to science. For it invites us to consider a pedagogic or ethical usage that a critique of enlightenment might derive from the contemplation of the scientific spirit. Such a critique might itself be regarded as a kind of exercise in judgement which would help us cast light on certain aspects of enlightenment itself. This is not a novel idea. The Stoics understood this function of science perfectly well. For them, the understanding of nature was not an end in itself so much as an aspect of ethical culture. For them and the other schools of Ancient philosophy, the contemplation of nature through physical theory had an ethical purport, being largely a question of learning to *relax* or to be reconciled with the world; of contemplating our insignificance in the world of causality and the endless cosmos (Hadot 1995: 87–8).

But we can think of the significance of science as education in a different way. We can say that the study of science – whether in the form of the history of science, Latourianism or whatever – itself belongs to the humanities in that such study functions as a schooling in the art of judgement, and a way of exemplifying or picturing by way of experience, the *creative* and perhaps unsettling aspects of reason. For that great rationalist, Emile Durkheim, in what are perhaps some rather uncharacteristic passages, the history of science had a useful pedagogic effect in the context of moral education generally in that it militated against simplistic attitudes towards the world – "simplicism" – and broadened the child's or student's capacities for judgement (Durkheim 1973: 262–3). For him, not the least of the pedagogic effects of the analysis of scientific reason was as a way of inducing countervailing tendencies to the general habit of simplifying processes of reasoning into common or rationalistic deductions. For Durkheim, the analysis of science was especially useful in this context, effectively because it served to open up the black boxes of reason, allowing the student "to see how science is studied, how the labour, time and trouble that study entails contrasts with . . . deductive improvisations" and to see that:

> knowledge is itself provisional and that tomorrow, perhaps, a new fact may be discovered that may put everything into question again . . . With the experimental method, abstract simplicism acknowledges its limitations and abdicates the absolute dominion it at first enjoyed. (ibid: 262–3)

Both historical epistemology and Latourian anti-foundationalism are good ways of using the example of natural science as a place of fieldwork in the cultivation of anti-simplicism. Such an ethos of anti-simplicism should have a bearing on the ways in which we regard science itself. For instance, it might function as a countervailing tendency to the sort of view of science that we find in all those abstract hagiographies of scientific genius that celebrate the irreversibility of great scientific discoveries and so forth. And it is likewise a countervailing tendency to those breathless celebrations of all things scientific or, their converse, those ironic postmodern debunkings of science. Adopting an ethos of anti-simplicism is to be wary of those philosophies which would seek to re-enchant the world through science wherein scientists are Western equivalents of Zen masters, specialists with spirit, sensualists with heart (Ross 1991: 43; cf. Weinberg 1996). These scientists – or rather, popularizers of science – tell us that science can help us to find the meaning of life. But if so, it would no longer be science but something else. Science would become theology. I think that not least of the uses of relativist and other kinds of ways of apparently subversive ways of thinking about science, including those of Latour, is that they provide us with a schooling in judgement that is strategic precisely in so far as it promotes the evasion of this kind of tendency; to prevent us becoming victims of an immature, romanticized "scientific culture" of this sort.

For at the end of the day we still need to agree with Max Weber that although science may be ethical in that it entails particular relations that the knower conceives with themselves as well as with the world, it is also, unlike religion, ethically *meaningless* in its more general consequences. That indeed is one of the great things about science, and any critique of scientific enlightenment needs to keep us conscious of it: "Who – aside from certain big children who are indeed found in the natural sciences – still believes that the findings of astronomy, biology, physics, or chemistry could teach us anything about the *meaning* of the world?" (Weber 1991a: 142; cf. Lassman and Velody 1989).

Ways of escape

The only form of enlightenment that is worth the candle in relation to science is that which provides us with an escape route from the blackmail either of the hagiography of all things scientific or from the blackmail of a pointless and gestural anti-science. Any critique of scientific enlightenment has to be conscious of the fact that science is already a form of critique, hence that the alternative of being "for" or "against" science (as in the misleading model of the "two cultures", or as with rationalist pictures of science more generally) is *itself* something from which a critique of scientific enlightenment should help us to escape, and by which the very success or failure of such a critique might even be measured.

The pictures of critical institutions such as science that we carry about in our heads are also, in the widest sense, *politically* important. It is naïve to suppose that we might do without such pictures altogether. The task is rather to complicate the pictures that we have, and to find ways of escape from those which have come to dominate our thoughts. From such pictures there derives a whole politics of truth, a politics which governs what we can and cannot say, even to and within ourselves. This is perhaps especially so with our pictures of that set of enterprises that we call natural science. The function of social theory and the social sciences in relation to the natural sciences is not least to open up some of the rigidities of that politics.

Chapter 3

Aspects of therapeutic enlightenment

Plasticity – Expertise: ethical and moral – An excursus on the sociology of professions – Ethical expertise again – Ethical subjection – The idea of aristocracy – Aristocracies of expertise – Exemplarity – Performativity – Normalization – Psychologization – Governing intentions – Utopian ethics

There is another politics of truth, a politics concerned with another kind of enlightenment; with the truths not of the natural world but of human identity, individuality, personality, conduct, and the *self*. How might a critique of enlightenment situate itself with regard to such a politics? In this chapter, I do not summarize the accounts of previous investigations into this field (Rieff 1966; Taylor 1989; de Swann 1990; especially Rose 1990 *passim*; Giddens 1991b), but, more selectively, outline instead the elements of a critical attitude towards such a politics of identity and the self and, via an analysis of what I label ethical subjection and of forms of expertise such as psychology, discuss some of the limits that might confront such a critical attitude.

The main emphasis of this chapter is already contained in its title; not self-enlightenment but therapeutic enlightenment. Instead of working out sociological and other kinds of theories of the self, a critical attitude to the kinds of enlightenment that we direct at ourselves needs to look at the forms of *authority* that have been constructed to arbitrate as to what the self actually is. I claim that any approach to such forms of authority actually requires critical perspectives that have elements in common with nominalist and anti-foundationalist outlooks; that such outlooks are actually the correlate of the kind of authority represented by therapeutic forms of enlightenment themselves. What a critique of enlightenment requires with regard to this field of the politics of subjectivity and selfhood is not another theory of the self, but the means to avoid the requirement for such a theory. The task is, rather, simply to map some of the forms of enlightenment that are already directed at selfhood. That would involve investigation of the extent to which the human sciences have *already* been engaged in the great project of discovering, liberating and managing the self. A critique of enlightenment might then be in a position to develop something like a strategic response to the contemporary politics of selfhood.

Plasticity

The very idea of self-enlightenment is dependent – to adapt an idea from Nietzsche – on "plastic power"; the ability of humans to transform themselves out of the past – "to heal wounds, to replace what has been lost, to recreate broken moulds" (Nietzsche 1983a: 62–3). The plasticity of humans, Nietzsche said, meant they had the power to forget the past, to overcome what would otherwise be intolerable to them. But we can also talk about plasticity in a more mundane sense than is implied in this rather heroic version. Humans are plastic in so far as they are capable of being influenced, persuaded, goaded, advised, succoured, educated, cared for, cured. Precisely because of the plasticity of their nature humans are eminently "governable"; their desires, their view of themselves, their very drives are amenable to the ministrations of authorities of all sorts.

Perhaps there are really two poles to such governability. On the one hand there are all the modern apparatuses for the government of conduct that impinge on the individual, as it were, from outside. Since the early modern period, Western European States have developed a panoply of means for the government of the conduct of individuals; or for what Foucault once termed the "conduct of conduct". Religious forms of regulation have dominated, but there have been other kinds; first, the development of those forms of knowledge centred on the means of governing the State as a population of citizens that are to be the object of a certain kind of pastoral authority, and second, the development of what Foucault, perhaps rather misleadingly, called "the disciplines" themselves, all those kinds of knowledge that were also focused on a problematic of human regulation: psychiatry, criminology, social work, psychology, the "human sciences" in the very broadest sense.

On the other hand, there is the pole of government that is focused if not simply on the self but on the *inward* direction of conduct. For the governability of humans does not exclude the propensity of humans to exert authority over themselves, to impose laws reflexively, to interpret conduct according to moral and ethical principles that are, so to speak, *self*-imposed. That too is part of plastic power; the ability to plumb resources from our inner selves as a means of dealing with, or even standing against, the outside world; what Foucault labelled the technology of the self (Martin, Gutman and Hutton 1988). Obviously the cultivation of such powers has a history of its own, and Weber's *Protestant Ethic* would be only the most celebrated chapter of such a history, although other prominent authors might include Jacob Burkhardt, Marcel Mauss and Foucault himself (cf. Pasquino 1986: 99–100).

These two poles are hard to disentangle, both theoretically and historically. Theoretically, the distinction between forms of government that work from outside the self and those which work from inside seems crude and unconvincing. But that is because it is not quite the right way to think about the distinction. It is not that the inward direction of conduct necessarily *originates* from within the human breast but that the main *object* of the workings of such a power is the inward orientation – the motivations, the self-interpretations, the wills – of individuals. Historically, the distinction is difficult to disentangle because, again, the two conceptions overlap. The work of Gerhard Oestreich, for instance, has indicated the extent to which sixteenth- and seventeenth-century legislation in the European States was directed at a policing of the population that ideologically owed something to the ethical disciplines of the Stoics, to charge the people with a discipline of work and frugality, constructing the citizen as agents able to work on themselves in autonomous, responsible ways (Oestreich 1982; Rose 1996: 77–8). Here, the government of populations might be said to meet up with principles derived ultimately from the technologies of the self. Perhaps we might say, then, that the "modernity" of self-enlightenment consists in the meeting of these two poles, those of government and the self.

A further – surely decisive – aspect to such a modernity lies with the intellectualization of self-enlightenment. In most societies in world history it was only the few that were able to devote themselves to the cultivation of selfhood. Forms of moral cultivation have in most societies been the concern only of élites, and the generalization of such forms of cultivation is really only a phenomenon of the modern West. Today, plastic power is a matter not only of statecraft but of business; the State, private agencies, companies, voluntary associations, professional organizations and individuals are all involved in its exercise. Such influences effectively give an intellectual shape to what was previously handled by most societies in terms of practices of socialization; through the family, education, the inculcation of habit, or through practical systems of pedagogy. Today, however, we have seen the intellectualization of such moral authority in that more and more professionals and experts of all kinds are claiming to fill the gaps of "natural" or "social" authority; by mobilizing specific knowledges directed at citizens and arguing in effect that the usual processes of socialization are insufficient to bring subjects to a full state of maturity without the mediation and ministrations of other, more specialized, powers. This kind of authority is what we can call the expertise of human conduct, or just *expertise* (Rose 1992c: 356–7).

Expertise: ethical and moral

The term expertise usually has a "technological" connotation; it conjures up people like scientists and engineers. But here I refer not to experts in "hard" technology but to the expertise of human conduct: the expertise that focuses, whether or not exclusively, on the cultivation of what might be described as the *personhood of persons*; the expertise of doctors, managers, social workers, lawyers, consultants and professionals and perhaps, above all, psychologists of various kinds and persuasions (Rose 1994). It is hard to be exact about how we measure the proportions of this expansion of the powers of expertise in this sense. This is not quite the same domain as that known to sociologists as the sociology of the professions. We may be more hindered than helped by the prevalence of the vocabulary of the professions and professionalization. This is because this vocabulary has been critical rather than nominalistic in its orientation towards expertise, and because – for good reasons of its own – it has sought to construct the objects of its concerns in a manner oriented towards the idea of a science of society rather than a critique of enlightenment.

Experts of human conduct elaborate forms of knowledge that take a specifically "technical" form; they are designed not just to "know" but to diagnose, change and transform the make-up of individuals. We usually tend to dissociate such expertise from technology because it seems as if there are rather "inhuman" connotations to the idea of a technology of human conduct. Rationalist theories of professionalization and expertise would certainly concur in this. Yet this terminology is useful in that it draws attention to the fact that humans are creatures who are capable by nature if not generally by opportunity of taking their *own* natures and capabilities as objects of transformation. Talking about technologies of expertise enables us to investigate the workings of various kinds of authority without taking a moral stand on their accompanying ideologies of care, humanism, benificence and so forth. Now, the ability *not* to take such a stand is pertinent precisely in so far as, especially in the postwar period, modern expertise has become typically "ethical" rather than being moral (Rose 1990: 255–8). I argue that producing a critique of moral expertise is one thing; a critique of ethical expertise is another. That is because ethical expertise is already enlightened about itself; it is *already* a critique of the powers of authority of expertise. Instead of being directive and authoritarian in form, modern expertise tends deliberately to emphasize the freedom and the choice of its subjects. In fact, if contemporary expertise were simply a question of incarceration and coercion there would not be much of a critical problem. But modern expertise rarely presumes even to be directive of activity; it seeks, rather, to cajole, to encourage, to affirm forms of subjectivity. It works by seeking to act on the ethical capacities of persons rather than seeking to perform acts of moralization on the basis of substantively "correct" forms of conduct. Instead of either applauding this kind of expertise as the saviour of humankind in a world of brutality and ruthless competition or dismissing it as so much ideology (cf. Rieff 1966; Halmos 1979; Edelman 1984), what is required is something akin to what Rose has described as a critical sociology directed at the question of freedom itself (Rose 1992a).

The distinction between moral and ethical expertise is meant to be heuristic rather than structural or morphological. Moral expertise focuses on more or less determinate ways of reforming human capacities, focusing its activities on a particular grouping of persons which it then seeks to reform, regulate, punish or reintegrate in various ways. Moral expertise, we might say, is other-directed in that the object is to work on and reform a constituency deemed to be outside of the normal run of things. Obviously, moral expertise has a history. And obviously this history is tied to the various techniques that have been available for isolating particularly problematic constituencies. Thus moral expertise is initially founded on the problematization of something like deviance; the criminal, the mad, the *immoral*. Technologies appropriate here might be procedural, such as the new forms of statistical reason that isolated the question of suicide as a moral problem in the early nineteenth century (Hacking 1990: 64–72). Or they might be institutional technologies such as the moral space of the asylum, which, as readers of Foucault know, came into existence at the end of the eighteenth century. The asylum was a kind of moral technology in that it was originally a communal space where one was literally reformed out of madness through the inculcation of certain moral ideals foremost among which were those of work, discipline, the organizational use of time, submission to medical authority, and moral solidarity in a community of others (Castel 1985: 256).

The point behind moral expertise is reformation; it seeks to change humans in accord with some or other normative view of what humans should be. For many this is already to invoke the diabolical powers of such expertise; but normalization is by no means an intrinsic evil. Nor should we be lead down the parallel path of social control theory at this point, for expertise is not simply a tale of the State and its legitimation of itself. As Castel insists in the context of psychiatry: "too much stress has been laid exclusively on the internment function of the asylum" (ibid: 257). It is true that for a science of society, the collapse of the utopian space of the asylum into simply a negative, custodial space is more than pertinent. But from the perspective of a nominalist account of expertise, it is the reformatory ideology that is important in itself. And, in this context, we should not make the mistake of assuming that moral control is the same thing as the coercion of carceralism or of social control. As Rose observes:

> The Nineteenth Century was to see the invention of the prison, the work-house and the lunatic asylum as apparatuses to re-model the character of those citizens who transgressed their part in the contract of civility. But civility was also instituted through strategies which attempted to *create* well-regulated liberty *through* freedom, to the extent that they sought to invent the conditions in which subjects themselves would enact the responsibilities that comprised their liberties: individuals would have to be equipped with a moral agency that would shape their conduct within a space that was necessarily indeterminate. (Rose 1992a: 6)

In sum, the distinction between moral and ethical forms of expertise is not simply that of an unenlightened versus an enlightened expertise; rather both represent different ways of inspiring others to enlightenment. The analysis of these kinds of expertise in such terms has been perhaps more hindered than helped by the prevalent critical discourse in the social sciences of professionalization.

An excursus on the sociology of professons

The sociology of the professions has opened up a rich seam of enquiry by investigating the strategies through which professional associations of various kinds have sought to make themselves indispensable within particular cognitive fields, and to enact procedures of moral and occupational enclosure around their activities. Typically, although it is obviously unfair to generalize too much, such sociologies focus on professions as interest-groups, enquiring into the ways, on the one hand, in which professions help to serve the given interests of particular classes and, on the other, how professions evolve specialized forms of discourse giving them hegemony over their various constituencies (Elliot 1972: 52–5; Johnson 1972: 57–8). Often, such emphases lead analysts of the professions into a rather critical approach to their subject matter, rejecting an earlier orthodoxy that tended to regard the professions as a benign counterweight to some of the more ruthless aspects of the capitalist mentality (cf. Abbott 1988; Larson 1991). Instead, the professions are seen as little systems of monopolization, having as their function as much the exclusion of outsiders from a certain monopoly of a cognitive domain as the protection of the best interests of the client (cf. Freidson 1970; cf. Jamous & Pelloile 1970).

Yet however insightful such analyses may have proved themselves to be, it is still the case that they miss some crucial aspects of what I call ethical expertise. Typically sociologies of the professions – concerned as they tend to be with delimiting the concept of the profession as sharply and rigorously as possible – tend either to play down or vastly exaggerate the overall scope of professional powers. If we just think of doctors, lawyers and the like, then professions barely seem all that important to our cultural present (Elliot 1972: 143). Yet nor do we live in anything amounting to such a grandiose concept as a "professional society" unless we were to extend the definition of a profession so far as to make it almost meaningless (cf. Perkin 1989). In that context, perhaps we need to make a distinction between the general cultural ethos of work in modern capitalist societies, and professionalism *per se*. Weber, for instance, thought it was a feature of modern Western societies that they were oriented towards the notion of a "vocation". The final few pages of *The Protestant Ethic and the Spirit of Capitalism* are largely devoted to this subject (Weber 1992b). It is not, as I mentioned earlier, just Protestantism that interests Weber and it is certainly not simply the causal "origins" of capitalism itself. It is rather that Weber thinks that modern "man" is committed to the very idea of the vocation or calling. We expect life to offer us a worldy opporunity to realize ourselves in some kind of work; that, in the widest sense, is the meaning of the famous "work ethic". In that, broadly cultural, sense, we might say, with Weber, that we live in something not unlike a professionalized world. But in that case, professionalism *per se* would be something else again; involving, at the very minimum, some kind of cognitive specialism or claim to such (Freidson 1986). In short, at the very least, the notion of professionalism needs to be separated from more general notions of vocationalism.

Even so, this distinction is not particularly revealing for our purposes when considering the particular question of the expertise of human conduct. Suppose we were to find ourselves finally able – after several decades of the attempt – to come up with a viable definition of a "profession"; one that was enough to satisfy all those in the debate over what exactly a profession is. Then all that would remain to do, surely, would be to count up the numbers. We would be able then to say that such-and-such a proportion of the population were involved in professional activities; and that, we imagine, might put us in a position to say something about the scope of professionalism as a form of power in our societies. Even so, such an exercise still would not tell us very much. For clearly it is not just a quantitative matter. We could count all the doctors, lawyers, architects and others and that might tell us something about the social scale of interest of expertise. It would tell us, in short, something about why professional powers might be of interest from the perspective of a "science of society" and that might be good. But it would not allow us even really to approach the question of professionalism from the perspective of a critique of enlightenment, not least because such a critique would be interested in the context of forms of expertise as styles of authority.

Before investigating further what a critical approach might mean in this context, let me likewise distinguish such an approach from one which would attempt to fit the expertise of conduct into a rationalist model; holding that expertise has infiltrated more and more into everyday existence (Larson 1984). In what he regards as a partial modification of the Weberian perspective, Habermas, for instance, writes of "an élitist splitting-off of expert cultures from contexts of communicative action in everyday life" entailing a "deformation" of modernity and a straightforward reduction in our capacities for freedom (Habermas 1987b: 330–1; cf. MacIntyre 1981: 85–6). But expertise is not necessarily – nor necessarily adversely – invasive of society. Expertise is not straightforwardly implicated in a malign rationalization of the world. Expertise is wholly different from what might be termed "technocratic" expertise; that is, all those "applied" professions – engineering, economics and so forth – that are concerned with something akin to an instrumental relation to the world. An engineer who builds a bad bridge may be a bad engineer, but is still an engineer; but a doctor who makes somebody sick is not just a bad doctor, but is someone who, in an important sense, is not in fact a doctor at all (Airaksinen 1994: 8–9). Nor, then, is the realm of ethical expertise even reducible to that of the professions. Expertise is often, even usually, professionalized; but not all professions constitute expertise in our sense of the term. And this has consequences for those concerned with the analysis and criticism of such forms of expertise. For if we regard expertise strictly in a rationalist way, then so we will be led down the road of – not surprisingly – a critique of such rationalism in the manner, say, of Habermas or unsubtle variations on the so-called iron-cage theme in the work of Weber. This is not to dismiss such conceptions out of hand. It is merely to say that the expertise of human conduct does not necessarily exist only on that, critically speaking, predictable terrain.

Ethical expertise again

That is not least because the difference between moral and ethical expertise is not one between coercion and freedom. The sociology of the professions or of rationalization might do quite well with moral expertise. But even if both are forms of authority which seek to act on human conduct in various ways, and to use the capacity and the desire for "freedom" of humans as a resource, ethical expertise could nonetheless be said to differ from moral expertise in that it makes a less clear distinction between the normal and the pathological, and that it provides no overt determinate content of what moral character should be. It is not that ethical expertise does not partake of a moral form of discourse at all; rather that its moral content is more formal than substantive. In ethical expertise it is the idea of duty that is important, not necessarily the particular content or shape that such duty is to take. That is especially so of all those disciplines that can be grouped together under the label of the "psy" complex of disciplines (Rose 1996). The expertise of counselling, consultancy, psychotherapy and others is less about moral tutelage than about urging people to look at themselves and to pay some attention to the conduct of their own conduct. Such expertise perhaps reflects something like a *flotation* in contemporary moral norms, entailing the opening up of what has been termed an "ethical space" in Western liberal societies (Gordon 1987; Rose 1992b: 144–5; Rose 1996: 99–100).

A fair number of writers have attempted to document this transformation. Perhaps its key text remains Foucault's *The History of Sexuality, volume 1* (Foucault 1976; cf. Castel 1973; Miller and Rose 1988; De Swaan 1990; Rose 1990; and for a feminist defense, Bell 1996). Its achievement was to have isolated and described in the domain of sexual regulation a blurring of the distinction between the normal and the pathological. Although they were barely mentioned in what is in many ways an unsatisfactory work, Freud and psychoanalysis served as Foucault's object of attention here. English – though not perhaps American – readers have often been rather surprised at this emphasis. But really what is of interest about psychoanalysis is not its penetration into society but that it is exemplary of ethical forms of expertise in general. Psychoanalysis, however esoteric in practice, is paradigmatic of the ethical turn in expertise at least in so far as it makes no hard and fast distinction between a category of sick people and a category of well people. For psychoanalysis, our pathology is everywhere within us and within all of us – such that it becomes difficult to speak straightforwardly of "pathology" at all. From the perspective of a critical sociology, psychoanalysis no doubt is not of great importance not least because there are not that many psychoanalysts about (Gellner 1985; cf. Berger 1965). Moreover, the critics of psychoanalysis have focused overwhelmingly on the question of theory and doctrines as opposed to the more mundane yet far more important question of technique. However, as a general rationality of expertise and as a model of authority, and above all as a technology of enlightenment, it is of fundamental interest (Miller & Rose 1994). For in psychoanalysis, the expert is an expert not least because of the mere fact of an ethical work performed on the self. The central notion here is that of the transference; the analysand identifies with the exemplary figure of the analyst and works through their problems *through* the figure of the analyst (Kendall & Crossley 1996: 189). But there is usually no specific moral guidance involved here. The psychoanalyst does not say "follow me" or "do as I say". In fact, the psychoanalyst does not really have to do anything, except *be* a psychoanalyst; and what that requires is a hard-won form of insight into the self; a form of insight that takes the form of an extended training – for all analysts have themselves been analysed.

The psychoanalyst certainly brings enlightenment, or presumes to do so; but it is not a moral form of enlightenment so much as an ethical one. For psychoanalysis we might say that it is just the *fact* of ethics that figures as a duty – the duty to ethics itself, the will to become ethical. Obviously, this form of enlightenment takes different forms depending on the version of analysis under consideration. Freud's own model of enlightenment was, perhaps, a rather grim form of maturity, encapsulated in his comment, admirably free from hubris, that his aim was merely to allow people to live with their own unhappiness. His successors have not all been quite so sanguine about their powers, and some have regarded if not psychoanalysis itself but the forms of expertise that have derived from it as nothing less than a kind technology of salvation (cf. Breuer and Freud 1953: 305; Rose 1990: 241).

But psychoanalysis is only really interesting to a critique of enlightenment from a restricted, strategic point of view. It is akin to a laboratory into which we might look to document the characteristics of ethical forms of expertise, and to witness such characteristics in something like pure, unadulterated form. And beyond psychoanalysis reside all the less grandiose forms of therapy; those that seek to enlighten the individual through a mass of petty techniques aimed at the ethics of the soul (Castel 1973; Rose 1990). These therapies are themselves forms of cultural interpretation in that they seek to be responsible for producing all sorts of attributes, attitudes and affects in persons.

I will come to consider such "psy" therapies further in due course. We shall see that what is distinctive to that approach is the emphasis on relations of authority. This emphasis can be clarified by way of a contrast with the interpretation of such therapies in the terms of a tautological sociology. Compare the views of Anthony Giddens on this score. He regards the therapies as a function of a turn towards reflexivity in the societies of late modernity. For Giddens, it is not just that there are objectively more risks in the world, but that we are ever more perpetually alert to risk, hence the institutional logic of late modern societies leads people to apply the principle of reflexivity to themselves (Giddens 1991b). This is a society of anxious selfhood, shame culture and therapy. For Giddens, people's personal troubles are not just the product of our living in an anomic world. Rather, Giddens paints a picture of individuals excavating their own souls in the name of reflexivity itself: "Therapy is not simply a means of coping with novel anxieties, but an expression of the reflexivity of the self" (Giddens 1991b: 34). Here reflexivity is the *explanans* as well as the *explanandum*.

But what Giddens portrays in epochal terms as a sociological phenomenon that pervades entire societies can instead be seen as being only the consequence of a modification of certain relations to the truth of the self in liberal, Western societies. This modification concerns the links between truth and *authority*; and what we might call new rationalities of truth. For when one is telling the truth about the soul, we see the emergence of a reflexive culture of truth among those authorities claiming the right to speak in the name of therapy. Giddens uses the therapies as part of the tools of his explanation of the reflexive turn whereas really they should be part of the *object* of his explanation; all those authorities that tell us that we are obliged to tell the truth about ourselves. Here authority turns inward upon itself in order to find a ground from which to speak (Foucault 1976: 66–7; Miller and Rose 1994).

If we are to situate ethical expertise in terms of its characteristics as a specific form of authority, it may be of some use to consider the place of this kind of authority in relation to other kinds. This should serve – for instance, by situating such kinds of ethical authority in a longer genealogy than is perhaps usual – to help us to distance the idea of ethical expertise from some of the pictures of it that might otherwise be tempting if rather too easy; for instance, those pictures that see all kinds of expertise as analogues of malign forms of coercion or social control. And who better to turn to for guidance in this task than to Max Weber, who pioneered the study of domination and authority in the social sciences? At this point, then, our study of expertise will have to take something of a theoretical, and then an historical, detour.

Ethical subjection

The kind of authority I am thinking of is not in the first instance the crude domination (or exploitation, or coercion) of humans by humans, but rather a form of domination – for reflexivity is not the new phenomenon suggested by Giddens' analyses – directed at the self by the self. We can call this form of domination ethical subjection. Whereas Weber argued that a science of culture needs to distinguish between three kinds of domination – tradition, charisma and bureaucracy – I suggest that we might do worse than to add a fourth. Ethical subjection is itself a means of legitimating certain kinds of conduct; it is a form of domination in so far as one dominates oneself. Reference to Weber is a little disingenuous here because he really had particular things in mind with his theory of domination. Nevertheless, such a reference point helps to clarify our view that modern ethical expertise draws on the tradition of a particular kind of authority, that is prior to the advent of modern *intellectualized* forms of ethical authority: that is, forms of authority established in the spirit of enlightenment (cf. Rose 1990: 217, Chapter 16 *passim*).

Ethical subjection operates on the "inwardness" of humans; that is, their conviction that they might find the authority for their own conduct from within themselves. Our pictures of such inwardness need to be purged from all the subjectivist categories of consciousness, conscience, identity, individualism and other such terms, even if it captures elements of all of these. Inwardness is not conventional as these are, but strictly cultural – we *invent* inwardness for ourselves. Nor is inwardness a psychological phenomenon; to invoke it is not to invoke a theory of subjectivity. Rather ethical subjection might be seen as a universal – "anthropological" – *propensity* of human beings but it is not a universal *property* as such; indeed, in history the availability of systematic forms of inwardness, in distinction from the prevailing values of a general culture, is probably a rarity. Ethical subjection requires the labour of culture for its existence. It includes all those forms of authority that are legitimated through an appeal to the duty owed to oneself. All rulers and authorities presumably say *obey me* because it is good to do so – hence all rule is "formally" ethical in that sense – but the ethic of inwardness also invokes what is really a specific kind of ethical motivation in saying *obey me because that is the way to be true to yourself*.

Examples of such ethical subjection would take a categorist of Weber's skill and erudition to document. They would include various secular systems of ethics of which the central case might plausibly be Stoicism. The Stoic sage was responsible only to himself, yet rather than being a world-denying ethic, Stoicism underpinned a culture of rule that held that – as part of one's very duty to oneself – one was obligated to dispense justice (Rist 1978: 263, 267). Or we might include the ethics of the Chinese *literati*, so memorably described by Weber himself. The inwardness of the gentlemen *literati* became functional at the point at which a feudal system was replaced by more centralizing powers. Thus Confucianism "provided the administrative personnel with essential qualifications; the imperial officials, in the exercise of local power, in which they replaced the lords and the nobles of the feudal system, needed to be endowed with qualities equivalent to those of their predecessors" (Granet 1975: 104; cf. Munro 1988: 156–7). For Weber, Confucianism was a kind of "status ethic"; but it was also an autonomous orientation towards the world, tied to particular techniques of conduct. A modern example might plausibly even come from that of modern professional ethics. Obviously, we can point to the reproduction of professions on particular class lines and so forth. But professions are not just expressions of class interests and in that sense they are not just expressive of prior social ethics; rather, they have a technical quality in that they represent organizational forms enshrining various deontological principles that organize inwardness (cf. Harris 1994: 106).

I want to suggest that ethical subjection is a peculiar principle of human domination in that it is simultaneously inward and impersonal. Weber's concepts of charisma and bureaucracy, although obviously directed at a different set of problems, are useful to set this notion of ethical subjection into some relief.

Weber probably assumed that all legitimate domination worked on what might be seen as an ethical basis. As Roth points out (Roth 1978: lxxxix), the term *Herrschaft* (domination) is used by Weber as an effective adaptation of the Kantian categorical imperative. Weber says: "*domination* will thus mean the situation in which the manifested will (*command*) of the *ruler* or rulers is meant to influence the conduct of one or more others (the *ruled*) and actually does influence it in such a way that their conduct to a socially relevant degree occurs as if the ruled had made the content of the command the maxim of their conduct for its very own sake" (Weber 1978, vol. 2: 946). In other words, for Weber, all legitimate domination takes an ethical form in so far as a condition of its legitimacy will be that those who are subjected to domination internalize the command as being of intrinsic value in its own right. Yet ethical subjection is a distinct form of domination. For although all forms of authority are in the widest sense "inward", they do not derive their force from inwardness as such; rather, the apposite orientations in conduct are maintained effectively by various forms of administration (patrimonialism, bureaucracy itself) and not by recourse to the self.

The exception is charisma which is, for Weber, ethical in a stronger, more specific sense. Weber writes of charisma as being a kind of inward, personal force that seizes the individual affectively rather than rationally. Charisma is like a conversion that takes over the whole individual and his conduct. Charisma is then inward but it is also personal; it relies on allegiance to a specific person, or surrogate, the charismatic leader. This means that charisma does not entail a duty to the self in a primary way; rather one has a duty to attend to one's own conduct, to one's own inwardness, in so far as one owes allegiance to the leader. Ethical subjection is and is not like charisma. It is like it because it operates as an inward power in the same specific sense, but it is unlike it because it does not operate in a personal way, but – like bureaucracy – through *impersonality*.

In fact ethical subjection is actually more akin to bureaucratic authority than to authority of the charismatic kind. It is impersonal in so far as it involves an *ascesis* directed at the self; a striving to discipline the self, to shape it in certain ways. Ethics of inwardness are, then, a hybrid form of the legitimation of conduct; striking ethically and inwardly yet operating according to a logic that is deliberately impersonal. Ethical subjectivation operates on something like *the will*; it attempts to make the will the slave of principles proper only to itself. What is aspired to – and this is analagous to the rule of the files in bureaucracy – is domination by a kind of impersonal force of the will. It entails the attempt to internalize duty and to make of duty an aspect of inwardness. This is why the language of the self and selfhood are not properly apposite for thinking about ethical subjection. Nor should we think of the ethical component here necessarily in terms of a retreat from the outside world into a private realm of the self. Rather ethical subjection is a way of acting upon the self, of *transforming it into a power*. What is at stake is not just the law of necessity but a striving for domination over the self, which is to say simultaneously for a certain kind of domination over our outside circumstances. No one has bettered the words of one of the great moral theorists of the nineteenth century, J-M Guyau, in arguing on this point:

> Duty will be reduced to the consciousness of a certain inward *power*, by nature superior to all other powers. To feel inwardly the greatest that one is *capable* of doing is really the first consciousness of what it is one's *duty* to do. Duty, from the point of view of the facts – metaphysical notions being left on one side – is a superabundance of life which demands to exercise, to impart itself. Duty has been too much interpreted until now as the sentiment of a *necessity* or *compulsion*. It is, above all, the sentiment of a *power*. (Guyau 1898: 91)

In Weber's work, forms of legitimate domination always have institutional analogues; legal rationalism is expressed in bureaucracy, traditionalism is expressed in patriarchalism and patrimonialism, charisma is expressed in various kinds of religious prophecy and caesaropapism. Can we locate an instititutional analogue for ethical subjection? Perhaps many would suggest themselves. Here I discuss a likely analogue that is interesting not least because it is curiously neglected as a historical force in Weber's own work – and that is aristocracy.

The idea of aristocracy

How is aristocratic power legitimated? Is there an ethical rationality that is characteristic of the aristocrat? Sociologists – with the celebrated exception of

Norbert Elias – have hardly overexerted themselves on this question (Elias 1983; cf. Campbell 1987). We shall find little evidence of a Weberian mechanism of allegiance propping up aristocratic power. In fact, we are faced with plenty of evidence that aristocracy works precisely on the basis of a rational contempt for the very issue of allegiance; and allegiance is legitimated through a contempt for the very idea of legitimation. Elias, for instance, describes the social ethos of the court aristocracy in terms of a sort of deontology of profligacy:

> We find a paradigmatic expression of this social ethos in an action of the Duc de Richelieu related by Taine. He gives his son a purse full of money so that he can learn to spend it like a *grand seigneur*, and when the young man brings the money back his father throws the purse out of the window before his very eyes. This is socialization in keeping with a social tradition that imprints on the individual the duty imposed on him by his rank to be prodigal. (Elias 1983: 67)

Yet the fact that such anti-bourgeois profligacy is considered a duty will obviously tell us something about the kind of allegiance that belongs to aristocratic power. Such power commands allegiance precisely because it *assumes* it rather than commands it as such. The superiority of the aristocrat is not based on claims that are simply traditional, rational or related to the assumption of exceptional powers. Rather the reason is that the aristocrat is supposed to be born to rule; rulership and aristocracy simply go together. In this sense a justification of aristocratic rule would be a contradiction in terms – the aristocrat simply *is* his own justification. Aristocratic domination is based not exactly on the consent of others to aristocratic rule so much as on the aristocrats' own consent to dominate. It is a consent that he owes to himself – and it is for this reason, albeit a kind of denial of a reason, that aristocratic domination is supposed to be legitimated in the eyes of others. Pierre Bourdieu expresses this in terms of an essentialism proper to the spirit of aristocracy:

> Aristocracies are essentialist. Regarding existence as an emanation of essence, they set no intrinsic value on the deeds and misdeeds enrolled in the records and registries of bureaucratic memory. They prize them only insofar as they clearly manifest, in the nuances of their manner, that their own inspiration is the perpetuating and celebrating of the essence by virtue of which they are accomplished. The same essentialism requires them to impose on themselves what their essence imposes upon them – *noblesse oblige* – to ask of themselves what no on else could ask, to "live up" to their own essence. (Bourdieu 1986: 24)

In short, because of this demand to live up to their own essence, the legitimation of aristocratic power is largely to be found within the aristocrat himself, in a certain stylization of ethical subjection through inwardness, in that well-known sensibility of an innate superiority. The aristocrat is not, however, necessarily just somebody born to rule but somebody with an essential "distance" – we might say, thinking again of Weber, an "inner distance". In other words, there is a strongly ascetic aspect to being an aristocrat. The historian J.C.D. Clark, insisting on the rationality of the aristocratic code, has characterized this stance in terms of what he calls the "social theory of élite hegemony". By this he means an ethic of inwardness governing the way in which – if one imagined oneself as a particular kind of person – we governed one's own conduct (Clark 1985: 95).

As Clark insists, there is much misunderstanding of aristocratic rule. Perhaps it seems to most – and especially if we take bureaucratic forms of authority as the norm – more or less irrational, the paradigm – no doubt precisely because it has a kind of inherent unjustifiability to it – of an anti-modern and certainly an anti-enlightened kind of authority. But this is misleading because the essentialism of aristocratic power is often misunderstood to be an essentialism by birth when in fact it is an essentialism by status (cf. Schalk 1986: 115–44). It is true that the aristocrat is necessarily someone of high birth, "born to rule". But that does not mean that high birth precludes education into our birthright. No one was ever born an aristocrat in the sense that to be one is enough to consider ourselves born to rule. Indeed where this comes to be the case, historians usually begin speaking of a decline (a better term might be moral implosion) of the aristocracy; and these are the periods during which we begin to see the proliferation of overt *justifications* of aristocracy – something that would have been anaethema in a truly aristocractic age.

In short, the inwardness of the aristocrat is derivative of a strict ethical subjection to the duties of rank. That is the *basis*, indeed, of aristocratic legitimation. The aristocrat is only someone who is fit to be obeyed in so far as he bears a sense of dignity – which is really only a term for the duty one owes to oneself. But this sense of a duty owed to oneself and to one's rank is held to have consequences for government. The aristocrat is a governor precisely because he belongs to a status community that is well-practised in the virtues necessary for government. The aristocrat's very distance is, in part, what fits him out for this task. As Tocqueville put it, "The nobles, placed so high above the people, could take the calm and benevolent interest in their welfare which a shepherd takes in his flock" (Tocqueville 1969: 13; quoted in Elster 1993: 109). Moreover, being an enduring status community, aristocracy itself is supposed to be above petty interests and the mean squabbles of democracy:

Nothing in the world is so fixed as an aristocracy. The mass of the people may be seduced by its ignorance or its passions; a king may be taken off his guard and induced to vacillate in his plans; and moreover, a king is not immortal. But an aristocratic body is too numerous to be caught, and yet so small that it does not easily yield to the intoxication of the thoughtless passion. An aristocratic body is a firm and enlightened man who never dies. (Tocqueville 1969: 230; quoted in Elster 1993: 108–9)

From the perspective of a critical attitude to enlightenment, this notion of an enlightened aristocracy is not quite as incongruous as it may initially seem from the perspective, for instance, of an epochal sociology or a critical theory of society. But care must be taken to distinguish the ethos of aristocracy from the status group composed of aristocrats *per se*. What I have all too briefly elaborated is something akin to a Platonic ideal of aristocracy, according to which rule of the self – a certain inward authority – is a condition for the rule of others; but it is a model that goes well beyond antiquated aristocratic communities *per se*. My argument is rather that what we call aristocracy is only the status-ethic version of a more general principle of inwardness as an authorization of domination or rule, a principle that may have its own variants in today's age of enlightenment.

Aristocracies of expertise

There are grounds for saying that at least one aspect of the genealogy of modern ethical expertise might be discovered in the heritage of the aristocratic spirit. In any case, what such a linkage would highlight would be that such expertise is as much a striving for ethical excellence and ethical exemplarity as it is for moral or knowledgeable "closure" on the part of particular status groups. Positing such a link would mean thinking even of the figure of the advisory professional as first and foremost a kind of ethical construction. The early notions of the professional were modelled on a notion of the "gentleman" who possessed an inner dignity and a distance from the immediate difficulties of the world. According to Joseph Jacob, the model of the ideal-typical gentleman dates from the early Renaissance, and its central text is Castiglione's *The Courtier* of 1561 (Jacob 1988: 117–23). Obviously the idea is modelled on that of nobility; with the difference that the gentleman's qualities can be the object of a deliberate pedagogy more or less separated from the question of our original status or rank at birth. Nevertheless the triumph of the notion of the gentleman was a triumph for the aristocratic principle of essence over existence. The notion carried the insistence that we can *learn* to inherit our essence.

The professional gentleman is supposed to be reserved and detached, practising a sort of "nonchalance which conceals all artistry" (ibid: 119). The expert obviously cultivates a form of inner distance from the immediate interests of their constituency; the ethical expert does not bear a straightforwardly "instrumental" relation to their work. By contrast, in a mere "occupation", one has no ethical or "inward" relation to one's tasks; one is, rather, "occupied" in a more or less passive sense. But the expert of conduct is involved in a symbiotic relation between the work that is performed in occupational acts and the work that is performed on the self; hence, here the ethical component of the work in hand is internal to the kind of work itself (cf. Airaksinen 1994: 8–9).

Expertise also shares with the idea of aristocracy something that is quite often pointed out: its insulation from ideologies of calculation and profitability. Clark's examples from the *ancién regime* in England are gambling, fox-hunting and duelling. These practices were integral to what it meant to be both an aristocrat and a "gentleman" (cf. Perkin 1991: 274). Again, these were not just sports or mere acts of consumption but ascetic stylizations of our honourability. Clark argues that duelling, for example, "is the best index to, and proof of, the survival and power of the aristocratic ideal as a code separate from, and ultimately superior to, the injunctions of law and religion. Each duel was a deliberate act of rebellion against both, and a gesture of contempt towards the prudent, rational, calculating values which plebeians might be thought necessarily to hold" (Clark 1985: 109; cf. Perkin 1989: cf. Perkin 1991: 237–52).

The point, overall, is that all too often we tend to have a picture of the ethics of professionalism and of aristocracy as being opposed, perhaps because the professional is often taken to be akin to a kind of bureaucrat. But the expert professional is really the opposite of a bureaucrat. They are rather somebody who has cultivated what is essential to them, virtuosi of ethical subjection. Hence the peculiar idea of the professional "vocation"; somebody who is "called" to their professional tasks. One would never need to be "called" just to be a petty bureaucrat. Rather the professional calling lies in a line of continuity with aristocratic paternalism. Perkin quite rightly insists that the:

> supposedly pre-industrial, aristocratic, anti-industrial attitudes propagated by the public schools and Oxbridge, which some historians … have blamed for the decline of the industrial spirit in England, were in fact the newly emergent social values of the reforming schoolmasters and dons whose disdain for industry and trade stemmed from their conviction that professional service was in every way superior to what they regarded as "money grabbing". (Perkin 1989: 119; cf. Clark 1985: 109)

Such attitudes were also a modification of aristocracy; but what they had in common was an emphasis on the principle of the government of one's own conduct as being a prerequisite for enacting one's duty of governing others. What was common to both was the ethic of inwardness itself.

Exemplarity

In any case, the analogy of expertise with aristocracy suggests both a similarity and a difference. Such an analogy suggests, first, that the emphasis on the dissemination of more or less rational forms of knowledge by expertise should not be of primary interest for our critical attitude to therapeutic enlightenment. *Rationalist* models of expertise will not get us very far in this respect. All expertise aims for the status of truth – the truth of the self – but what is less important than the dogma that is inherent to such forms of truth is the ethical fabrication of those who are to be the masters or guardians of such kinds of truth. Ethical experts are not just virtuosi of certain kinds of reason, but practical virtuosi of the self, living embodiments of ethical doctrine. In other words, to understand the epistemological make-up of expertise entails looking at the ethical make-up of the *proponents* of expertise; at "personality" in ethical expertise, and at all those forms of ethical subjection that experts practise upon themselves in order to establish themselves as authorities of conduct. That means that, as well as looking at the ideology of the "psy" disciplines, at education, at all those areas of "applied knowledge", attention needs to be given to the ethical make-up of the proponents of knowledge – teachers, social workers, therapists, managers – as exemplars of the expertise in question.

If forms of expertise are not generally reducible to rational ideologies, and if ethical expertise is embodied in the habitus of the practitioners rather than any belief system or set of ideas, this is not simply to attribute to expertise a practical rather than a rational status. For expertise is really a rational technology for *disseminating* ethical qualities and attributes. Again, psychoanalysis might form the paradigmatic example (although others might be replicated from business and management, education, the psychotherapies, and various kinds of consultancies and therapeutic rationalities). In psychoanalysis, the analysand identifies with the analyst, and imbibes thereby some of the ethical qualities of the analyst; the analysand learns in a practical context what it is to adopt the ethical attitudes of one who has been psychoanalysed. Or take the example of educational ideology. Ethical truth is learned but not necessarily formulated, recounted or theorized. Therapeutic enlightenment is not the rationalization of conduct, nor the corrosion of the "ethicality" of the world. It is rather the attempt to embody such ethicality in rational form, by relating it to particular systems of truth.

Expertise is not, then, the effect of more or less anonymous processes of rationalization. Far from being rationalistic in its provenance, it acts, more often than not, according to procedures of "prestigious imitation" wherein the constituency is supposed to learn from the practical example provided by the habits of the experts; and the work that modern experts perform on themselves in order to cultivate inwardness may just be exemplary of the ethical work of inwardness that their constituency is also supposed to perform. This means that a critique of self-enlightenment needs to begin with those aristocrats of selfhood, the experts themselves, rather than with formal ideologies of self-enlightenment. As Ian Hunter puts it: "the ethical dimension of culture is not founded in a universal moral or historical self-consciousness – whether that of 'man', or the 'universal class'. Instead it must be seen as a product of the specific ethical practice through which a minority of ethical athletes have shaped a relation to the self as the subject of moral action" (Hunter 1988: 99). Ethics derive from minority practices of those designated or who designate themselves with ethical authority. But, for all its aristocratism of origin, ethical subjection may easily have *democratic* implications; for the premise is that the ethical forms purveyed in various forms of expertise are actually widely transferable and that the expert corps are the medium for that transferral.

So professions and experts may have a special morality; but this does not make them an "out group" as such if that means that they have a different or an alien morality – rather, they have an *exemplary* morality, one which is held up for others to imitate (cf. Williams 1995: 193). The democratization of ethical subjection has been labelled "proto-expertise", meaning the way in which people become "experts of themselves" (cf. de Swaan 1990). And, with expertise, one is only the master of others in so far as this is exemplary for the ways in which they can be masters of themselves. What is at stake is not so much a particular kind of subjectivity with a specific content but the establishment of relations of authority over the self and over others, such that – if we are an expert – the way in which we are an authority over ourselves informs the way we can be an authority over others.

Performativity

The association of ethical expertise with aristocracy via practices of ethical subjection is meant to reveal differences as well as similarities. Above all, the difference is that expertise is intended as a form of enlightenment; it involves specialized languages and forms of knowledge that are supposed not just to guide a way of life but to tell and reveal a particular kind of *truth* (Rose 1990).

Expert corps might, then, be seen as specialized speech communities, utilizing secondary speech genres that are at some remove from the discourses of everyday life (Bakhtin 1986: 72; cf. Bourdieu 1988: 63–4). But they are so removed only in order to work on everyday life to more effect; in any case, such removal does not necessarily signal a claim to detachment. Rather, we might say that the detachment of such speech genres is the price we pay for their *involvement*, their very ability to gain a purchase on everyday life (cf. Elias 1978). Moreover, there is seepage between specialism and constituency; the constituents absorb the language of the specialists and turn it to their own account. Such genres are, no doubt, characterized by particular styles and by particular modes of addressivity; that is, they are addressed in certain ways to certain people and, no doubt, in some manner actually contribute to the ways in which we understand those who are addressed and how they understand themselves. Forms of expertise – moral or ethical – typically operate through forms of classification which do as much to produce as to reflect existing kinds of individual difference (cf. Douglas & Hull 1992). In that sense, such speech genres are not merely the exclusive property of some professional community but act on and are drawn on by both the professional community and its constituency. What is at stake is something like the performative effects of language on people, whether professional, expert or public; that is, the ways in which authorities of various kinds induce us to conceive of ourselves and to act in certain ways. All authoritative speech functions in this way. "All speech," says J.G.A. Pocock, "is performative in the sense that it does things to people. It redefines them in their own perceptions, in those of others, and by restricting the conceptual universes in which they are perceived" (Pocock 1984: 39). Quite so. But perhaps we might think of various of the professions and forms of expertise as those agencies which have turned such performativity into a specialized vocation and tied to specific claims to truth; in short, as something like vocational technologies of enlightenment.

Normalization

To say that forms of expertise use knowledges and truths to act on their constituencies is to say, in effect, that expertise seeks to be a form of *normalization*. In other words, all expertise, whether moral or ethical, seeks to bring certain human capacities into alignment with certain systems of truth. For many, to designate expertise as such is immediately to open the way for a critique of expertise. But things are more difficult than this; and that is for two reasons. The first is because normalization is not intrinsically bad; the second because, as I shall argue in relation to the so-called "psy" disciplines, expertise is oriented to the truth of the self and is not just attributable to false knowledge or ideology. Taken together these make straightforwardly dismissive critiques of expertise – in terms of social control, or whatever – doubly difficult.

All expertise, it would seem, attempts to modify a situation. Expertise is almost by definition curative; it seeks to ameliorate, change, enlighten, liberate. In this sense, all expertise ultimately refers to a *medical* model. And this is not surprising, especially if we consider the extent to which the image of medicine was important for the Enlightenment itself (Gay 1966). But, contrary to the critical traditions of most sociology, normalization is not intrinsically a bad thing; that the medical model normalizes should not be regarded as indicative of a betrayal of its enlightenment roots (Illich 1976; cf. Canguilhem 1989). Certainly, it is necessary to expose the limits of the argument that holds that we live in something like a medicalized society, in which our daily lives are administered through expert-assisted problems (Rose 1990: 257; cf. Bauman 1991: 213–14).

Medicine normalizes. But what does it normalize? More or less straightforward *vital norms* are of importance here; broken legs, lung diseases and so forth are clearly – for the individual concerned – negative states when compared to their absence. Indeed, we are tempted to say, with Canguilhem, that it is the body itself that is normative, the body itself that dictates what norms are proper to medicine. The body sets its own norms of optimal functioning. When these are impaired, the doctor sides with the body in its struggle to restore optimality, even if it is impossible to return fully to the "normal" state (Canguilhem 1989). This means that medicine is not a "science", in the conventional sense of that term, but a way of using certain kinds of clinical truth to take sides on the part of the human individual. But problems arise when we move away from such areas of agreement over vital norms, and when medicine is tempted to tread in territories beyond the vital norms of the individual. For instance, there is a world of difference between the doctor acting in the interests of the normativity of the body, and expertise acting in the interests of a norm that has been "discovered" in a population. What is the relation between individual vital norms and the norms of a population? In fact, what is at stake is quite a different understanding of the normal itself. Ian Hacking tells us that:

> As a word, "normal' . . . acquired its present most common meaning only in the 1820s. The normal was one of a pair. Its opposite was the pathological and for a short time its domain was chiefly medical. Then it moved into the sphere of – almost everything. People, behaviour, states of affairs, diplomatic relations, molecules: all these may be normal or abnormal. (Hacking 1990: 160)

Things are further complicated by the fact that, as Hacking shows, there is an ambiguity about what we mean by normality. There is a conservative sense in which the normal just is whatever is normal; and there is a more prospective sense in which the normal is a desired state (ibid: 168–9). Then there are ambiguities about how the normal should itself be determined, and – even more problematic – how the range of abnormalities are to be judged (Canguilhem 1989: 237–56). What is an acceptable range of abnormality? Is abnormality the same as pathology? But in spite of the host of ambiguities surrounding the term, the point is that from the perspective of power, the normal is an immeasurably useful concept. Certainly the idea of normality is central to the proliferation of expertise. It provides a sort of flag or standard around which a multitude of "practical human sciences" seek to orientate themselves: criminology, psychology, pedagogy, social work; in short, what Foucault called "the disciplines". "For the marks that once indicated status, privilege and affiliation were increasingly replaced – or at least supplemented – by a whole range of degrees of normality indicating membership of a homogeneous social body but also playing a part in classification, hierarchization and the distribution of rank" (Foucault 1979: 184). But just because such disciplines normalize does not make them intrinsically bad, not least because there may be wide agreement and transparency concerning the assumptions and procedures behind such normalization.

If, in general, medicine works in the interests of our general norms this is both because, when it comes to the body, and even when it comes to the population, there is a remarkable amount of *agreement* about the values we wish to pursue and because there are technical means for stabilizing such agreement. We wish to retain the autonomy and longevity of our bodies, and are usually prepared to submit to the medical profession in so far as this is the case. Likewise, populations might generally be expected to agree on the desirability of prophylactic measures such as sanitary regulation or inoculation campaigns. The problem arises when there is less agreement as to what those norms should be, and when expertise is dogged by a certain technical insufficiency. Such is the case with ethical expertise in general and most obviously with psychological expertise in particular; where there are both less generally agreed norms and less technical sufficiency of operations. And that is the point. It is not the existence of ethical expertise that is interesting – for such means of governing conduct are, as we have seen, not necessarily so novel. Rather what is significant is the characteristic of certain modern kinds of expertise to seek to tie themselves to the pursuit of intellectual kinds of enlightenment. Hence, in turn, the fundamental importance of psychology and the "psy" disciplines as a provocation for the very problematic of a critical attitude to enlightenment. For if medicine seeks to normalize vital norms, what do the "psy" disciplines seek to normalize?

Psychologization

Psychology is a professional discipline but it is no more a straightforwardly "scientific" one than is medicine. Since Wundt's establishment of the first psychological laboratory in 1879, psychology has viewed itself as an autonomous discipline with its own domain (Danziger 1990: 17). But psychology, in a wider sense, is also a form of expertise, not just as a discipline but in terms of the way in which psychological concepts and notions have invaded terrains outside the discipline of psychology proper: in medicine, social work, various forms of consultancy – all those domains which one historian has labelled the "psy complex" (Rose 1985, Rose 1990, Rose 1996). For some critics, this very dissemination of the "psy" disciplines into society has lead to worries that we have embraced a regime of psychic "law and order". For some, psychology, in this wide sense of the term, is synonymous with personal enlightenment itself; for others it is wholly antithetical to it. Perhaps this ambivalence is internal to "psy" itself. As Canguilhem put it in the context of French psychology: one road from the institute of psychology leads up to the intellectualism of the Sorbonne, the other down to the prefecture of police (Canguilhem 1980).

The first critical problem presented by psychology for a critical attitude to enlightenment is that there is an intrinsic and obvious difficulty when it comes to reaching agreement over the status of mental norms; and even that, for some critics, to impose a mental norm can go against what it means to have a vital norm at all. Whatever the scientific pretensions of psychology, it is limited by the very object of its analysis: on the one hand, its territory cannot be directly observed and, on the other, one of the symptoms of infraction of a psychological norm may be that one has no idea of the infraction – which has, then, to be referred solely to the interpretation of the "experts". This means that there is always the risk in psychology – hence, in the other human sciences, the suspicion of its diabolical character – that in seeking to impose mental norms it is basically an instrument of social control. Psychology always and necessarily runs this risk. And although psychology may claim its authority from medicine, in fact it can never straightforwardly do so. Whereas organic medicine can at least claim to derive its norms from the vital order of the body and from thence transferring such norms to populations, psychology typically reverses this logic and – as Rose insists – derives its conception of its object from statistical norms found in populations (Rose 1985: 229):

> To derive a theory of normality from a conception of the normativity of a life process and the incidence of a pathology is one thing. To derive a theory of normality from the normativity of a statistical average and the incidence of variations from it is another ... Health, for the psychology of the individual, is not so much life in the silence of the organs as life in the silence of authorities. (ibid: 231)

But does this mean we have to criticize psychology as falsehood or ideology? That would make things easier, but it is not a realistic path for a critique of therapeutic enlightenment. We can expose the limits of psychological reason and we can criticize or refute particular elements or tendencies of psychological knowledge and methodology. But a critique of psychological therapeutics *as such* is an unrealistic proposition. The limitations on psychology are necessary, and not just the product of the ignorance or hubris of psychologists. It is naïve to be opposed *in principle* to forms of specialized knowledges such as those of doctors, teachers or psychologists. It is not that the disciplines are themselves intrinsically tyrannical but that they need to be subjected to the "discipline" of the citizens themselves (Walzer 1983: 290). But this is not so easy as we might imagine; especially in the case of psychology, and not just because of the notorious opacity of mental facts, but rather because of the particular kind of intervention that is proper to psychology.

I argued in the previous chapter that science is a form not just of reflection or representation but of intervention (Hacking 1983a). If science *intervenes* with its subject matter, the mode of operation of expertise is *interference* with its constituency. Again, I will focus on psychology; not because we live in a psychologized society, but only because psychology can be considered to be the "central case" of enlightened ethical expertise. Psychology is not a "science of man" in the sense of an objective, neutral discipline. Rather, psychology "makes up" people (Hacking 1986; Rose 1996: 13). That is to say that forms of expertise like psychology interfere with their subject matter and interact with people's own conceptions of self. Indeed, psychological expertise is only the paradigmatic example of a discipline that invents what Hacking calls "moral kinds"; a discipline that exists in a dynamic relation to its subject matter, perhaps promoting the very forms of behaviour that it is designed to discover out there in the world and subject to its standards of normality. Critics often point out that there is a kind of circularity or looping-effect in operation between the ways in which people conceive of themselves and the forms of expertise that are brought about to conceive of them. Old-fashioned labelling theory used to hold that people were labelled by agencies, such as psychiatry, and then gradually people came to recognize themselves in the label; in other words, the labels provided by expertise functioned as self-fulfilling devices (Scheff 1966). The point about the label was that it took over the whole self. The notion of making up people is not so different. Except that in contrast to labelling theory, the process of construction of moral kinds is not necessarily a malign, ideological act. It is not that the label is false. Rather there is a self-fulfilling aspect to making up people. Hacking calls this dynamic nominalism:

> The claim of dynamic nominalism is not that there was a kind of person who came increasingly to be recognized by bureaucrats or by students of human nature but rather that a kind of person came into being at the same time as the kind itself was being invented. In some cases, that is, our classifications and our classes conspire to emerge hand in hand, each egging the other on. (Hacking 1986: 228)

This means that – in contrast to labelling theory – it will not do to use ideology-critique as a means of criticizing psychology in particular and ethical expertise in general. Psychology is not straightforwardly "ideological" in this sense. For we cannot say with any certainty that expertise is wrong, "true" or "false". We can *disapprove* of expertise on a moral level but not decisively falsify its "findings" on an epistemological one; and that is simply because it is one of the notorious characteristics of expertise to bring into existence what it is describing. This fact alone means that special methods of criticism are required when it comes to the technologies of self-enlightenment; methods which do not necessarily pitch some alternative truth of the self against the truths told by the "psy" disciplines but which attempt, for instance, to disrupt some of their certainties through "critical histories" of expertise (Rose 1996: 41).

All this means that there are good reasons for some kinds of anti-foundationalism and nominalism with regard to psychological authority. But there may also be dangers to such an outlook. For there is a further question to ask at this point. What is the *ontology* of such expertise? What aspect of humans does expertise "make up"? Many forms of critique in the human sciences have come to grief over this question. It would be misleading to suggest that what is made up is the self, subjectivity or identity as such. For that implies that we would ourselves know what the self is, in the form, say, of a general theory of the self. But on the other hand, it is theoretical hubris to suggest that forms of expertise *wholly* make up persons; that is to *equate* the self with the effects of expertise. One of the difficulties with some accounts that are inspired by Foucault's work, for example, is that they can sometimes look as if they are contributions to a complete description of modern personhood, identity or subjectivity. We sometimes even hear nonsense to the effect that Foucault has a *theory* of the "modern subject" to offer us, even though Foucault's problematic was not critical sociology but the philosophical critique of enlightenment. A similar story could be told of all those postmodern debunkings of selfhood; they likewise often convey the impression that in contrast to established notions of identity and so forth, they themselves are really "in the know" about the true nature of the self. As regards expertise, and to avoid precisely this kind of interpretative hubris, we need instead a more limited notion of the "ontology" of its concerns. A good candidate, which we adapt loosely from the work of Ian Hacking, is that of intentions.

Governing intentions

To invoke intentions is to take a deliberately restricted view. Intentions are not everything. They are not motives, subjectivity, consciousness, identity or the self. Intentions, says Anscombe, are answers to "why questions"; responses given to others or ourselves about what we have done or will do (Anscombe 1966: 24–6). This means that intentions are accounts rather than desires, which means that they are essentially ethical, involving questions of obligation and interpretations of "ought". Anscombe insists that we can only have an intentional action under a description: "The description of what we are interested in is a type of description that would not exist if our question of 'why' did not" (ibid: 83). There is no such thing, then, as an "interior" intention, and we need to distance ourselves from a certain view of intentions which holds that they are somehow the products of our well-springs of interiority: in other words, that intentions come straightforwardly from within us (cf. Mills 1963 for a celebrated sociological version of this argument). The question would then be: where do our practices for the description of intention come from? Obviously from many sources. But we are not indulging in the hubris of the theorization of subjectivity if we say that one of the functions of ethical expertise of all kinds, and of the "psy" disciplines in particular, is to provide us with such vocabularies and the scope for their coherence. This perspective also helps us to avoid an overblown emphasis on the self as the effect of power. Our intentions are governed, intellectualized – but not necessarily *controlled* or determined by expertise; they are shaped, cajoled, *directed* but not crushed. We can just as well see ethical expertise as generative of a greater latitude in the scope of our intentions as opposed to a restriction of such latitude. As Hacking observes: "When new intentions become open to me, because new descriptions, new concepts, become available to me, I live in a new world of opportunities" (Hacking 1995a: 236).

On the other hand, one of the effects of expertise is more typically to claim a monopoly on our vocabularies of intention. By no means a complete monopoly, and besides there are many different kinds of psychology. Nevertheless, there is a monopolization *tendency* within the very logic of psychology in that it seeks to fix intentions into the logic of a more or less scientific truth. Psychology is not just a way of describing intention but aspires to be a form of enlightenment. The fact that intentions are up for grabs with regard to possibilities of description means that there is such a thing as a politics of intentions. Psychology does not erode the lifeworld, construct the self, or impose a monolithic view of human subjectivity on the flux of conduct; but it *does* have a tendency to corrode the possibilities for such a politics of intentions.

Consider, very briefly, the politics of psychotherapy, which concerns itself, above all, with the recovery and manipulation of memories of intentions – whether of those analysed or of others. As Hacking shows in his book on multiple personality disorder, there is no possibility of a scientific account of explanations of memories of child abuse (Hacking 1992c; Hacking 1995a; cf. Hacking 1995b). Hacking writes about what he calls "memoro-politics"; "a politics of the secret, of the forgotten event that can be turned, if only by strange falshbacks, into something monumental" (Hacking 1995a: 214). In fact, says Hacking, memories – like the past – are essentially indeterminate. Hacking glosses Anscombe's work to defend the view that the past is in fact changeable from the perspective of the present. There is a logical aspect to this. "Old actions under new descriptions may be re-experienced in memory ... As we change our understanding and sensibility, the past becomes filled with intentional actions, that, in a certain sense, were not there when they were performed" (ibid: 249–50). In other words, the past – in so far as it is a past conditioned by descriptions of intention – can actually be changed by the practices and preoccupations of the present.

The point is not that an open memoro-politics has been replaced by a more restrictive politics based on the findings of psychotherapy; for, as Hacking insists, memoro-politics is itself the product of an initial problematization of memory in the human sciences (ibid: 213). It is rather that such a politics is as much a question of ethics as it is of science or truth. Or rather it is a question of an ethics *of truth*. The very indeterminacy of memory makes moral demands on us. Expertise both promotes and thereby delimits our capacities for such ethical invention: that is, to curb our capacities for increasing the number of things we can do intentionally. Thus, to continue with an example from Hacking, the contemporary "pardoning" of court-martialled Great War deserters on the grounds that they were suffering from a particular kind of illness – "post-traumatic stress disorder" – did not increase the things that the soldiers could have done intentionally but decreases them. As Hacking comments: "I think I might be proud that my ancestor had the wit to try to desert, the most rational thing to do, under the circumstances" (ibid: 116). What counts here is that memory is an ethical matter. Particular intentional actions can be viewed under particular kinds of description; but in balancing such descriptions – even in the past – is an ethical consideration. The deserters may have been suffering from post-traumatic stress disorder; but whether we prefer that description to a description in terms of a sensible flight from danger in the midst of an absurd campaign is an ethical not a scientific matter.

This, then, suggests a possible focus for a critique of enlightenment with regard to the ethics of expertise. The critical aim would not be to denounce the "psychologization of man" or to hint darkly at the complicities of psychology with power, but to conduct analyses which are designed to hold open the door for an ethical interpretation of intentional action; not to denounce practices of ethical subjection but to make their renewal a possibility. But, as the philosophers would say, from what "ground" would such a critique take its authority?

Utopian ethics

The fact that expertise interrelates with its subject matter is not necessarily a reason for despair. The idea that there could be forms of society which did not have forms of ethical authority at all is a chimera, and I have done my best to show that ethical subjection is itself rather a *basic* – if hardly universal – form of domination. A critique of enlightenment directed at ethical expertise might be regarded only as a positive science of authority, one concerned only with the "how" of authority, and not tempted – in softening it up for critique – to reduce all authority, as so often occurs in the social sciences, to the category of authoritarian*ism* (cf. Watt 1982). Thus merely to *problematize* authority might in itself be seen as an aspect of enlightenment.

But if this kind of enlightenment is just an exit, what is written on the door? At the beginning of this chapter, I mentioned the question of ethical expertise in the context of the contemporary politics of the self. Today there are numerous accounts and genealogies of selfhood which attempt to outline the definitive theories of subjectivity, or to isolate the specificities of the modern view of the soul (Carrithers, Collins and Lukes 1985; Taylor 1989; Giddens 1991b). A critique of therapeutic enlightenment, as I see it, would not need to commit itself to adding to such accounts. It should not seek to provide a realist theory of the self, although in the next chapter I shall look briefly at the question of certain – aesthetic – regulatory ideals that might be measured against the modern self. Nevertheless, the realism of a critique of enlightenment need not commit us to any certainties concerning the truths of the self, subjectivity, identity or personhood. This would not be because the critique of enlightenment is opposed in principle to such projects. Indeed, having no theory of subjectivity of its own, it does nothing to refute them. Nor is it necessarily to take the form of some postmodern fashion that, almost as a matter of honour, always celebrates the diasporic character of selfhood or identity wherever it finds it. On the contrary; fissured, multiple identities are not generally pleasant to experience and such melancholy celebrations are all too often the product of the romantic fantasies of self so often indulged by intellectuals, especially those who like to regard themselves as being marginalized in some or other way. A more worthwhile critical attitude would be directed, in any case, to a very different end. Its agnosticism about the self is a matter of a certain utopianism about the self; the self *might* be able to choose its own substance, its own freedom, its own descriptions. Such a view is utopian in the strong, deliberate, *ethical* sense; it is completely unrealistic, even undesirable. But it is a yardstick for measuring the forms of enlightenment that are directed at the self and for thus gaining a certain distance from them. In short it is a kind of *active* – restricted, strategic – utopianism, a means of directing criticism at the present.

Such a distantiation is also the opposite of the view – often associated, regrettably, with Foucault's work – that holds that selves are just the functions of power or discourse or whatever. A critical attitude to enlightenment may be grounded in a utopian vision of human capacities; but it might often give its *subject matter* and – for that very reason – the gloss of dystopia. By emphasizing the extent to which our selves are governed by psychological discourse or by expertise, we reassert the right or rather the will *not* to be so governed. Critiques of enlightenment are performative in that they themselves, in their very enactment, serve to assert such rights. But the verdicts which are characteristic of such critiques are not in the form of sociological descriptions but the diagnoses of a tendency. In short, a critique of enlightenment directed at the ethics of expertise is itself *ethical* rather than scientific or programmatic. And if its motto, at least with regard to contemporary expertise, is indeed the Nietzschean one of a *war on psychology*, this is not itself a morality or a worldview. We can kill psychology in the name of enlightenment and still go to a psychologist to sort out our problems *and* still believe that psychologists are telling us something of the order of a truth about ourselves. The critique of therapeutic enlightenment is not, then, necessarily a summons to live without psychology. Nor is it a philosophy or worldview that holds that contingency is our *essence* (cf. Rorty 1989). On the contrary, its aim is to dramatize the possibility of contingency which – no doubt being essentially *rare* – requires such restricted methods to bring it into consciousness *as* a possibility. What defines the anti-foundational aspect of such a perspective is not a scepticism with regard to the unity of the self so much as a certain, nominalistic attitude to various kinds of *authority* over the self; an anti-foundationalism about authority that implies a sort of background foundationalism with regard to the very existence and desirability of *ethics*.

The critical attitude to enlightenment has to insert itself inside such an ethical space; it might be seen as an enterprise that is directed at bringing about effects that are also *affects*. Such a habit of critique might function not as an alternative "theory" of the self but as an exhortation to expand the horizon of our judgement with regard to our capacities; not to give up hope or to say that our contingency has been reduced to discipline or something abstract and faceless such as "power", but to dramatize the contingency that – whatever its difficulty – exists as the very basis of the very possibility of the invention, re-invention and redescription of our ethical capacities.

For many sceptics and critics this will not be enough; they will demand some kind of alternative model or theory to oppose to therapeutic authority. The next chapter no doubt illustrates, among other things, the difficulties – if perhaps the inevitability, the irresistibility – of such a view.

Chapter 4

Aspects of aesthetic enlightenment

Aesthetic morality – Aestheticism – Art as ideology – Art and the ethics of truth – Aesthetic truth – The new – Creativity and freedom – The ethic of the aesthetic – On willing what cannot be willed – Aesthetic responsibility – Teaching freedom

Social critics, epistemologists and depressed or unhappy people all have tendencies to worry about therapeutic enlightenment. What accounts for their worries is not least the suspicion that they are being fed dogma or pseudo-science in the name of enlightenment. Perhaps what is worrying is not that therapists and their ilk seek to erect themselves as authorities over conduct – for as we saw, there is a long tradition of that – so much as the tendency to claim legitimacy for therapeutic kinds of authority from intellectual doctrines about the nature of humans. It is the fact that therapeutic enlightenment often entails an intellectual claim for a moral evaluation of conduct that is worrying.

This worry can provide us with an initial point of entry into the question of aesthetic enlightenment. Hitherto in social theory and the social sciences, the question of the status of art has been raised, broadly speaking, in two contexts: either as evidence or as the object of a critique. As evidence, developments in the sphere of art can be used to illustrate wider trends in society or culture; thus, for instance, the emergence of aesthetic practices which transgress boundaries of high and low culture might provide evidence, for some, that we have entered into a postmodern cultural environment. In terms of critique, sociologists and others have had some fun in debunking the pretentious strategies and naïve ideologies of the artworld; a particular target here is the notion of disinterestedness or the autonomy of the work of art. Neither of these approaches is particularly concerned with the issue of aesthetic enlightenment as such; the first because the issue is not particularly relevant, the second because of an innate scepticism about the tying together of art and enlightnment at all. But our worry about therapeutic enlightenment can serve to show that the question of aesthetic enlightenment should not be bypassed or taken for granted so easily. Put simply, that is because the idea of the aesthetic can be used to provide a model of autonomy that can be contrasted – whether as a concrete alternative or as a rather abstract regulative idea – with the therapeutic ideal. This means entering into a discussion of what Michel Foucault called the aesthetics of existence.

I aim to show that the idea of an aesthetics of existence is interesting if not necessarily entirely coherent; it certainly begs some further questions. Nevertheless, there is something obligatory about it *as* a question. The notion is designed to function, in effect, as a model of autonomy; that is, a model of freedom, and of enlightenment, one that may even be substantively contrasted with that of the therapeutic ideal. But if the very notion of aesthetic enlightenment is to be taken at all seriously, it is necessary to enquire further into the kind of work that the notion of the "aesthetic" is being asked to do. That is why I give some space in this chapter to consideration of what is by now a hackneyed and probably a laughable question: What is art? But such an enquiry is all the more pertinent – if not for "aesthetic" reasons as such – in that for generations of thinkers the field of art has been a key site for thinking about questions of freedom, autonomy and enlightenment more generally. As in the notion of an aesthetics of existence itself, the notion of the aesthetic has been used as a kind of metaphor for freedom, of a desirable state; hence it is not surprising that there have been debates as to whether it is legitimate to apply aesthetic principles, however these are defined, to other spheres of life – as, for instance, in contemporary theory opinions are divided as to whether an aesthetic model of politics might be a good or a bad thing (Lyotard & Thébaud 1985; Eagleton 1990).

This chapter does not come up with a philosophical theory of art that would legitimize the aesthetic model as a paradigm of enlightenment. Yet, in outlining what is in many ways quite a traditional view of the artistic enterprise, it does offer some reasons as to why the quest for such a paradigm in art has been *tempting* for so many. It even goes some way towards concurring with this kind of quest. However, the very last thing that this chapter advocates is any form of aesthetic*ism*. I say that the critical uses of the model of art are not of a direct kind (describing oneself as an artist, practising this or that specific kind of art, writing in an "arty" way and so on) but, conversely, that the *existence* of art as an activity might have the useful function of being able to tell us some things about the impossible character of enlightenment and the impossible character of autonomy and freedom itself. This, then, is what might be called a *functional* rather than a normative view of art in relation to enlightenment. But before entering on such considerations, let us begin with the more manageable topic of the aesthetics of existence.

Aesthetic morality

In some of his last writings and interviews, Foucault often mentioned the idea of an aesthetics of existence. In many ways, it is rather an obscure concept and writers have been divided about its coherence and utility. Some have certainly regarded it as a rather irrationalist notion, one directed perhaps against the very ideal of a rationally oriented enlightenment.

The concept appears perhaps most prominently in Foucault's discussion of personal sexual ethics in one of his last books, *The Use of Pleasure* (Foucault 1986). Here it signified the idea of the creation of a style of life without recourse to the fixity of moral codes on the one hand, or epistemological guarantees on the other. Foucault presumably regarded this as being a question of aesthetics as opposed to anything else in so far as what is at stake is an autonomization of life according to a certain creative *style*. Thus "classical antiquity's moral reflection was not directed towards a codification of acts, nor towards a hermeneutics of the subject, but toward a stylization of attitudes and an aesthetics of existence" (ibid: 93). By talking about aesthetics in this way, Foucault was talking about at least three things. One very general thing, namely a principle of invention, singularity and creativity; and two more specific, if negative, things – namely, the possibility of fabricating a sense of self-identity with as little recourse as possible to either moral codes, on the one hand, or forms of knowledge, on the other. Indeed, the idea of an aesthetics of existence could be glossed simply as a stylization of existence without recourse to moral codes or epistemological norms.

Thus in Antiquity, in contrast to the world of early Christianity, techniques of the self, says Foucault, did not take the form of the fabrication of identity through moral codes but rather through an aesthetic fabrication of existence.

> This elaboration of one's own life as a personal work of art, even if it obeyed collective canons, was at the centre, it seems to me, of moral experience, of the moral will, in Antiquity; whereas in Christianity, with the religion of the text, the idea of God's will and the principle of obedience, morality took much more the form of a code of rules. Only certain ascetic practices were more closely linked to the exercise of a personal liberty. (Foucault 1989: 311)

A moral code is not the same thing as a morality. Foucault was unhappy with the idea of a moral code but his aesthetics is clearly a question of a morality, albeit a negative one – a kind of doctrineless, self-imposed doctrine of how to live.

Such an aesthetic model of existence is not something that is meant to be based on a scientific knowledge of the self. Hence my claim that it could be regarded as being opposed to therapeutic kinds of authority. Rather, its aesthetic character is given by its opposition to the concept; or, in fact, it is a domain where concepts are – in the Kantian sense – indeterminate. So unlike the modern era where, in Foucault's view, the truth of the self is most usually given through a discourse of desire centred on a psychological or a psychoanalytic style of knowledge – that is, through therapeutic enlightenment – the aesthetics of existence repudiates the grounding of our lives in epistemological form. "The relation to truth was a structural, instrumental, and ontological condition for establishing the individual as a moderate subject leading a life of moderation; it was not an epistemological condition enabling the individual to recognize himself in his singularity as a desiring subject and to purify himself of the desire that was thus brought to light" (Foucault 1986a: 89). The aesthetics of existence is, in other words, a notion that takes us away from all those injunctions that we should seek the truth of ourselves once and for all and then act or base our sense of identity on the basis of that truth. Aesthetic morality should be its own yardstick, regardless of the so-called sciences of the self.

Aestheticism

This idea of an aesthetic morality was not necessarily akin to some postmodern injunction to become aesthetic*ist* in a narrow sense. It was not necessarily or exclusively an injunction to live what would be commonly seen as an artistic life; the life, for instance, of the bohemian, the dandy, Noel Coward or today's new laddish *avant-garde* artists. The significance of art is not to be understood in terms of a compensation for life. Rather, what is at stake is an aestheticisation *of* life. "The idea of a *bios* as a material for an aesthetic piece of art is something which fascinates me" (Foucault 1984b: 348). Foucault was thinking here of the *techne ton biou* of classical antiquity, a *techne* not exactly of the self as such, but of life (only later, with the Stoics and the Epicureans did the arts of existence begin to centre on the self).

Once again there is a Nietzschean echo. It is not a question of devoting one's life to art – be that painting, writing or just posing about as an aesthete – but of creating a singular art for one's life. Perhaps there is something of an historical tale to be told here. No doubt from Foucault's viewpoint the development in modern times of a form of power centred precisely on the forces of life – viz *bio-power* – served to undermine the idea that life might be the object of an art. In the French version of his "Genealogy of Ethics" interview, Foucault elaborated on this theme, implying that the aesthetics of existence in the modern world – as it reappears in the Renaissance – appears as an implicit affront to the pastoral power that had been developing in the Christian Middle Ages (1984d: 629–30; cf. Foucault 1984b: 370). And later, from the end of the eighteenth century, the notion of the "life of the artist" took on a certain importance as against the ideologies of "interest" and egoism that were characteristic of bourgeois techniques of the self; "the 'artistic life', 'dandyism', were constituted from the techniques of self that were characteristic of bourgeois culture" (Foucault 1984d: 629). Here, the notion of the "life of the artist" acted as a practical exemplification of the fact that art belongs to life, and life to art (Flynn 1988: 117). In art, the life of the creative spirit becomes exemplary of what it is to live, to be creative, to invent in general. Hence the world of art was a privileged field for the expression of what might be termed the values of life.

Surely, such a form of enlightenment is bound to founder in contradictions; not least in the fact that the aesthetic rejection of the world is only made possible by the existence of the world as it is, the world rejected by the aesthete. In other words, it is always tempting to read aestheticism as an essentially compensatory attitude to the subjective fate of modernity. That is not necessarily to dismiss aestheticism as an ethical attitude. Far from it. Weber, for instance, was most preoccupied with aestheticism in just this sense: as a reaction to the rationalizing forces of modernity (Weber 1991b). But Weber saw aestheticism as more than merely a compensatory attitude to life in a disenchanted world. For a time, he was friendly with the mystic and poet Stefan George, leader of the so-called Cosmic Circle (Green 1974: 73–4; Scaff 1989: 106–8). For Weber, to embrace the aesthetic sphere as a form of life was to revolt against the "liberal historicist" notion of progress. Weber himself was uneasy with such notions of progress, and it is possible to see his own work in terms of what has been called an aesthetics of adaptation: that is, a certain way of living with the fact that there can be no demonstrably scientific ideals in life but recognizing, rather, that such ideals have to be our own creations (see ibid: 82). But Weber also recognized that a more uncompromising aesthetics of protest was also a viable, even rational, option in the modern world, and such was Stefan George's attitude, which consisted of a wholesale rejection of the world in a life devoted to art.

The interesting thing about Weber's views here, in so far as they can be reconstructed at all, is actually the extent to which he has *sympathy* with George's position. For Weber, the kind of aestheticism represented by George was not simply a compensatory revolt against the spirit of modernity; rather, it was a rational response to that spirit, and aestheticism itself was a rationalizing force in so far as it sought to make the principles proper to art constitutive of the conduct of life as such. Not that Weber was sold on George's ideas, which he referred to as entailing merely prophecy without any content (ibid: 107). But he recognized them as being in their own way a rational response to the forces of modern culture, and that such an escape from the world was not a form of self-indulgence but one which, in a sense, mirrored in its asceticism that which it sought to escape. As Scaff puts it: "So for Weber, as for Nietzsche, capitalist modernity is *ascetic*; asceticism is not only our "fate" but our "fatality". The consequences of its release into the world leave us with the demand of calling forth our own ideals from within ourselves, of transvaluing our values. In this view, anything else is weakness" (ibid: 89).

Such a critical orientation perhaps opens up a certain space for thinking about aestheticism as a form of enlightenment. This is not least because of its emphasis on the ethical *laboriousness* of aestheticism; "we know of no great artist who has ever done anything but serve his work and only his work" (Weber 1991a: 137). We tend to think of aestheticism as being a *reaction* to the puritanical forces of modernity (cf. Johnson 1969). We think of Huysmans' languid, entirely self-indulgent hero of *A Rebours*, or of the characters of *La Bohème*. But there is a difference between the ethics of aestheticism and bohemianism. We only have to look at the life of Oscar Wilde to see a rigorous ascetic sensibility at work. Far from being some camp sort of dilettante, Wilde was the conscious and consciously exemplary embodiment of a rigorous aesthetic virtuosity; a living instance of the fact that the embodiment of the aesthetic cannot be something rationally formulated but has to be just such a living instance. Or there is Baudelaire. In *The Painter of Modern Life*, Baudelaire famously depicted the artist Constantin Guys as a dandy. But a dandy in the mid-nineteenth century was not a bohemian but an ascetic type. "The specific duty of the dandy consists particularly in that cold exterior resulting from the unshakeable determination to remain unmoved; one is reminded of a latent fire, whose existence is merely suspected, and which, if it wanted to, but it does not, could burst forth in all its brightness" (Baudelaire 1992: 422). And Baudelaire says:

> Contrary to what a lot of thoughtless people seem to believe, dandyism is not even an excessive delight in clothes and material elegance ... It is, above all, the burning desire to create a personal form of originality, within the external limits of social conventions ... Clearly, then, dandyism in certain respects comes close to spirituality and to stoicism, but a dandy can never be a vulgar man. (ibid: 420–1; cf. Foucault 1984a: 41–2)

Where do such considerations leave us? To invoke the examples of Wilde, Baudelaire and the like might be regarded as endorsing the rather dubious view that the aesthetic form of life is the highest form of life, that the aesthetics of existence should become the object of a concrete morality. That would amount to an aesthetic*ist* understanding of aesthetic enlightenment. Even Foucault himself appears on occasion to flirt with this kind of view, for instance when he asks: "Why should the lamp or the house be an art object, but not our life?" (Foucault 1984b: 350). Even if such a view might veer in the direction of a rather dubious aestheticism, when taken in itself, the idea of an aesthetic of existence does not necessarily imply any injunction to lead an *artistic* life as such; or rather, we need to insist that the artistic life need not be necessarily reducible to the life of someone who is avowedly an "artist". Nor is it a question of saying that somehow Wilde and the others are sociologically "symptomatic" of certain features of modernity (cf. Rieff 1983). It is rather that Wilde and the others might better be seen as exemplary embodiments of a regulative ideal in ethics. This is not to be necessarily aesthetic*ist*, nor even to valorize the aesthetic life itself; rather these are instances of people who have sought to give themselves the autonomous moral law, outside of existing moral or epistemological norms. They are individual embodiments or reference points for a certain ideal of enlightenment; not literal models but regulative ideals or exemplae which disclose at least that the will to autonomize ourselves outside of moral or epistemological norms is a cultural or "anthropological" *possibility* in an age of enlightenment. Foucault, then, *invokes* the possibility of an aesthetics of existence – one which would have, very deliberately, little to do with, for instance, therapeutic models of ethical subjection – but he does not provide us with an aesthetic "theory" of such forms of existence.

Nevertheless, the question still remains as to what kind of enlightenment such figures are embodying. Which in turn, as I signalled at the beginning of this chapter, requires an enquiry into the nature of that sphere of practices that we conventionally call "art" itself.

Art as ideology

Such an enquiry is really quite hampered by prevailing trends in those social sciences that have bothered to turn their attentions to art. Consideration of these, however quickly, will assist us in clarifying what might be specific to a critique of aesthetic enlightenment that would have a place in social theory but be the opposite of a sociologistic enterprise. For example, the sociology of art, such as it exists, has been overwhelmingly critical and epochal in orientation. Key candidates for exposure have been the idea that art is not connected to politics or society, the myth of the creative genius, and the idea of a high art that is insulated from popular culture or the other, "lower", arts (Wolff 1981). Such critiques are all very well; they are no doubt an integral aspect of a certain kind of rather resentful sociological enlightenment about art. What they tend to overlook, however, is the question of art itself as a positive practice of enlightenment; what might be described as the internal normativity of aesthetic enlightenment.

No doubt the important work of Pierre Bourdieu – which I use as a foil in some of what follows – is a partial exception here. Bourdieu does produce something like a *critique* of art, but for him what is interesting is precisely its status as a candidate for a certain kind of enlightenment. We might say that art is for him at the centre of the idea of a critique of enlightenment because, precisely, art is an example of a basically *false* kind of enlightenment. For Bourdieu, the sociology of art should be right at the centre of the enterprise of sociology for reason of a paradox; because art is a form of power that is based precisely on the fact that it is *not* a form of power. Art attracts the sociologist in Bourdieu precisely in so far as it sets itself up as being immune from sociological explanation. In that sense, art is a sort of test case for the viability of any sociology at all. For what could possibly be more vulgar and outside all of the fundamental rules of etiquette in art than to seek to explain the existence of art sociologically? Bourdieu clearly relishes this challenge. His target is really the Kantian view of the creation of artworks in terms of "autonomy", devoid of all interest. He loathes this doctrine because he takes it as a matter of principle that artworks serve to legitimate given structurings of interest. But Bourdieu is very keen not to be regarded as the proponent of a vulgar, reductionist (Marxist) view of art. It is not that the notion of aesthetic autonomy has an elective affinity with the ideological tenets of a bourgeois society obsessed with the values of individualism, but that art is a means of "symbolic violence" upon those who are excluded from it (Bourdieu 1986: 4–5; Bourdieu 1991: 37; Bourdieu 1993: 222).

Bourdieu is a useful foil here because, in contrast to his perspective, I shall argue below that a modified version of the notion of disinterestedness is indispensable for understanding aesthetic enlightenment. This will require, however, that we abandon the interpretation of aesthetic practices exclusively in terms of ideology or equivalent notions such as the very idea of a *critique* of art. Bourdieu's analyses leave a satisfying effect for all of those – one suspects not just those ostensibly deprived of cultural capital – who have ever felt alienated or disenchanted by the esotericism of the art world, even if the initial effects of this can seem to pall and become repetitive after a while. Bourdieu's is a formalist theory in so far as he posits an aesthetic field in which agents are placed at varying distances from each other; the sociological component being a certain homology between the space of social positions of artists and the space of aesthetic positions themselves. But the effect is a criticism of the whole field, indeed of the field as such. For the fact is that Bourdieu's account of art is simply inconclusive at a normative or critical level. It has the pretensions of a critique of art but fails to live up to this in so far as it offers no grounds for any distinction between good and bad art. Bourdieu vigorously contests the numerous ways in which various kinds of art seek to deny the social moment in art, yet his theory is clearly unable to envisage the possibility of an art that was not tied to its social conditions. Hence, Bourdieu's critique looks much more radical than it really is. And when we turn to look at some of Bourdieu's more normative reflections on the artworld, we quickly see the weakness of his position; lauding, as he does, the view of "free exchange" in art, and the kind of politically oriented work of an intellectual and academic like Hans Haacke, which is to say a kind of art that, having little "autonomy" of its own – being always directed at making a specific intellectual point – is itself "ideological" rather than strictly speaking aesthetic in orientation, and is perhaps even itself derivative of what is implicitly a sociological critique of art (Bourdieu and Haacke 1995).

None of this would really matter all that much except to make the point that perhaps the main goal of the sociology of art should not be to debunk art but to find a way of escaping the dilemmas of hostile or knowing *critique per se.*

For there may be ways to approach the social domain of art which have little in common with the repetitive canons of a hostile critique of art. This would involve not the repetitive attempt to accuse art of concealing things or of performing covert acts of symbolic domination but of simply reconstructing and outlining the limits of the aesthetic enterprise itself.

Art and the ethics of truth

Art is indeed not, as Bourdieu would insist with us, the product of inspiration or genius; we need, rather, to think of the production of works of art as a segregated kind of practice for producing certain kinds of truth; as an autonomous aspect of enlightenment. Generations of philosophers and others have sought a more profound, stranger truth in art. The critique of aesthetic enlightenment would do better to go in the opposite direction. A common limitation of much philosophical discussion of art is that in making of art a question of truth it often tends to make of art a kind of non-rational truth as in some versions of the Heideggerian tradition (Heidegger 1975; cf. Derrida 1987: 2–3, 5–9). In any case philosophy often teaches us that art discloses, or promises, another kind of truth. But such analyses often fail to capture what is mundane and actually quite rational about the pursuit of aesthetic truth. That this is not by way of a rationalist or "knowledgeable" truth will be obvious enough. "The real difference between art and science lies in the *specific form* in which they give us the same object in quite different ways; art in the form of 'seeing', and 'perceiving' or 'feeling', science in the form of *knowledge* (in the strict sense, by concepts)" (Althusser 1984: 175; cf. Deleuze 1981: 39; Deleuze and Guattari 1991: 163–99). So what sort of thing is this aesthetic kind of truth?

Our only recourse in answering this question is to look again at categories of autonomy and disinterestedness. There is some support for this kind of approach these days, but usually only from rather eccentric quarters. If neither purist philosophy nor sociological critique are, for all their respective merits, quite appropriate for a critique of art as enlightenment, then it cannot be surprising that perhaps the exemplar of the kind of approach we are looking for can be found in the work of a thinker who adopted a dialectical approach to these questions. Theodor Adorno tried to hold together a paradox; that is to say that modern art – sociologically conditioned as it was – might really be autonomous, even emancipatory. Adorno certainly held art to be socially conditioned. "Autonomy, art's growing independence from society, is a function of the bourgeois consciousness of freedom, which in turn is tied up with a specific social structure" (Adorno 1984: 320). But he recognized that the fact of the social conditioning of art in itself does not get us very far down the line of saying anything particularly interesting about art. "The fact that it is the function of bourgeois art to have no function does not disprove the idea that bourgeois art has no function" (ibid: 322). Adorno's viewpoint represents a minimal move but a necessary one; and one that is rarely taken with any seriousness in either sociology or philosophy today. Adorno recognized that autonomy and society were not necessasrily in contradiction; or rather that the contradiction was internal to the normativity of modern art itself. But it is not so much that modern art *is* autonomous, but that its normative *spirit* is one of autonomization; hence, the conventional connection of aesthetic practices with the ideal of freedom, and hence the utopian element implicit in the very idea of art.

Needless to say, much ink has been spilled in debunking the autonomizing, enlightening pretensions of the vision of aesthetic autonomy – and not, by any means, just by vulgar sociologists. What is generally overlooked is the extent to which the bourgeois category of disinterestedness is actually a question of an *ethos*. It is not so much that disinterestedness actually exists but that, as an aspiration, it can be the object of a form of restricted, ethical work, a means of rationalizing all of one's conduct in a particular way. Disinterestedness – the attempt to have a comportment towards the beautiful that is devoid of all ulterior references to function – requires a kind of *ascetic* commitment; it is the "liberation of ourselves for the release of what has proper worth only in itself" (Heidegger 1981: 109). It is the exercise of disinterested comportment that allows for the realization of the so-called autonomy of the work of art. This means that it is not just a question of asserting that the artworld is a domain of works that *are* disinterested, or which exist autonomously in a literal sense. It is rather that the aesthetic *spirit* is a critical spirit which is oriented towards disinterestedness; that the production of works of art, as an aspiration, takes the form of a practical reflection on the possibility of autonomy. That alone would amount to a good reason for saying that a reflection on the aesthetic spirit has to be part of any reflection on the characteristics of enlightenment.

Aesthetic truth

Perhaps it is precisely in so far as art is an insulated, otherwordly activity – one that does not flow seamlessly into all aspects of life, one that is in effect a specialized enterprise – that it can be seen as being more generally symbolic or exemplary of autonomy at all. In that sense, we need to think of what Bourdieu calls the "pure aesthetic" not as some kind of ideology but as a restricted ethical invention or achievement. Can we draw up a picture of this pure aesthetic?

At least since the time of Kant, art has been associated with ideals of freedom and autonomy in various ways. Art may be symbolic of autonomy in a "constructive" sense, that is, in terms of the freedom attributed to the artist, or in an "ethical" sense, that is, in terms of the autonomy that the appreciation of art confers on the consumer of art works (Podro 1982: 5–6). Philosophers will no doubt continue to debate the relative merits of this or that view of autonomy attached to the making or appreciation of works of art. But in thinking about the idea of an aesthetic of enlightenment, it may be as well to take a less nuanced view. This quite deliberate lack of nuance, this cultivation of a certain naïvety with regard to this question of "what is art?" is necessary in that "with this query we enter a domain of conceptual enquiry where native speakers are poor guides: *they* are lost themselves" (Danto 1964: 575).

Let us just assume that we know what "art" – bourgeois, modern art – is. It is pictures, sculptures, novels, poems, plays, musical compositions and so forth. In other words all those "objects" – types or tokens – that are just conventionally called *art* as opposed to anything else. We need to listen to our everyday grammar on such matters. All art in this sense is bourgeois art just in a conventional (rather than a critical) sense; and the advantage of this term is that it happily subsumes other supposedly more nuanced categories – modernist, postmodern, conceptual, *avant-garde* – quite easily within it. Bourgeois art is just that kind of art which is held to have its own value, regardless of other sources of input, influence or authority. This is not to negate the social aspect of art as such; and everybody knows, especially sociologists, that there have been traditions of art which were subjected to outside forms of authority. We know that the work of quattrocento artists was determined not solely by the aesthetic conscience of the artist but by the terms of contracts which specified what the painter was to paint, when the painting was to be delivered, and which colours the painter was to use (Baxandall 1972: 6–8). We know that Alexander Pope had his work corrected in public by his patron, Lord Halifax (Schucking 1966: 27; cf. Bourdieu 1971: 163). We know that most artworks in history have been subordinated to religious, mythological or mystical ends as opposed to "pure" aesthetic purposes; and that such a phenomenon of a "pure aesthetic" is a modern invention (Bourdieu 1993). And so forth.

None of this means, however, that modern principles of criticism cannot be applied retrospectively to past traditions of art, *as if* they inhabited something like a pure aesthetic. After all, it is possible to "criticize" premodern forms of art; and indeed to recognize such forms as pertaining to the category of art in the first place. In other words, the argument from the historical specificity of modern, "autonomous" art does not really do the critical work it is often thought to be doing. Merely because something is historically specific, or had to be invented, does not mean that it cannot be applied as a retrospective principle; nor that it has no right to exist at all. If, as is the case, it is only within our bourgeois modernity that any idea of an autonomous aesthetic sphere has become a possibility, this should not lead us into a knowing critique of such an idea of autonomy, but rather a critical exploration of its grammar.

The modern artwork is something that aspires to a certain autonomy. Deleuze and Guattari put a nice twist on this rather hackneyed notion by arguing glibly that the fundamental problem of the modern artist is simply to

111

make the artwork "stand up on its own" (Deleuze & Guattari 1991: 164). In the modern, bourgeois period artworks are supposed, in so far as they are artworks and not anything else, to be unique, unrepeatable, beyond cliché; or, at least, if one is committed to being an "artist" as opposed to being anything else, such values are what one aspires to achieve even if one never succeeds. So this is not to say that all works of art actually do succeed in standing up on their own, but rather that the aspiration to do so is integral to the very idea of what we might rather pretentiously call the "artistic aspect" of the work of art. In other words, an art gallery may be full of works of art that may as well be called works of art by virtue of the conventional fact of their very inclusion on display in an art gallery; but what they all aspire to is the status of standing up on their own, producing – as Deleuze and Guattari put it – percepts and affects proper to themselves. Again, the point can be made that, to those who object that Egyptian art, or Romanesque sculpture, or Russian iconic art would not qualify as art on this definition, we can respond that the artistic aspect of any work can be made available to later generations; in other words, that these things – whatever their ideological origins – can be turned into what we now call art in so far as people contemplate them as freestanding objects. Oddly enough, it could even be said that the work of art could exist more autonomously in societies where its status as a work of art was merely a byproduct of its status as a work of religious devotion or a political statement. In these instances the work of art existed as a work of art essentially as a byproduct of its other functions, whereas in modern societies, where art is held to be ideally autonomous, the very idea of such autonomy is constantly held up for critique.

So this problem of making the work stand up on its own confronts every artist *qua* "artist". The advantage of this rather glib language is to gain a certain distance from another kind of claim, which is to say that the artwork is or aspires to be autonomous from society, patronage, the church, use-values or whatever; standing up on its own does not quite mean autonomy in the usual sense, that is, autonomy from social interests. All these things can be included in the work of art, but the "truth" of the work of art has to be based only on whatever is proper to itself: that is, as an *emergent* product of all the diverse things that have gone into it. The work of art might be seen as a sort of lash-up of diverse resources and materials that – unlike the products of science – are intended to stand on their own without connecting up to anything else, either in time or space. Thus works of art aspire to a peculiar, autonomous kind of "durability". Even the Forth Bridge has a use-value which is quite specific: to cross the river Forth. But Picasso's *Portrait of Kahnweiler*, whatever the incredible complexity of its constitutive "process", is the result of a problematization that dictates that, whatever else is going on, whatever the immediate problems of process or "research" that are encountered on the way, it should stand up on its own (cf. Baxandall 1985: 39–40).

The new

Closely tied to the autonomizing ethos of enlightened, bourgeois art – whether modern, postmodern or whatever – is the principle of "the new". "Make it new," said Ezra Pound. But it would be a mistake to regard this principle as exclusive to *avant-garde* movements in art. What is problematically at stake in the sphere of all modern, bourgeois art as distinct (resorting to an unfashionable contrast) from that of "culture" or "entertainment" more generally – is the will to produce the new; and in that sense all art in modernity has aspired to the status of what we now tend to think of as *avant-garde* art. Whether we are talking about modernity or postmodernity, the *avant-garde*, the neo-*avant-garde*, conceptualism, or whatever, the disclosure of the new is what counts as the measure of the "truth" of a work of art.

This is a staple notion within continental philosophy. "The establishment of truth in the work is the bringing forth of a being such as never was before and will never come to be again" (Heidegger 1975: 62). But if only the category of the new were an unproblematic one, as some postmodern philosophers like Lyotard appear to think. For him, it seems as if all experimental, Duchampian and conceptual art is by definition conforming to the new; if it is iconoclastic then it is new (Lyotard 1984b; cf. Lyotard 1992: 16–25). Yet the problem of art today – as with all bourgeois art, even well before today or even yesterday – is that of finding a novel form of the new itself; of finding the new in a world where novelty is itself a commercial watchword. This is one of the lasting concerns of Adorno and Horkheimer's *Dialectic of Enlightenment*; the critique of the category of the new in the culture industries and hence the search for a kind of authentic or workable concept of the new. How do we create the new in a cultural environment in which the new is itself an object of fetishization? Adorno and Horkheimer are probably wrong about Orson Welles; but the principle is right. "Whenever Orson Welles offends against the tricks of the trade, he is forgiven because his departures from the norm are regarded as calculated mutations which serve all the more strongly to confirm the validity of the system" (Adorno and Horkheimer 1986: 129). For the new is not simply that which stakes a claim to difference or which noisily inaugurates a new style; perhaps the new can only come forth deceptively by masquerading perhaps as something which is not new at all.

As Adorno urges, determining what is or is not new is not an easy business: "The new is necessarily abstract ... The new is a blind spot, as empty as perfect thisness" (ibid: 30). Moreover, the new cannot be defined in any substantive terms at all: "The new is the longing for the new, not the new itself" (Adorno 1984: 47). Everything would be perfectly straightforward if it were only a question of finding the rules and then breaking them. Bourdieu has made this a central theme of his sociology of art. But because he views art as a social institution rather than as a general problematic of the new, Bourdieu seems to be tempted into reducing all art to the facile breaking of the rules –

which in turn leads him to endorse forms of art which in their conceptualism are certainly more innocuous, predictable and aesthetically ineffective than his own progressively motivated intellectualism would like him to think (Bourdieu and Haacke 1995). But he is right to urge that breaking the rules often amounts to the first and most predictable of all the rules of art. Lyotard commits the same, if opposite, mistake when he appears to endorse just about everything that proclaims itself as *avant-garde* (see Lyotard 1984a, postscript). It is trivially true that experimentation is part of the vocation of art in the modern era; but it is not the case that we know necessarily what experiment actually is, that is, in advance of experiment itself. The form of the new has to be related to a content; it is not just a matter of the new as form – that anything that is experimental is thereby new. And things can only be done once in art – once you have signed and exhibited your urinal, there is little point in repeating the exercise too often; unless – as with the Borges story about translating *Don Quixote*, Warhol's soup cans, or Bacon's endless popes, or indeed Duchamp's own repeat of his urinal exhibit, or Avdei Ter Oganyan's broken and repaired repeat version of 1993 – the repetition is itself to become an aspect of the articulation of the meaning of the new.

Obviously it would serve us well to be able to draw up an inventory of the different ways in which different styles of art have related themselves to the new. This would not be an analysis of aesthetic revolutions or of the way different groups and schools of artists broke from the past in the search for distinction; it would rather be a question of studying the different ways through which the new is sought out and produced. The problem of the new is not linked specifically to the *avant-garde* but to modern art as such; that is, all modern art that seeks a break with what it sees as "tradition". John Berger put it well when he observed that in fact what comes to be known as art in the modern period is actually work that broke free of tradition and produced work diametrically opposed to the values of traditional art or just the conventional, academic art of the age (Berger 1972: 109). But this question of the new does not have to be seen in Berger's rather romantic terms any more than in the terms of Bourdieu's rather reductionist cynicism about art. Perhaps the terms posed by Henri Focillon are the most apposite; for him, the artwork seeks to embody a sort of freestanding time, involving a manufacturing of a temporality that stands outside of the normal processes of isochronal time and on the basis of which the artist *inserts* a new time and a new environment into his age (Focillon, 1992: 139, 154):

> The history of form in Raphael – whose life we have come to look on as a model of perfect happiness – reveals serious crises. His time held out to him the most diverse images, the most flagrant contradictions. And, deep within himself, he gave way again and again to a ductility of instinct and a lack of resolution that remained with him until at long last he boldly inserted into his age a new time and a new environment.

If it is to stake a claim *as* a work of art as opposed to anything else, the artwork does indeed need to surprise us in so far as it should represent something we have not witnessed before; and one relatively uncontroversial standard for assessing paintings, for example, would be that each time we stand before a really good painting, we would be seeing it differently; it would continue to surprise us. Matisse, for instance, famously said of a Cézanne in his possession: "I have owned it for 37 years. I know this canvas rather well, although I hope not completely." Perhaps this kind of newness can be contrasted with those kinds of (modern, postmodern, conceptual) art that parade their newness, that make a fetish out of their novelty (cf. Elster 1983: 82–4). Does this mean that we have to condemn postmodern or neo-conceptualist forms of art?

There are really two problems here. The first is that, as Elster insists, modern, postmodern, or neo-*avant-garde*, conceptual art always runs the risk of losing its autonomy, indeed of becoming an *intellectual* or philosophical form of expression as opposed to a specifically aesthetic one. The response to this might be to insist along with Francis Bacon or Alberto Giacometti that such forms of art parade their novelty without disclosing it, or at least that this is a danger that intellectualist forms of aesthetic activity always tend to run. As Giacommetti said of the abstract art of his day: "The artists of today want only to explain their own subjective feelings instead of copying nature faithfully. Seeking for originality, they lose it. Seeking the new, they repeat the old. That is true above all of abstract art."

The second problem has to do with cliché. Perhaps what is to be avoided most of all is the turning of the new simply into a cliché, something predictable even in its unpredictability. The quest for the new is particularly beset by this problem of the cliché: "modern painting is besieged, overrun by photos and clichés which are installed already on the canvas before the painter has begun his work. In effect, it would be a mistake to think that the painter works on a white and virgin surface" (Deleuze 1981: 14; cf. 58–9). The new itself can be a cliché as someone like Bourdieu is all too aware, as in all those embarrassingly self-conscious attempts at subversion, wickedness and shock that, for him, almost seem to constitute the artistic enterprise *per se*.

So the production of the new can fail. But the point is that with modern and with *avant-garde* art and neo-*avant-garde* art the production of the new has become the "normal" – we might almost say the "traditional" – form of all artistic production. But in any case, the history of the rise of the *avant-garde*, neo-*avant-garde* and pseudo-*avant-garde* has less to do with the reformulations of the big questions of art and life than to do with the rather more localized question of finding different ways of producing the new (cf. Bürger 1984). What is always at stake in aesthetic kinds of enlightenment is just this question of the new *as a problem*, with the "modern" component of works of art comprising simply the attempt to find an "answer" to such a problem in the context of particular situations and traditions (cf. Baxandall 1985: 35).

Creativity and freedom

I said earlier that this was to be among other things a functional view of art. I meant that we should not expect to be able to transfer aesthetic principles beyond the specialized sphere of art as such. The idea of the aesthetic is at best a regulatory ideal that can be used, perhaps, as a kind of measure in relation to other practices – as I suggested in relation to Foucault's ideal of an aesthetic of existence – but not as a substantive principle beyond the artworld itself. The existence of the artworld, on this view, serves a kind of ethical *function* in being the place which specializes in producing autonomy, producing the new – a specialized domain of enlightenment with rules that it invents for itself. In fact, perhaps that is the best definition of the aesthetic sphere; the place not for the exercise of artistic conventions, but the place where new conventions are explored. In that sense, the "function" of modern art is not to say this or that, but just to exist as a specialized space for the invention of conventions.

Perhaps there is a positive function for art here – or so it could be argued. This would amount to a strong kind of functionalism in relation to art. Perhaps art itself works on human capacities in particular ways; perhaps in that sense, art does have a direct moral function. Aesthetic experimentation teaches us moral things. As Stanley Cavell argues, modernist art is not about the exploration of conventions but about undoing the tyranny of convention: "Artists are people who know how . . . to make objects in response to which we are enabled, but also fated, to explore and educate and enjoy and chastise our capacities as they stand. Underlying the tyranny of convention is the tyranny of nature" (Cavell 1979; cf. Greenberg 1965). That may indeed be so. But my argument does not necessarily imply such a strong interpretation of the functions of art as this. I settle for a weaker version. There is a moral lesson in art but this does not just lie in the substantive contents of artworks; rather it is what the *ethos* of the production of art can tell us that is important for a critical attitude to enlightenment. That moral lesson concerns the status of freedom.

The ethic of the aesthetic

We can understand this question of freedom initially in quite a literal sense. That is to say, artists are themselves people who – ideal-typically – enjoy (if that is the right word) an exemplary kind of freedom. It is not only that such artists are supposedly free to do as they please, but rather that the logic of the aesthetic field typically invites strategies that are as far removed from any kind of ethical naturalism as possible. Ethics of aesthetic existence have, then, a certain fascination not just for gossips and the curious but for anyone interested in a utopian or counter-factual ethics, for artists are so frequently those who seek to stylize themselves at the limits of the possible. What can be fascinating in ethical terms can be grist to the mill of a knowing, critical sociology; but the perspective I advocate here is really the reverse of that of someone like Bourdieu who would characterize all aesthetic strategies in terms of competition within the artistic field. For equally the artistic field can be regarded as an arena for experimenting with the question of freedom.

So, in part, this question of aesthetic freedom is just a question of the social role of the artist, as someone who exemplifies a particular form of libertarian attitude, as signified, for instance, by the predicament of the successful modern artist who enjoys what is really an *exemplary* freedom. "Because he is able to experience himself in a way that is impossible for other people, he is able to experience in a more fundamental, original way than they can ... He is one of those heroes we are supposed to worship, for he has overcome fate through creativity" (Kuspit 1993: 2). But it is also more than that. For Elster, the creation of works of art entails forms of action that are the products of necessity and constraint, but − as he puts it − of *necessities chosen freely* (Elster 1983: 80). As such, the activity of art is exemplary of practices of freedom in general; the activity of art represents the activity of choice within constraints, but art merely adds the aspiration that the contraints are freely chosen. Art, then, might be said to represent a sort of pure zone of freedom, not in so far as there are no constraints at all but in so far as, in art, one is free to *choose* one's own constraints and the boundaries within which one is to work. The production of artworks, then, is a kind of practice of freedom; not the "anything goes" of outrageousness or bohemenianism but the deliberative choice of constraints and the stylized production of particular aesthetic "products". Indeed, what practices of the artworld disclose to anyone wishing to think about the question of freedom is precisely that enlightenment in general, even if we take a negative conception of it, is never just a matter of the absence of constraints but of the shaping or stylization of constraints. The example of aesthetic enlightenment discloses to us that the accomplishment of freedom has an ascetic aspect.

This kind of issue is more or less completely obscured by the tradition − not just proper to sociology − of a sociological critique of ideologies of creativity. Sociologists have certainly made it a matter of honour to confront and refute this idea wherever they have found it (Bourdieu 1971; Elias 1994; Bourdieu 1995). Typically they have been outraged at the ways in which artists have sought to make the act of creation something uniquely belonging to themselves and undermining those other forces (traditions, markets, other workers and artists) that have gone into the production of artworks. Here, for example, is the sculptor Barbara Hepworth talking about her assistants, Dicon, Norman and George:

> They don't know what I'm doing ... No − Dicon, Norman and George are my good friends and extra hands. I couldn't do so much if I had to do all

the carving from beginning to end, because it takes such a long time . . . They have come to know, instinctively, what I'm aiming at, because we've worked together for so long. But all the really delicate stages are my own . . . And they are all highly skilled in their various ways. Their intuition is splendid – I think because they're not artists themselves. (Bowness 1971: 9)

On the one hand, we might want to respond to this by debunking the ideology of creativity that lies behind it. And we would be helped here by Hepworth's evident unease with a situation in which most of her work is actually done by other people and her resort to the mystical category of the "artist" to mark the correct boundaries. Plenty of similar examples might be considered along similar lines, especially from the world of painting (Rembrandt, late Matisse, late de Kooning). Yet, on the other hand, there is more to this kind of situation than just an ideological cover-up. For what people like Hepworth are responding to, in accounting for their work in this kind of way, is precisely the problem of their responsibility for the creation of what is new. For if the artwork is autonomous, who or what is responsible for it?

I shall say that this question of responsibility is an ethical *problem*. The sphere of art is of interest for those concerned with the ethics of freedom not least because that sphere tells us something about freedom in general which is that we have to evade responsibility for it. That is because to will freedom is, as with the will to create the aesthetic, something that cannot be willed without paradox.

On willing what cannot be willed

In his delightful discussion of "willing what cannot be willed", Jon Elster argues that a feature of any artistic activity is that the artist must not be seen to be trying too hard; and if anything, the artwork should be like a byproduct of the artist's activity (Elster 1983). Elster's central image is that of Trajan's column which – with its miniscule details and carvings that cannot be seen without binoculars – impresses the masses precisely because it does not try to impress, precisely in so far as it has an overt contempt for the audience. The awe of the masses was a byproduct, but was not ostensibly part of the intention of the makers of the column. Hence the column impresses simply because it makes no effort to impress (Elster 1983: 68; citing Veyne 1976: 676). For Elster, all true art has to be like this because, if we suspect that the artist is trying to impress us, our attention will be drawn to something other than the artwork itself, for instance the artist themselves; in other words, the work of art will not have an independent or autonomous existence but will merely be the product of a subjective intention (instead of being "utterly satisfying . . . utterly impressive"; Elster 1983: 77). In this sense, the problem of conceptual art is that it seems – in intellectualizing about the artwork, as with those visual artists who insist on providing us with written notes about their intentions in their work – to be willing what cannot be willed, attempting to bring about the artistic aspect of the work of art directly rather than as a by-product. The response, if we really want to make something autonomous, has to be at least to *act* as if we do not will it. This *negative* endeavour provides us with the epitome of the ethic of the aesthetic.

This might seem to take us in the opposite direction from all those post-modern denigrations of the figure of the artist. But it is not that the artist does or does not matter but only that the very logic of the bourgeois aesthetic field dictates that the question of responsibility for the artwork will always be an open and contentious one. We might even say that what makes art interesting from an ethical point of view is precisely this question; and that the aesthetic sphere might become an interesting empirical laboratory for those concerned to map the evolution of ethics of enlightenment since the time of the Enlightenment itself. So in fact, this question of aesthetic responsibility is a problem in a positive sense, an obstacle – rather in the manner in which the French tradition of the history of science speaks of epistemological "obstacles", and in the face of which we have to respond necessarily with a certain degree of creativity. The point is not that aesthetic criticism needs to take account of the author or the creator but only that all paradigms of aesthetic production have to confront this question of aesthetic responsibility, and especially so in the case of "purist" theories of aesthetic production. It might be possible to read all the apparently pretentious strategies of bourgeois artists in this way; not so much as an aspect of the psychological tendencies of irritating self-designated artistic types but as part of a kind of ethical genre of the aesthetic field.

Take for example the most famous instance of such a genre: the romantic conception of genius. From the viewpoint of a sociological critique the idea of the genius is one of the most absurd ideas ever imagined; as if thought and creativity could come from nowhere, or from what amounts to the same thing – just from the heads of particular individuals. But the category of the genius is also one novel and economic way of *solving* the problem of aesthetic responsibility in the context of the production of pure, autonomous works. The genius serves to promote a notion of the artwork as being entirely autonomous – a pure aesthetic, in Bourdieu's terms. Far from drawing attention to the artist, the category of the genius actually serves the function of drawing attention to the work because it signifies the extent to which the artist is *not* responsible for the work but is – on the contrary – a victim of the work. The work attaches itself to some poor innocent, the artist, and then proceeds to torment him, to kill him, to drive him to drink and so forth. We need, then, to reverse our usual understanding of the relation between the artist and the work. It is nonsense to explain the work on the basis of the artist's inner psychology; but it makes perfect sense to look at the artist's life as an aspect of the autonomization of the work. The artist's life is an *instrument* in that autonomization; and, for the artist at least, there is one rule – autonomize the work by absolving yourself of responsibility for it. In other words, the "problem" for the modern, bourgeois artist is actually to demonstrate that he is the one that does *not* create but, if anything, is the object, even the victim, of a kind of anonymous and autonomous *force* of creativity.

So if there are grounds for including an analysis of the artist in relation to the work, this is not on the grounds of a causal relation to be posited between the two. They are rather in parallel; not with all writers and artists, but many have seemed to work on themselves, to turn themselves into a work of art in parallel with their art. Foucault makes this case in the extreme when he observes of Raymond Roussel that his major work was not just his books but "himself in the process of writing his books":

> The private life of an individual, his sexual preference, and his work are interrelated not because his work translates his sexual life, but because the work includes the whole life as well as the text. The work is more than the work: the subject who is writing is part of the work. (Ruas 1986: 184; cf. Foucault 1984c)

In such cases, what is at stake is not just the generation of romantic stories to enhance the notoriety, and hence the marketability, of the artist in question but rather something of the order of an ascetic enterprise. Artists work on themselves precisely in order to show that they are victims of art rather than the source of it – hence, the better to autonomize the artworks for which they are deemed "responsible".

Again, consider in this context an entertaining, modern example, the painter Francis Bacon; surely not only Britain's greatest artistic export of the twentieth century but also its most accomplished proponent of a stylized aesthetic of existence. Bacon was the paradigm of the aesthetic personality; not because he was an "aesthete" but because he devoted himself with a wholehearted commitment to living out at all times the life of the artist. Bacon drank, gambled away fortunes, talked endlessly, loved dramatically, drank and drank all the more – and painted. It is pointless to dismiss the interest in the legend of Bacon's life as prurience; rather, his cultivation of himself was at the centre of his art. "I worked on myself," said Bacon, "to be as unnatural as I could" (quoted in Farson 1993: 20). Some studies of Bacon assume that he is trying to tell us something or other – something or other that might be amenable to psychoanalytic forms of explanation – about the modern self or identity (van Alphen 1992; but cf. Adams 1996). Moreover, to those who are not afraid to speculate, Bacon's homosexuality clearly made him an outsider and, for many, this alone is almost sufficient in the making of a great artist. Posed in these terms the notion of Bacon's life having anything to do with his art is already clearly ridiculous merely on statistical grounds (not all homosexuals who dislike their mothers become artists with Bacon's abilities). More common are those studies which simply recount Bacon's exploits with a certain awe (Farson 1993; Sinclair 1993; Peppiatt 1996). Such studies attempt to get behind the mask that was Bacon, but this is clearly a misguided enterprise. Rather Bacon's life was clearly an aesthetic creation in itself, in parallel to his art. John McEwen compared Bacon to a Baudelairean dandy. "This Byronic aspect to his nature had something to do with a complete absence of sentimentality, a recklessness, a bleak rationality, an awareness that his lack of religious faith was in itself despair and also an intense animalism" (quoted in Sinclair 1993: 310).

But instead of romanticizing the lifestyles of people like Bacon, it is possible to see them as quite rational stylizations of aesthetic personality; that is, as ascetic "solutions" to various problems of creative responsibility. Bacon sought simply to create his life in parallel with his art. On the one hand, he cultivated a sensibility that was designed *not* to impress. He was not like Stefan George: living out an aesthetic life in accordance with the values of art. Or at least, art for Bacon was the site of a pure nihilism, if an extraordinarily creative one. He always professed the most direct, hardly aesthetic*ist*, attitude to his work as if the fact that he produced art was a kind of byproduct of a biological need. His interest, he said, was in images, and that was all. There was something biological but not really aesthetic about it. "I'm just trying to make images as accurately off my nervous system as I can. I don't even know what half of them mean. I'm not saying anything" (Sylvester 1980: 82). Images impacted upon our drives, and that was all: more he could not say. Those who have criticized Bacon for, at times, not taking a sufficiently intellectual attitude towards his own creative work have missed the point about his aesthetic strategy. For the artist cannot know about the work, for then he would be responsible for it, whereas the whole object of the exercise is to make oneself literally irresponsible so that the work is enabled to stand on its own. On the other hand, in stylizing his life in a certain way, Bacon – the empirical individual – was rather deliberately *not drawing attention to himself*; on the contrary: he was hiding behind his art, since all he was in life and work was his art. There is no Bacon that is "responsible" for the work since there is no Bacon beyond Bacon the artist who invented himself as a work of art. With Bacon there is no "Bacon" but only the work. Again, what is at stake in this logic – and logic it is – is an attempt to absolve oneself of responsibility for what one is doing, in the rightful interests of the autonomy of the work. And hence what is required of a critique of aesthetic enlightenment is not so much a critique of models of aesthetic charisma but a constructivism of different models of aesthetic personality, a constructivism that would regard such models as solutions to problems of autonomization rather than merely as so many forms of escapism or self-indulgence.

I think we could do worse than to regard the strategies of people like Bacon as so many ways of attempting to solve the problem of willing what cannot be willed. Bacon knew that in order to invent conventions one has to invent the convention of oneself in such a way so as to cease being responsible for the conventions that one has created. The result was that Bacon now appears to us as the epitome of the entirely free spirit. We cannot know what such freedom must have cost him personally. We can only say that his efforts amount to a kind of living parable of freedom in general; it has to be worked at, cultivated, but if it is *willed*, proclaimed, theorized: all will turn to dust. The only people that can pronounce on our freedoms – just as with our arts – are future generations.

Aesthetic responsibility

At the beginning of this chapter I promised to say something about why any of this talk about the aesthetic should be of any interest to anybody concerned with the question of enlightenment. My discussioin of aesthetic responsibility may seem only to have clouded this issue further. In spite of what I have said about freedom and art, I do not want to say that we can somehow derive a theory of freedom *from* art. On the contrary, I think that our discussion points us in the opposite direction – away from an aesthetic*ist* appropriation of the aesthetic. This is in some contrast to the work of some of those in the social sciences who regard, albeit in overtly opposing ways, the idea of the aesthetic precisely as a seductive one that *might* somehow act as a model for their endeavours. These range, albeit in different ways, from postmodernists such as Lyotard to liberal-Marxists such as Habermas; the one regarding the aesthetic as an exemplary space for considering questions of judgement, the other regarding it as a space of redemption and reconciliation. Yet others have regarded the aesthetic sphere as a place of escape from the tyranny of enlightenment; hence those movements, even in the social sciences. One thinks above all of the work of Georg Simmel as well as many strands of avowedly postmodern or anti-foundationalist social science, which have sought to take an aesthetic point of view on social life (Frisby 1985; Maffesoli 1985).

The aim of this chapter, on the other hand, has been to indicate that, in contrast to many of the emphases of such perspectives, the pursuit of the aesthetic – as Foucault saw – can be regarded as an *aspect* of enlightenment. But the lesson attached to this is strictly *negative*; art, indeed, being the paradigm or rather the limit-case of negative enlightenment, the self-criticism of criticism, as such. For if – precisely as we saw from the discussion of aesthetic responsibility – aesthetic autonomy is likely to be the byproduct of our concerns and cannot be directly "willed", then we cannot ever expect to derive a particular content of the aesthetic as a model of enlightenment on the basis of aesthetic practices themselves. That is the paradox of aesthetic enlightenment. Those who *say* that they are artists or who claim to be using artistic principles in their work, and – worse – those who *intellectualize* about such principles: these are always the most embarrassing kinds of people. This means that, addressing the significance of art as regulative ideal, the ethics of aesthetic conduct is an intrinsically *negative* affair; a paradigm-instance of the negativity of enlightenment itself because no doubt it is the same with enlightenment; we have to take care how it is willed and those who proclaim the true and final way to freedom or autonomy, whether of individuals or communities – those who claim to know what enlightenment is – are perhaps the most dangerous of all.

With regard to the sphere of art itself, I think that this means that any form of analysis that aspired to the status of a critique of aesthetic enlightenment would be concerned to show the ways in which art functions as a kind of regulatory ideal; which is not to say that we can apply aesthetic principles to other forms of life beyond the aesthetic sphere but that the aesthetic sphere is a place where certain principles are given exemplary, because insulated, form. Moreover, such principles are intrinsically ethical. Art is a place where the creativity of what is new and the production of autonomy take on an exemplary importance precisely in so far as those are the problems that intrinsically confront all artists in so far as they are artists as opposed to anything else such as shopkeepers, teachers, dockers or gymnasts. And the last thing that is involved in the production of works of art – which is another reason for the uneasy status of all forms of conceptualism in art – is the (philosophical) application of an *aesthetics*. It has been a commonplace since Hegel to argue that the production of works of art and the theory of aesthetics do not go together, even that the existence of aesthetics might be symptomatic of something like the death of art itself. Those who would attempt therefore to *apply* aesthetic principles to other kinds of activity beyond the aesthetic sphere are on intrinsically difficult ground. Hence the moral to be drawn from a critique of the aesthetic sphere is that no lessons from the aesthetic sphere can be straightforwardly applied anywhere else. The aesthetic sphere, like the work of art itself, if it is to stand as an emblem of enlightenment, has to stand alone.

This strictly negative principle can, however, be given something of a minimal positive form. It is, crudely speaking, an embodiment of Foucault's principle that, even if everything is not bad, then "everything is dangerous". Recalling Cavell, it is not just nature but conventions themselves that are to be mistrusted, for conventions are, in the end, themselves an aspect of nature. Put somewhat less gnomically, we can say that the example of aesthetic enlightenment exhorts us to adopt a strictly *nominalist* view of freedom. The point about freedom is that we cannot know what it is in advance; freedom has to be produced, in a way that is analogous to the production of aesthetic conventions – new conventions have to be found. We can never stop with a finished view of freedom; and the recognition that freedom is an ever-unfinished business is integral to the pursuit of freedom itself. The artworld exists as institutional testimony to the unfinished work of freedom *as* something that is, definitively unfinished.

Teaching freedom

But can such a negative attitude to freedom and enlightenment be cultivated? Can it be *taught*? Because of all the quite conventional associations of freedom and autonomy with the question of the aesthetic, it is not surprising that generations of philosophers have thought that one way to teach freedom might be on the basis of a specifically *aesthetic* education. This has usually taken a positive form: such philosophers have traditionally attempted to give a specific content to what they mean by the aesthetic. Such for instance have been the dreams of all those who, since Freidrich Schiller, have been drawn to the ideology of the aesthetic in terms of beauty and other substantive concepts associated specifically with the aesthetic sphere. For Schiller, aesthetics is important precisely because of its educational potential. Beauty is related to freedom – "it is only through beauty that man makes his way to freedom" (Schiller 1967: 9): because freedom is expressed in an inner unity of the human being, a unity that has been split assunder in the present age (ibid: 33); and because the way to such unity is through education in aesthetics, that is, fine art providing an education through beauty (ibid: 55). Beauty, for Schiller, is a great reconciliatory force; melting beauty for those who are tense, energizing beauty for those who are relaxed, each leading the sensous to thought and the spiritual to sense. In Beauty, all limitations, constraints and contingencies are forgotten.

Few today now subscribe to the idea of an aesthetic education specifically in Schiller's sense. What has art necessarily got to do with beauty anyway? That does not mean that the idea was itself incoherent, for instance when seen in terms not of philosophy but as an ethical practice (Hunter 1988: 81). Not incoherent, but faced with difficulties nonetheless; as if aesthetic enlightenment might consist in substantive principles that could be taught, or known in advance of the actual, experimental, difficult practices of aesthetic production. Such specific aesthetic programmes – those which take the aesthetic domain itself as their terrain of education – tend to run up against the paradox of the aesthetic; that its nature cannot be known in advance, that there are inevitably problems entailed in *teaching* specific aesthetic principles. From what I have said in this chapter it is obvious that a critique of aesthetic enlightenment would lead us to a view that is very unexciting aesthetically; that the very idea of aesthetic*ist* proselytization should be held in some disregard, if not distaste, not least out of a certain healthy respect – in both senses, admiration and fear – for the integrity and autonomy of the aesthetic sphere itself. But that is not necessarily to abandon the very idea of an aesthetic education altogether.

Chapter 5

Questioning enlightenment: ethics of truth in Foucault and Weber

Foucault and the question of criticism – Max Weber and the 'science of man' – Weber and Foucault as critics of enlightenment

As Ian Hunter shows in his book *Culture and Government*, the Schillerian ideal of aesthetic education is by no means dead, even if it may be so in its nineteenth-century, romantic form (Hunter 1988). The aesthetic sphere itself – the world of literature and the arts – is generally held up as the best place to learn a certain kind of enlightenment; a matter less of thinking of the aesthetic as a regulatory ideal so much as claiming it as the privileged site of certain kinds of enlightening moral experience. If the model of such aesthetic education is rarely these days that of the "well-rounded person", the bottom-line remains that good habits of subjectivity are best learned in relation to studiousness within the aesthetic field itself.

Such a viewpoint is likely, if anything, to be strengthened by demands to introduce more generalized forms of education, especially in the universities. The arts disciplines have a track-record of being oriented to developing the general, critical capacities of students rather than merely filling them with specific kinds of knowledge. But as we saw in the last chapter, there is no reason to equate the regulative values of the aesthetic exclusively with the aesthetic field as such (in fact there may be some good reasons for *not* doing so); hence we are not forced to cede exclusive rights to aesthetic education to the aesthetic disciplines themselves. And in the light of that thought, I now want to make some claims for social theory and the social sciences as places where, loosely speaking, a surrogate for an aesthetic education in the form of a critique of enlightenment might have a home as well. I do not do this through a general theory of aesthetic education. Rather, I take a much easier option and sketch interpretive pictures of the work of two thinkers who can be regarded as exemplary of the kind of outlook that I am advocating. Both

Max Weber and Michel Foucault, I argue, were ethical thinkers rather than proponents of a science of society. They exemplify in their work a kind of thought that while being obviously oriented to social issues is not, in any orthodox sense, "sociological" but which has, if anything, an ethical character. I hold them up as paragons of what an interesting – that is, a quizzical rather than a nomological – social theory can look like. In drawing these little pictures it is also possible to show that a critical attitude to enlightenment is not something that has to be invented; rather, it already exists and has done for some time, even wholly outside the latter-day rubric of postmodernism or iconoclastic anti-foundationalism.

I do not say that either Foucault or Weber offer us a model of aesthetic education in any direct or literal sense. Yet each worked for effects that were more than just "scientific". Both wanted their work to be dialogic in the sense that it would transform those who heard or read it; in other words, both were *teachers* striving for a reimagination of themselves and others; and both used the resources of a critical attitude to enlightenment as an instrument for doing so. In a different way, each now possesses a kind of aesthetic status in their own right. Both are often held up as exemplars of particular styles of doing social thought, styles which their proper names themselves embody such that we might say they themselves are the incarnations of an aesthetic value, able to stand up on its own. This means that a picture of the thought of thinkers such as these – in spite of all their massive differences – should not take the form of commentary whereby a particular methodology is disclosed for others to copy, but should more resemble an image of something unique and unrepeatable, if perhaps inspiring.

Foucault and the question of criticism

Was Foucault's thought an example of an aesthetic education? Perhaps in only rather a minimal sense; that of a philosophy of transformation or becoming. Foucault's thought was full of the idea that the function of intellectual work includes a kind of work that we perform on the self, if only to get free of ourselves. Foucault says of his own work on this point: "For me intellectual work is related to what you could call aestheticism, meaning transforming yourself ... This transformation of oneself by one's own knowledge is, I think, rather close to the aesthetic experience. Why should a painter work if he is not transformed by his own painting?" (Foucault 1988: 14). Perhaps in a peculiar way, then, and in so far as a body of work such as that of Foucault is addressed to others as well as himself, his philosophy is like a branch of aesthetic education, even if it does not educate through reflection on any specifically aesthetic materials; painting, music, literature or whatever. Perhaps Foucault's whole philosophy could be seen as entailing the practice of attempting to transform ourselves and others, a kind of artistic will to power through individuation: "For the attitude of modernity, the high value of the present is indissociable from a desperate eagerness to reimagine it, to imagine it otherwise than it is, and to transform it not by destroying it but by grasping it in what it is" (Foucault 1984a: 41; cf. Deleuze 1990: 135, 154).

Foucault was not a "master-thinker" in the sense of being someone who should be or can be followed. His work was enlightening in so far as it was indicative of a certain – and certainly viable, if not reproducible – approach to a critique of enlightenment. Foucault was a philosopher. He can be useful either directly (for those at work in various problems in philosophy or in the field of the history of the social sciences) or otherwise as, in Deleuze's terms, a "mediator" for those working in other disciplines (Deleuze 1992). In so far as he is a mediator, we may have to do a certain amount of violence to Foucault's work if we want to appropriate it. That is especially so with regard to the science of society, for what would be unquestionably absurd would be any attempt to appropriate Foucault straightforwardly and unproblematically to the project of sociology. Foucault's problematic is not centred on society. His work has nothing to say on the subject of the structure of societies, on identity, on selfhood – in short on all those things in relation to which his work is so often held to be relevant. That is not to say that it cannot be relevant; only that we have to translate certain aspects of that work into other idioms in order to make it so (cf. Dean 1994).

Foucault's work is centred on a particular problematic. But this is not power or the subject or discourse or whatever. Foucault was much more interested in *freedom*, which is to say ethics – and, of course, enlightenment.

Foucault's project in moral philosophy – if we can call it that – has been nicely described as an attempt to think through the question of subjectivation without recourse to any notion of the subject (Deleuze 1988: 101; Deleuze 1990: 154). For Foucault, an ethical form of life is something that is derived almost against the demands of biological or social life. This concern is no doubt the source of the import of the Stoics in Foucault's conception of the ethical life. For Foucault, the Stoics did not just produce an ideology designed to enable resistance against the negative forces of life; theirs was a positive problematization of existence. Although the Stoics used biological theories as a basis of their ideas, the whole point of their practical measures was to transcend the necessities of biological and other kinds of fate; a way of conceiving of ethics without conceiving of ethics in the form of an interiority. Such too was Foucault's problematic (cf. Hadot 1995: 206–13). That, too, was why he distinguished between an ethical elaboration of existence and a moral code (cf. Chapter 3, above). Whereas a moral code is analagous to a set of laws determining conduct, an ethical relation is one of a carefully fashioned freedom. Indeed, in Foucault's work there are traces of something even so crude as a dialectic between moral codes and ethical technologies; some eras, some societies privilege the code, others privilege ethics and techniques of the self. It is more than a little unlikely that Foucault was really thinking of drawing up a general typology of ethical and moral injunctions in history. Nevertheless, it does seem as if he was prepared to draw up broad analogies between periods that were subjected to varieties of ethical intensification. It is in this vein that he compares the Roman–Hellenistic period to the contemporary era in which he sees similarly a need for an autonomous ethics other than one founded on a scientific knowledge of the self, desire or the unconscious.

There are many distinctions abroad between ethics and morals. I think that Foucault had a certain limited amount in common with Anglo-Saxon philosophers such as Bernard Williams in arguing that morality or the moral code was but a part of the totality of ethical considerations. For Williams, the territory of ethics is given by the Socratic question of how we should live; in contrast to this the domain of moral obligation forms but a sub-system of ethics, albeit one which can often seem to stand in for the totality. This widening of the very territory of ethics has the effect, for Williams, of delimiting the claims of philosophy itself which, he thinks, is in no position to provide the master rationale of our ethical choices. At best, for Williams, philosophy legislates for a certain confidence in ethics, but not for ethical conviction or certainty. Perhaps an aspect of such confidence can come by way of what Williams calls the "relativism of distance": that is, a kind of relativism that makes ethical confrontation "notional" as opposed to real. Some of Foucault's studies of ethics, late in his career, might come under the heading of a certain relativism of distance in this sense (Williams 1985: 162; Williams 1993).

What appealed to Foucault in classical ethics was, no doubt, not their feasibility in the present but precisely their distance from any kind of moral codification. Morals are governed by codes of interdictions, sets of commands that determine correct and incorrect conduct. From this derives a certain conception of moral life as being an essentially constraining affair, with morals appearing as external to the individual. Against this picture, Foucault proposed a conception of ethics as entailing something like constitutive rules of conduct as opposed to regulative ones. An ethics is a rule or series of rules imposed on the self; a voluntarily willed submission to some kind of authority, a discipline practised in the name of freedom. It was not that there was no question of obligation in classical ethics. In this sense, Williams' and Foucault's distinctions cut across each other somewhat. Where Williams sees a distinction between ethical conduct and questions of moral obligation, Foucault would place a separation between systems of constraint and forms of obligation imposed on the self. But this obligation had to come from within; it was a kind of ethical boot-strapping of obligation. Hence Foucault's notion of ethics: not as an intrinsically other-directed activity, but as a kind of duty that we owe to ourselves.

Foucault's conception of ethics was not, however, of a decisionist kind: that is, of the sort addressed by Williams under the heading of an existentialist choice to lead a certain kind of life by force of the will alone. As Williams observes, "ethical conviction, like any other form of *being convinced*, must have some aspect of passivity to it, must in some sense come to you ... You could not have an ethical conviction, and be conscious that it was the product of a decision, unless that decision itself appeared inescapable" (Williams 1985: 169). But the model was not one of an isolated freedom in the face of existence but rather a submission to some kind of force that lay outside oneself. In this sense, Foucault's conception of ethics does meet Williams' requirement that an ethical conception must somehow go "outside of the self". Hence the rather remarkable sense of an atmosphere of obligation inherent in Foucault's conception of ethics, albeit a sort of extra-moral obligation – it is an ethics of conviction and, in that sense, a usage of Kantian obligation *against* the sub-system of morality.

It is not surprising that Foucault was tempted to resort to an aesthetic principle as a weapon against such an idea of morality. In his last lectures at the Collège de France, Foucault – as Thomas Flynn tells us – posed himself the-question of the role of Cynicism in the modern West. Perhaps this is an example of an aesthetic principle at work in ethics. The original cynics surely developed something like an aesthetic of existence, and they did so out of a minority-Socratic tradition. Plato's *Laches*, Flynn tells us, was a turning-point in styles of parrhesia or truth-telling. The authority of Socrates in the dialogue stems not from his technical knowledge but from a certain stylistic alignment of his *logos*, his doctrines, and his *bios*, his mode of life. This alignment constituted a style of existence that was irreducible merely to the actual – stated – doctrines of Socrates. There is an important aspect to this; what is at stake is not adherence to a doctrine but an ongoing transformation of one's existence, an openness to truth and life (Flynn 1988: 108–9). In other words, one might say that the condition of such a beautiful existence is not a will to moral closure, a once-and-for-all defining of principles, but a will to *movement*, a practical philosophy of becoming. Maintaining this sense of movement or openness is a matter of discipline and asceticism; it is the opposite of an anarchistic, free-flowing or irresponsible existence. Movement is a difficult, ascetic business.

Foucault, Flynn says, takes the Cynics to be the early epitome of such a style of aesthetic existence in the West. The deliberately and calculatedly unconventional lifestyle of the cynic allowed for a very specific kind of truth-telling: a life lived as a "scandal of truth". What this involved appears to have been an extension to the point of parody of the Platonic tradition as applied to our whole life; hence, an absence of dissemblance, the deliberate attainment of dishonour through poverty, the rejection of social conventions, and so on (ibid: 110–11). Flynn glosses an interesting point that Foucault is supposed to have made in these last lectures, and this gives us some clue to the role that an aesthetics of intellectual existence had for him. Flynn says: "Foucault notes that this approach was considerably weakened once philosophy became the *métier* of professors and that the last such philosophic hero was probably Goethe's Faust: 'Exit Faust and enter the revolutionary'" (ibid: 110). Foucault, on the other hand, preferred the model of Faust.

This means at the very least that we cannot be surprised that Foucault's is hardly an ordinary philosophy. Foucault would no doubt hold philosophy to understand itself as a spiritual exercise in the context of "existence" rather than as a philosophical "discourse" as such. There is an "anthropological" element to such a concern; for Foucault's object of attention here is not society or modernity but the status of "man": human nature, and above all *enlightened "man"*. Those who complain that Foucault has no theory of human nature are both right and wrong. They are wrong at least in so far as there is a minimal anthropology at work in Foucault. He believes that humans have certain capabilities that interest him, even if such capabilities are not to be found universally across all human societies. Not least of these capabilities is that of taking human nature as itself an object of work; humans are those beings that strive to make themselves free, to fashion their freedom. And that is the extent to which those who hold that Foucault had no theory of human nature are right. Such an absence was really strategic. The game involves assuming that nothing is fundamental or permanent to human nature, to make our enquiries themselves an aspect of a quest for freedom; and in that sense, if it is an anthropology, we might describe it as a *negative anthropology*. Foucault's work is itself ethical. It is more an exercise on the territory of human nature than a series of propositions *about* human nature; and in that sense it will do little good to treat Foucault as if he were a "scientist" of some sort and seek to prove, as if it were against him, that really such a thing as human nature does exist.

If one looks at Foucault's work one will find that this question of freedom crops up again and again. But because Foucault does not have a positive definition of what freedom is, we merely have a series of studies concerned with the construction of freedom; that is, because he is a nominalist about freedom, he takes what we would call in our terminology a realist orientation towards it. But such studies are also a critique of enlightenment in so far as analysing the diverse ways in which humans have sought to fabricate their freedoms means that the limits of such constructions need to be illuminated. Hence, for instance, Foucault analyses the freeing of the mad, the severing of their chains, and the invention of the moral space of the asylum partly in terms of the advent of a new form of freedom, but also in terms of a critique of such a construction (Foucault 1971). It is not that Foucault preferred chains and water treatments to the moral freedom of the asylum; it is rather that all freedom is regulated, there is no pure freedom, hence the critique of freedom must be an aspect of the pursuit of freedom itself. And we can say that Foucault's strategic nominalism about such categories as freedom or human nature also makes him something of a utopian in that he holds out for the possibility of a freedom that is entirely free of determination or a human nature that might entirely make itself. But such utopianism is a regulatory ideal; it conditions what can be said, and acts as a principle of criticism rather than a necessarily realistic telos.

Foucault's main concern, then, was not really with society or the self or the subject but with this issue of freedom, which is to say ultimately with a critique of enlightenment. Take, as a more extensive illustration, the category of governmentality which was of such importance in Foucault's work and in that of some of those who have been influenced by him (Burchell, Gordon and Miller 1991; Foucault 1991a; Rose & Miller 1992). Perhaps the key to this perspective is that it opens up a space for thinking of political power without reflex recourse to the category of the State. It is not that the State is irrelevant, merely that we do not *begin* necessarily with the question of the State. Rather, government is exercised at all levels of the social hierarchy; it does not just derive from the State or some central, sovereign point. Foucault's original paradigm or founding example here is that of the Greeks, as when he describes Xenophon's principle of the isomorphism of the arts of government: "governing oneself, managing one's estate, and participating in the administration of the city were three practices of the same type" (Foucault 1986: 76). The task becomes to draw up a series of descriptions of the different rationalities and techniques by which humans have been governed in differing eras.

As far as Foucault was concerned, we do not govern unless we are confronted with a field of forces across which to "dispose" our government; anything else would be merely coercion or domination. Freedom is a constant theme of Foucault's studies of government; hence the frequent invocation of a sort of reciprocity operating between the government of ourselves and the government of others. Thus, for Aristotle, the goodness of the individual was contributory to the well-being of the city: "The individual's attitude towards himself, the way in which he ensured his own freedom with regard to himself, and the form of supremacy he maintained over himself were a contributing element to the well-being and good order of the city" (ibid: 79). *Enkrateia*, self-mastery: this implied a certain freedom with respect to the self, a freedom from the debasement of all relations of slavery. "But this freedom was more than a non-enslavement, more than an emancipation that would make the individual independent of any exterior or interior constraint; in its full, positive form, it was a power that one brought to bear on oneself in the power that one exercised over others" (ibid: 80). Government implies, in this sense, a certain balance between the government of oneself and the persuasion and consent over others. It seems, then, that the notion of government, in this wide sense, is very much tied to the idea of an elaboration of relations of freedom in our conduct towards oneself and others. The theme of government thus actually signals this concern for freedom.

So what happens when this concern for freedom, this principle, is specified in the context of modern Western political rationality? Foucault's aspiration was not anything approximating to the order of a "science of society"; it is much more a contribution to a cultural science centred on the question of freedom. But what concerns him are not the political philosophies of freedom that have been dreamed up in the minds of the great thinkers of the West but the practical rationalities, the problematizations and the positive forms taken by freedom; hence his concern with "practical" texts which are themselves the objects of a "practice" (ibid: 12). In short, his concern for freedom took the form of a kind of negative anthropology of the capability of freedom in the modern West, and an investigation into what has been called modern *formulae* of freedom: that is, freedom in the light of its formation, as a principle of rule rather than a negative postulate of political philosophy (cf. Rose 1992a). And this means that when Foucault considers such instances as the political rationalities of liberalism and neo-liberalism, he is many miles distant from the philosophical themes that are usually associated with such topics, just as he is a long way from wishing to say that liberalism is the successful "doctrine" underlying all political aspirations in the West. It is not a question of documenting the triumphs of liberalism and its offshoots but of interrogating liberal and neo-liberal preoccupations for what they can inform our interests in an historico-philosophical anthropology.

The theme of liberalism is of interest from the viewpoint of Foucault's critique of enlightenment not because it is all-pervasive but, on the contrary, because of its status as an *invention*; that is, because of the rather extraordinary "novelty" of its intentions. This means that the idea of a kind of quasi-sociological Foucauldian "approach" to questions of liberal and other kinds of government is something of an absurdity. Liberalism is interesting not in a sociological way, but because of its status as a kind of ethical experiment. Everyone seems to know what liberalism is, but when we attempt to define it there always follows trouble. In invoking the notion of a liberal mentality of *government*, the identity of liberalism moves from being described, as is all too typical, as a kind of anti-State theory or an absence of government, to being associated with a certain – positive – *style* of government. That is why so many analyses of modern governmentality focus on the emergence of liberalism; they are seeking to show that liberalism entails a new sensitivity to the techniques and mechanisms of government (Burchell, Gordon & Miller 1991).

There is, for instance, the "problem space" of early liberalism; this centred on the fabrication of a realm of civil society, a free space of agonism and interaction.

This problem-space is an open-ended space of real politico-technical invention, of a governmental constructivism. Liberalism sets limits to what government can know or do *vis-à-vis* a civil society that must none the less be governed even if, as in the most radical proposals, it is sometimes maintained that civil society or the nation is entirely capable of governing itself and does not require a State. (Burchell 1993)

In other words, what we call civil society, the distinction between public and private in early liberalism, is not a natural development consequent on a certain stage of the development of capitalism, but the product of a constructive series of problematizations of the proper spaces and limits of government. Liberalism here appears as a sort of *experimental* rationality; it is a "crucial" experiment in the history of rationalities of government, an experiment that, even if it was ever successful in the first place, has never been straightforwardly replicated. But then that is not the point, and history is not reversible; and, besides, it is the experimental attitude that is important not as to whether we can write either the "real history" of liberalism or whether we wish definitively to assess the sum import of liberalism in relation to other political rationalities (socialism, for example) in the West. So the point is not as to whether liberalism, in this particular sense, has indeed defined the political aspirations of the West; nor is the game to found a full-scale sociological perspective on the basis of this notion of governmentality; the idea is more with an anthropological investigation into "governed man" than with the formulation of new rules for political sociology.

In fact, the point is both a cultural and an ethical one. Culturally speaking, the interest of liberalism lies in the fact that it represents a political technology designed to act on the very capacities of freedom in humans. It offers a challenge for those who would wish to analyse the ways in which freedom is given a practical form and a political resonance in our societies. Ethically speaking, and here we see why the perspective entails a negative anthropology, the object is to achieve a certain pathos of distance *vis-à-vis* the forms of freedom that confront us as necessary and desirable. It is precisely because freedom is such a universal – unquestionable aspiration – that we must remorselessly and dispassionately genealogize the varied forms of freedom that are offered today. For freedom does not exist beyond the practical forms that it takes. So in gaining an ethical distance from freedom, we are not repudiating it but, if anything, the reverse: we are "dedicated" to freedom in the Weberian sense.

But is Foucault in any sense endorsing liberalism? Methodologically speaking the answer has to be no, in that he uses none of the tools of liberal sociology or philosophy to analyse liberalism itself. Above all, in Foucault's work there is no recourse to any notion of a public/private division. Indeed, the *raison d'être* of the concept of governmentality really centres on the need to find a concept that will not reduce the question of power to that specifically of *public* power, and above all the State.

One of the important effects of these studies is to transmute what is perhaps our normal understanding of the territory of the political. It is as if this territory becomes in one sense contracted and in another sense expanded. Studies of governmentality contract the domain of the political in so far as they tend to aver that the State and the narrowly "political" states of wrangling that dispute around it is not all that exists within politics. By shifting the perspective away from politics as such to the much more apparantly heteroclite sphere of the government in conduct in general, these studies are typically concerned with only at best the governmentalization of the State. These studies take a leaf out of some of the post-Kuhnian, logistically-inclined sociology of science; the State is, at best, an important "centre of calculation" – but what needs to be analysed is the way that this centre appears out of the periphery rather than the internal activities of the centre itself (Rose and Miller 1992). On the other hand, by the same gesture the territory of the political becomes expanded because now there are no apparant limits to what can be considered *as* political since almost by definition any kind of government of conduct can come to seem politically motivated.

To many critics, such a perspective has made Foucault appear to be rather anti-liberal because apparently committed to a kind of paranoia concerning the all-pervasiveness of power. Others have even claimed that Foucault's interest in neo-liberalism actually made him something of a neo-liberal. There is no evidence for these kinds of interpretation. And yet in some respects Foucault is indeed a liberal – if a peculiar sort. Foucault's studies might be seen to adopt a form of enlightenment that is designed to give space to a certain voluntarism. Rather than conceiving of humans as cultural dopes – or, rather, dopes of discourse – studies of governmentality actually presume that humans are voluntaristic creatures or, at least, creatures capable of voluntarism. When Foucault talks about the *arts* of government, he means it quite literally – that forms of government are themselves *cultural* creations. Rationalities of government have to be invented; and they can become undone just as easily. All this is up to the will of humans; not necessarily a will that is directed in any particular way – just the will to govern and be governed.

But was Foucault, then, not against the very idea of government, just as he was supposed by so many to be against the very idea of power? Perhaps it is rather that Foucault regarded enlightenment as entailing only a critique of the very possibility of a form of government that acts in the name of truth. Indeed, Foucault glossed the notion of critique as "the art of not being governed so much" (Foucault 1996: 384):

> And if governmentalization is really this movement concerned with sub-jugating individuals in the very reality of a social practice by mechanisms of power that appeal to a truth, I will say that critique is the movement through which the subject gives itself the right to question truth concerning its power effects and to question power about its discourses of truth. Critique will be the art of voluntary inservitude, of reflective indocility. The essential function of critique would be that of desubjectification in the game of what one could call, in a word, the politics of truth. (Foucault 1996: 386)

This critical attitude does not, then, consist of a blanket rejection of the idea either of truth or of government, but only the will to critique both in the name of enlightened government itself; in short, in the name of freedom. The function of such critique would not be to impose another game of truth on government but simply to keep alive the recognition that we are governed in the name of truth; hence the on-going – if impossible, utopian, counterfactual – project of desubjectification.

But is that all? Or might there not be some more general principles at stake in these studies? Perhaps we might distinguish three.

First, there is what could be called the realist principle of *destiny*. Foucault's whole problematic was oriented to the analysis of what is given to us as if it were by necessity. In other words, its subject matter was not just anything and everything but, above all, those things which seem to be given to us as more or less indispensable. Humanism itself might be an example. It is a mistake to regard Foucault as being some kind of kneejerk anti-humanist; rather, because humanism is given to us as a kind of obligation it is asking for the perspective of a critique of enlightenment to be brought against it. Foucault's question was always "What is our destiny?" and consequently "Does it have to be our destiny?" This is, in a peculiar way, a realist principle in so far as what is studied is conditioned by what gives itself to us in the form of necessity. That might be, to take an example from an earlier chapter, psychology, for instance; for who could be against the enlightened aims of psychological knowledge? But that does not mean that, in the terms of a science of society, we live in a "psychological society" as such. Foucault's realism relates to certain kinds of object; not to saying that only some kinds of object are important. In other words, this realism is strategic, restricted, ethical.

Second, there is what could be called a principle of *clarity*. This is not a term that is usually associated with Foucault's work; but clarity does not mean common sense or that everything should make sense in the manner of that most difficult of subjects, Anglo-Saxon analytical philosophy. On the contrary, a striving for clarity means putting everything up for grabs, for leaving nothing immune from interrogation. The principle of clarity does not mean writing in a clear way but never assuming that we have the full meaning of our actions; it is the principle that "nothing is fundamental" which should, perhaps, be interpreted not to mean that nothing *is* fundamental (for who could say that?) but to proceed *as if* nothing were fundamental. Again, criticism here takes more of an ethical than a propositional or nomological form.

Third, there is something like a principle of *dignity* which informs the engagement of those who carry out this kind of criticism with regard to their subject matter. Dignity does not mean standoffishness or a refusal of commitment, but an ethical work of distantiation. That is an aspect of any critique of enlightenment; the attempt to distance ourselves, to make something strange, be that – as in the case of Foucault's work – madness, medicine, liberalism, sexuality or whatever. This is strictly an ethical – which is to say, a deliberately restricted – dignity; we cultivate such a thing only in order to be able to return to the world again, and return to it in a different way. The aim is not to dictate to judgement; to say do this or do that, to insist that certain kinds of analysis have necessary kinds of consequence or call on particular kinds of energies. Rather, the aim is merely to cultivate a certain latitude for judgement itself; to sow, as Nietzsche had it, the seeds of judgement. For, perhaps, at the end of the day, that is all that any critique of enlightenment entails: endless exercises in judgement.

For what is all this for, if not only to provoke judgement, which means to provoke worries about judgement? In fact, such a style of critique might be seen as cultivating aspects of what Williams has called ethical *confidence*; the ability to live in maturity and dignity with our ethical existence. He is worth quoting in full (Williams 1985: 171):

> The truth is that the basic question is how to live and what to do; ethical considerations are relevant to this; and the amount of time and human energy to be spent in reflecting on these considerations are relevant to this; and the amount of time and human energy to be spent in reflecting on these considerations must itself depend on what, from the perspective of the critical life we actually have, we count as a life worth living and what is likely to produce people who find life worth living. One question we have to answer is how people, or enough people, can come to possess a practical confidence that, particularly granted both the need for reflection and its pervasive presence in our world will come from strength and not from the weakness of self-deception and dogmatism. (Confidence is not the same as optimism; it could rest on what Nietzsche called the pessimism of strength.)

Obviously we cannot *teach* confidence in this sense; but we can seek to cultivate it through reflection, taking as our main task the constant deconstruction of self-deception and dogmatism which means, correlatively, that it would be a nonsense – or, at least, just a mistake, but a big mistake too – to understand the critique of enlightenment itself, including and especially Foucault's contribution to it, in just such terms of dogmatism and self-deception. Hence at the end of the day, a critical attitude to enlightenment is itself anthropological, at least in rather a restricted sense. It seeks to work in a certain way on the human faculty of judgement; not dictating to it, but only exercising it, perhaps to its limit.

The conditions for this are clear. We need, said Foucault, to escape from the blackmail of being for or against enlightenment, for or against modernity; not least in order to resurrect for today's conditions some of the principles of enlightenment as *ethos*. Enlightenment is not a doctrine but an attitude, the will to keep ourselves on the move, to find a way out of our predicaments (Foucault 1984a). One of the features of such an enlightenment would be a kind of manic attentiveness to enlightenment itself; enlightenment would be as much the object as the medium of such an attitude.

I have insisted that Foucault was not a sociologist in that he has no theory of society. But, in a sense, such a judgement is misleading because it assumes that the task of sociological thought is itself *necessarily* oriented to being a "science of society". But that is not necessarily the case, and especially if we are not sociologists but social theorists oriented to the question of enlightenment. And if we look at the work of that paradigm of all social theorists, Max Weber, it is easy to see that even that discipline might partake of some of the aspects of a critique of enlightenment. Needless to say, we find nothing of the order of an explicit or substantive aesthetic paradigm in Weber's work. But such a thing would, in any case, be to will what cannot be willed, and Weber's aesthetic credentials should be left to subsequent judgements. In any case, with the idea of a cultural science, it can be argued that Weber meant something a little more than just the study of humans in so far as the development of institutions and conventions. Rather the principle of culture was the aim as well as just the medium of Weber's work; the invention of cultural beings that were human in so far as they were, like the artist, beyond the constraints of nature. In that sense, Weber's problematic centred on the possibility of a cultural form of enlightenment: it was simultaneously concerned even with the idea of a critique of enlightenment.

Max Weber and the "science of man"

If we are to believe that it is not unenlightening to go through Weber in order to think fruitfully about enlightenment and ethics today, then we need, from the outset, to make sure that we have got the *right* Weber. And the Weber we want is much more the scientist of "man" than he is scientist of society. There is a certain amount of agreement on this question in the flood of recent writings on Weber; an agreement that can be rather obscured by the continuing question as to what, if anything, Weber owes to neo-Kantianism (cf. Hennis 1988, 1996; Schroeder 1992; Turner 1992). Besides, everybody knows that Weber only rarely if ever spoke of sociology as an autonomous discipline, and that his preferred term was the *Kulturwissenschaften*, the sciences of culture; and hence that Weber's concern was with the cultural aspects of "man": that is, not with some kind of cultural "sphere" but only – in perhaps a restricted sense – "man" *in so far as* he is a cultural being (Turner 1992: 43).

Weber has come down to modern sociology in part as a methodologist who stressed the importance of meaningful action in the study of human affairs. This is a good place to start, then, if we want to show that Weber was not a sociologist in the sense of a "scientist of society" but a proponent of a cultural science and a practitioner of the critique of enlightenment.

Certainly Weber, in his methodological writings, attaches importance to the interpretation of action. "Sociology (in the sense in which this highly ambiguous word is used here) is a science concerning itself with the interpretive understanding of social action ... We shall speak of 'action' in so far as the acting individual attaches a subjective meaning to his behaviour" (Weber 1978, vol. 1: 4). On the basis of such statements have stemmed entire traditions and controversies in the social sciences as when, for example, Jack Douglas insisted on the role of interpretation against Durkheim's apparently "objectivist" understanding of suicide. Human beings, the story goes, mean what they do, so to understand what they do we need to know what they mean. But perhaps there is a misunderstanding of Weber's own intentions here. For in an odd sort of way, Weber's problematic was not directed at meaningful action at all but to what he regarded as the causes of its demise in the West. In other words, the existence of meaningful action did not signify simply the precondition of a general methodological principle for Weber, but rather a substantive domain of social investigation in its own right. Meaningful action, for Weber, implies the presence of a personal element in relations of authority and association among humans, and where this personal relation is missing, or is obliterated, so Weber "falls silent" – although it is a very pregnant silence, one which determines the whole character of his sociology. The German critic, Wilhelm Hennis, has argued that, in the light of this preoccupation, we need to see Weber's sociology as being inherently – if productively – *restricted*. "This restricted conception of 'his' sociology is consistently related to the actual material involved; where there is nothing 'personal' to register Weber falls silent, and gets no further than unfulfilled intentions" (Hennis 1988: 100). Hennis adds: "We often encounter in Weber's work the curious word 'ethically neutral' (*anethisch*) – not unethical or anti-ethical, but ethically *neutral*. A prime concept of an ethically neutral institution was for Weber the market. Domination through a constellation of interests had an ethically neutral character, that is, it was not susceptible to ethical interpretation. This resistance, opacity, of the world in which we are 'placed' to ethical interpretation is the 'fate' with which Weber's work struggles" (ibid: 102).

We can quarrel with Hennis as to the extent to which Weber should be seen as a critic of the modern world in this sense (Gordon 1987; Turner 1992: 47). One way to address that problem is to focus on the prophetic or epical moment in Weber's work. That is the kind of moment we experience at the end of *The Protestant Ethic and the Spirit of Capitalism* where Weber talks about specialists without spirit and hedonists without heart as being the ethical types of the modern world of bureaucracy and legal-rational administration (Weber 1992b: 182–3). This is clearly not a straightforward sociological description of what humans will become, but is more like a warning that exists solely in order that it should not come about. In that sense, it is the reverse of the prophetic functions of Marxism, which prophesied in order that things *should* come about. That after all is what is at the very heart of the ethic of ideal-typical characterization: the exaggeration of aspects of reality. A cultural science is, as Turner says, intrinsically *polemical*; and we might add that part of its existence entails a restricted exaggeration in contextually confined contexts. The very possibility of such an epical "exaggeration" is given by the fact that Weber certainly supposed that humans were ethical animals: that is, not animals that were necessarily and always ethical, but animals capable of ethical conduct, capable of imposing logics of meaning on their actions in the world.

Weber was also preoccupied with the extent to which ethical possibilities and capabilities had been eclipsed in the modern world and hence, implicitly, with creating the conditions for the development of further possibilities and capabilities. This is the great theme of destiny as it appears in Weber. And Wolfgang Mommsen, for instance, has argued that Weber's so-called pessimism is a kind of prophetic warning, a deliberately dystopian engagement with the present, perhaps designed to act on our current conception of time in the name of another time to come. Indeed, Weber's whole intention is to invoke countervailing tendencies against what seems to be our fate:

> In this respect, the gloomy prognostications on the future petrification of the Western world, which are to be found so often in Weber's work, are not really to be understood as material statements about the finite nature of history, but rather as prophetic warnings designed to call forth forces to counter what seemed under given circumstances to be the greatest danger for Western man. (Mommsen 1987: 50)

In the name of what is such criticism undertaken? Weber is not the beginning – a "founding father" – of a value-free interpretative sociology but is rather at the end of a tradition of essentially *political* discourse that runs back to Aristotle (Hennis 1988; cf. Weber 1994a: 16). For these thinkers – Machiavelli, Rousseau, Tocqueville – what was at stake in the "sciences of man" was neither the establishment of the conditions for the optimal functioning of the human sciences nor the attainment of happiness for men and others but the determination of the optimal conditions for the emergence of particular *qualitative* types of human being. The task here is not to describe moral norms but to illuminate the conditions for something like ethical excellence within the particularized value-spheres of modern life. Weber himself was in little doubt which kinds of human beings were to his taste. In this context, Hennis draws attention to one of the key passages to be found in Weber's *Wissenschafstlehre*: "Without exception every order of social relations (however constituted) is, if one wishes to *evaluate* it, ultimately to be examined in terms of the human type (*menschlichen Typus*) to which it, by way of external or internal (motivational) selection, provides the optimal chances of becoming the dominant type" (Hennis 1988: 60; cf. for the original translation, Weber 1949: 27). Hennis is also fond of referring to Weber's inaugural address of 1895: "The question which stirs us as we think beyond the grave of our own generation is not the *well-being* human beings will enjoy in the future but what kind of people they will *be*, and it is this same question which underlies all work in political economy. We do not want to breed well-being in people, but rather those characteristics which we think of as constituting the human greatness and nobility of our nature" (Weber 1994a).

If Weber was a sociologist at all then this was for an historical reason; because this political question had been made more complex by the invention of social relations pertaining between the State and the individual. By Weber's day, the conditions for an autonomous politics had – even for a minority – passed away. Above all, the coordinating factor in political life had effectively ceased to be a conception of the State. "In the background of the possibilities of human development there was in fact for Weber – and to this extent he is a 'sociologist' – 'society', especially in its economic form … It was no longer the state that was crucial for the full development of humanity, in that manner that Rousseau had sought to classically formulate it" (Hennis 1988: 193). "The central point of 'practical', 'moral' and 'social' sciences is no longer the political community – in modern terms the state as *societas perfecta cum imperio*; in its place there appears *society* in its ideal form, *societas perfecta sine imperio*, constituted by those who are in principle free and equal. 'Society', with the market as an ideal type of sociability in which power and influence are freely competed for, delineates the extreme bounds for human action" (ibid: 108–9).

The opacity of the world meant, for Weber, that it was more than a little difficult to know what ethical pay-off to expect from the sciences themselves. For what might one hope from the cultural sciences? At the end of "Science as a Vocation", Weber wrote that one of the – apparently rather limited objectives – of the social sciences is to help people to gain *clarity*. Very often this has been taken to mean something like technical feasibility or some equivalent. But such clarity relates not just to a kind of technicist illumination of the "best methods" in a given situation; it also relates to giving an account of the ethical consequences of our convictions. Thus "we can force the individual, or at least we can help him, to give himself an *account of the ultimate meaning of his own conduct*" (Weber 1991a: 152). In other words, it is not just that the social sciences deal in things called ethics; rather, such sciences are *themselves* ethical. Not in that they preach this or that substantive form of ethics; but rather that they seek to bring about a change in the relation that a practitioner of such sciences has with their own meaningful actions, seeking to call into question those actions without laying down blueprints as to what should otherwise "be done". What better description could there be of the ethical aims of a cultural science? Not to provide us with an ethics but to force us to recognize our own ethical convictions, to enable us to give an account of ourselves.

So far I have merely glossed some senses in which Weber might be distanced from the sociological project in the name of a cultural "science of man". I do not think we can say that Weber adopts anything like a negative anthropology as such, but his work is animated – not least in central concepts such as charisma – by an ethical concern with the possibilities of human creativity, the ability of humans to impose values on the world. If Weber had an ethical concept that was at the heart of the values that oriented his work, it was that of conviction. Weber had absolutely no interest in the re-enchantment of a disenchanted world, but he was interested in the possibility of conviction in the face of a moral reality sundered by a variety of conflicting life-orders. Sometimes this motif in Weber is criticized as an obsession with "greatness" but that is not to do Weber much justice unless we substantially widen what is usually meant by greatness. Weber's interests did not lie solely in the valorization of the charismatic leader; his model was rather those political animals that are able to act on and within the world, and in the process moulding the world in their own image, shaping it to their ends. In that sense, as Turner insists, Weber's idea of politics is exemplary for the way in which he wants to valorize conduct in general; "not that it is in the political sphere that human beings construct and reveal their identities, but that the ordeal to which the politician subjects herself is the exemplary ideal" (Turner 1992: 146).

For everywhere Weber is obsessed with this question: How can we have conviction and personality given the objective developmental tendencies of the world? In the realm, at least, of politics, we might assume that fundamental convictions are paramount requirements for any kind of action that is not just going to be a cynical living "off" the main activity of politics itself. Weber was clearly not against conviction *per se*, even conviction of the strategically futile kind. Honigsheim writes of Weber's admiration for the Poles who resisted Bismarck's "silly language policies": "they are people whom we are trying to rob of their culture, and yet they fight against it, heroically and ready for death. He loved them for this" (Honigsheim 1968: 10). But, specificallly in the sphere of politics, an ethic of conviction was not – paradoxically – the way to carry conviction; for those who espouse an ethic of conviction "cannot bear the ethical irrationality of the world" (Weber 1994b: 361). Rather one was more or less obligated – perhaps even as a matter of conviction – towards an ethic of responsibility: that is, one which measured the consequences of one's own actions. But Weber's concern was not merely with bringing idealists to their senses and outlining a more "realistic" or pragmatic way to conduct politics; his view was that the value-sphere of politics imposes an ethic of responsibility on those who occupy its confines. Politics is ultimately about the disposition of the means of legitimate violence in the State: "Anyone who makes a pact with the means of violence, for whatever purpose – and every politician does this – is at the mercy of its specific consequences ... Anyone wishing to practise politics of any kind, and especially anyone who wishes to make a profession of politics, has to be conscious of these ethical paradoxes and of his responsibility for what may become of *himself* under pressure from them. He is becoming involved, I repeat, with the diabolical powers that lurk in all violence" (ibid: 364–5). But this does not mean that all conviction is impossible. Rather, it means that one must act on one's convictions in politics according to an ethic of responsibility. Such is the tragedy and the pathos of politics: to feel when responsibility reaches its limits. Then it is up to our judgement as to whether we wish, finally, to make a stand for our convictions. "On the other hand it is immensely moving when a mature person (whether old or young) who feels with his whole soul the responsibility he bears for the real consequences of his actions, and who acts on the basis of an ethics of responsibility, says at some point 'Here I stand, I can do no other' ", and in this ultimate sense – "the ethics of conviction and the ethics of responsibility are not absolute opposites" (ibid: 367–8).

Weber's *ethical* problematic could be said to centre, then, on this issue of conviction. In itself, the world may be ethically irrational or, at least, indeterminate; but the world is ethically rational in so far as people make it so, since people give meaning to the world with their own actions. We can see how far this takes us from a view which is still quite current which is that Weber's import is to have developed an idealist theory of the development, including the origins, of modern capitalism. This is the view that would put *The Protestant Ethic and the Spirit of Capitalism* as Weber's *chef d'oeuvre*. In fact, this view gets things the wrong way round. Weber is interested in what might be called the anthropological effects of capitalism. To be sure, capitalism is possibly the most fateful force of modern life; and Weber is interested in the ethical consequences of that fact. Weber's point, however, is not that the possibilities of conviction are extinguished in the modern world. It is not just a tale of how ethics became impossible first under capitalism, then under bureaucracy. Weber's point is rather that the modern capitalist world entails a kind of ethical impulsion; it promotes the demand for an ethics of conviction just as, almost in the same stroke, it thwarts such a demand (cf. Turner 1992: 173).

The Calvinists are, for Weber, at the origins of modern ethics of conviction. The significance of the Calvinists was that they invented the modern form of "vocation": that is, they linked the notion of the vocation – the calling – to worldly activity. For Calvin the calling had an intrinsically ascetic aspect, set against one's natural inclinations or character. "Vocation is the office or station in which God places us for his employment, not for our enjoyment; it is a special burden taken on as our only spiritual hope and purpose, not for personal fulfilment" (Goldman 1988: 39). But the Calvinist calling is not a passive *fate* to which we must submit; rather, it forms the condition of a kind of *service* to some kind of higher good (Goldman 1988: 45).

This notion of the calling was, for Weber, central to the "attitude" or ethos that was to allow for the development of modern capitalism. There is no *need* for such a calling today. Weber was not such an idealist thinker as to believe that capitalism would fall apart without the calling to motivate human beings. Rather, what Marx described as the dull compulsion of economic life is perfectly sufficient to keep us locked into our everyday forms of conduct. But the idea of the duty in the calling, Weber says, still haunts our lives "like a ghost of formerly religious beliefs" (Weber 1992b: 182). We might find it reactivated in certain specific contexts, but otherwise it *is* just a ghost. Rather than giving meaning to our life through an ascetic commitment, far more common is a retreat into subjectivism – something which Weber saw as the corollary of, the reaction to, rationalization itself. "Precisely the ultimate and most sublime values have retreated from public life either into the transcendental realm of mystic life or into the brotherliness of direct and personal human relations" (Weber 1991b: 155). But the matter does not end there, in spite of Weber's own protestations that his is purely an "historical" discussion, without presuming to trespass with judgements. For Weber's message was surely precisely that we must meet the spirit of capitalism with the appropriate weapons; and that is not a privatized subjectivism but a form of conviction or asceticism. Weber's work was situated around the problematic of such ascetic convictions: "Because of its matter-of-fact clarity about the self and the world, asceticism oriented toward the here-and-now is better able than other-worldly or mystical alternatives to work out an acceptable *modus vivendi* with the existing order" (Scaff 1989: 170).

This does not mean that Weber's sociology should be seen as having anything remotely to do with all those sociologies and philosophies of the self that are rather in vogue today. For Weber, the self is a territory over which we fight the battles of our convictions; but it is not in itself the end of the analysis. The idea of a whole self or a fulfilled self is wholly alien to Weber's concerns and he was the opposite of a romantic theorist of *Bildung* (Turner 1992: 36–40). Ethics do not *derive* from the self; rather it is, if anything, the other way around. It is our ethics that chain us to particular images of selfhood. Modern ethics tie our notions of conviction to the self. Hence, Weber's constant resort to the langauge of inwardness, which is simultaneously an onslaught on the language of psychology. Normatively speaking, Weber is not interested in the self, but in something radically opposed to it: *personality*. And here is where the theme of dignity surfaces in his work which is concerned not with the average individual but with the conditions making for the possibility of personality within any particular life-order. Weber was obsessed with cultivating the "inner distance" required for dignity (Owen 1991; Schroeder 1991; cf. Weber 1991c: 393); which also means the distance required for judgement. And Weber's thought, as much as if not more than can be said of that of Foucault – is all about the Nietzschean demand for sowing the seeds of judgement in a difficult, democratic age (Hennis 1988: 188; Hennis 1991).

So if the idea of ethics in Weber relates to the duty that one owes to oneself, this does not presuppose a concern with anything like the kinds of sociology of the self that are currently fashionable. Indeed, one of Weber's great uses is that he enables us to be able to bypass these issues with both clarity and an ease of conscience. It is a key aspect of Weber's ethical problematic to formulate the conditions for freeing the self of the self. Hennis regards this as a characteristic Weberian valorization of "dedication" (*Hingabe*) over "self-preservation" (Hennis 1988: 197). We hardly need to recite the famous paragraphs of Weber's "Science as a Vocation" with their invocation of a spirit of devotion to the work at hand, without recourse to romanticism or self-indulgence. "Ladies and gentlemen. In the field of science only he who is devoted *solely* to the work in hand has 'personality'" (Weber 1991a). The notion of personality takes on all the more of an intellectual pathos in the context of its tremendous distance from any psychological notion; a distance that is mixed with a deliberate proximity.

In fact, Weber frequently invokes apparently psychological concepts against psychology. But personality refers to the person who has escaped the self. If Weber's ethics are – at least on the lines outlined by Hennis – effectively Aristotelian, his notion of personality can be described as Kantian. For Kant and Weber, freedom is defined by an absence of reliance on either external constraint or inner affect or emotion; the man of personality is free in so far not as he acts without reference to values but as he freely *submits* to values of his own choosing (Goldman 1988: 142–3). In the *Critique of Practical Reason*, Kant says the following concerning the law of duty: "It can be nothing less than *personality*, i.e. the freedom and independence from the mechanism of the whole of nature, at the same time regarded as a capacity of a being whose particularity is namely pure practical laws given by its own reason" (quoted in ibid: 121). Ethical personality has nothing to do with selfhood; it is posed in opposition to it (cf. Schroeder 1991).

What are we to make of all of this, aside from merely indicating, as others have done, the distance that separates Weber's idea of a cultural science from the notion of a science of society? The response to this question should serve to indicate the extent to which Weber's work can actually be regarded as being paradigmatic of a critical analytics of enlightenment.

Weber saw, as few have appreciated since, the extent to which the forms of reason that traversed the present were implicated in problems of morality and identity. He also found a way of living with the simultaneous recognition that we could not go back or turn our back on enlightenment reason, yet that such reason was not in itself the origin of any ethical solutions to the world. Moreover, Weber built the entirety of his cultural science precisely on that problem. It is certainly misleading to contend that Weber was the proponent of a philosophical sociology centred on the concept of a monolithic rationalization of the world; in other words, that he was a thinker of a merely gestural anti-enlightenment. Weber's notion of rationalization does not partake of the form of a dialectic pertaining between the progress of reason and the subjective faculties of humans. Weber's point is quite different; it is that rationalization has *no consequences* for the ethical subjectivity of humanity and that we delude ourselves if we think it does. Hence, as we have seen, rather than pursue the chimera of a newer, better, more rounded subjectivity Weber set off in pursuit of something that was beyond science: the conviction of personality. In that context, Scaff is right to say that Weber's project is to seek ascetic ways of escape – enlightenment in Foucault's sense – from the predicament of the temptations of a subjectivist culture.

Weber's example also helps us to short-circuit any easy links between ethics and politics. Commentators have had a bad time attempting to account for Weber's political dispositions. For some he was a precursor of totalitarianism, for others a liberal progressive, for others a liberal in despair. One thing for sure is that, for Weber, political enlightenment is, as Turner puts it, an *ordeal* rather than a project in any straightforward sense. He was not exactly a liberal in despair but a proponent of an ethics of the will, a sort of strange or peculiar liberalism. Hennis writes: "If Weber were a Liberal then his Liberalism was of a curious kind, a very peculiar Liberalism. If we have to give him a label, then we could talk of a voluntaristic Liberalism, more properly perhaps of a liberal *voluntarism* closely bound to freedom" (Hennis 1988: 186). What characterizes this voluntarism for Hennis is a certain attitude to time, one wholly proper to a critique of enlightenment in so far as it represents what might be described as an ethical reaction to easy, meliorist models of progress. "Weber has absolutely no faith in *time*, it is solely the *will* of men and women that we can rely upon" (Hennis 1988: 185). As against Marxism which lays bets on time, or a liberalism which puts faith in the logic of "progress", Weber's view is that it is all up to us to create the conditions of our own freedom. In the context of the Russian revolution he writes of "the determined *will* of a nation not to be governed like a flock of sheep" (Weber 1994c: 69); Weber's cultural task was to seek evidence of the renewability of this will wherever he looked.

Foucault and Weber as critics of enlightenment

It would be difficult to claim that Weber's work is centred, as with that of Foucault, on a problematic of a specifically *negative* enlightenment. Whereas Foucault refuses any specific content for enlightenment, Weber has some very specific – and usually rather unpleasant – things to say about German identity, the German State and so forth (e.g. Weber 1994a: 15). And yet there are in Weber's work hallmarks of a critique of enlightenment; that constant concern to diagnose what is singular about the present age, and a concern to discover a "way out" or a way forward from that present; a concern that perhaps has particular meaning today as a weapon against romantic understandings of what such a way out might involve.

Nor – reverting to the theme with which I began this chapter – could anyone in their right mind happily say that Weber's work inclines towards the ideal of an aesthetic education in any direct or literal sense. As I mentioned in Chapter 4, if anything, Weber was critical of any attempt to aestheticize the moral life. But Weber's commitment to the ideal of "man" as a cultural being was in a sense an aesthetic commitment, albeit one that had little to do with the Schillerian model of aesthetic education (cf. Turner 1992: 47–50). Moreover, his commitment to a cultural science that was ethical rather than simply normative also places his work in a genealogy of aesthetic education in that the aim is to change the individual's conception of their own conduct; to transform the individual in the interests of clarity and personality. Weber's insistence that cultural science could not map directly on to the values of moral codes, as well as his reserve about the powers of science to inform conduct, make him at least an ally, an exemplar, of all those who have struggled with the idea of an aesthetic of existence itself. Indeed, testimony about Weber itself indicates this. Not that he was a rounded individual in the Schillerian sense, but that he was somebody who – though he had "nothing of the artist in him" – had learned to hold together, to stylize in an ascetic way, albeit at an enormous tension, the fibres of his life (cf. Green 1974: 145).

Weber's own example, then, may legitimately be said to have an aesthetic value. Weber's was an aesthetic of intellectual existence that might still be of exemplary value to the social sciences – indeed, looking at the way those disciplines construct their heritage, obviously is so. Scrutiny of Weber's work is itself an exercise in judgement, one that is of aesthetic value not in making us whole, well-rounded persons but – as with his resolute insistence that the social sciences have to be cultural sciences concerned with the "quality" of human beings – in questioning our very meaning of what it is to be human in the present. That is exactly the same aesthetic "effect" that is to be found in Foucault's work (Owen 1995; cf. Gordon 1987); and in each case, such an effect is a long way from the positivistic "results" to which the social sciences and social theory are apparently supposed to aspire, just as it is a long way from all kinds of aesthetic education that are based on some determinate category of aesthetic, subjective experience. Social theories of desubjectification do not parade their "aesthetic" credentials; indeed, to do so would be self-defeating. Nevertheless, forms of social theory such as those of Foucault or Weber are defensible as surrogate forms of aesthetic education: that is, as instruments of transformation, provocative to thought, catalytic of judgement, exemplary of the intrinsic difficulties of enlightenment.

Not that this is to suggest, finally, that there are too many substantive or positive similarities between Weber and Foucault (cf. Owen 1994). It is not a question of one of those embarrassing assimilations of two entirely different thinkers, nor of putting each on an equal pedestal – not least, since it is fairly obvious that Weber has and will pass into history as a far greater intellectual figure than Foucault. Perhaps there *are* similarities between them, but they are not similarities of opinion, method or results – nor even that they were both Nietzscheans – but similarities of scope. Whereas Foucault's problematic was freedom, Weber's centred on the question of conviction. But in very different ways both adopted the perspective of a "science of reality" designed to highlight the extent to which humans were cultural beings, and to designate the extent to which they might be more so. Both centred their work on problematics that were at once anthropological and ethical. In doing so both effectively elided that split between being for or against enlightenment, for or against reason, or, in today's critical argot, for or against modernity or post-modernity. Both were intellectuals concerned fundamentally, if in different ways, with the nature and functions of the intellectual calling itself: that is, with the question of the very ethics of enlightenment. Both were exceptional, even in a sense "prophetic"; perhaps not saints or artists but certainly "philosophers" in Nietzsche's affirmative sense (Nietzsche 1983b: 159). But does that mean that a critique of enlightenment and a valorization of the cultural aspects of "man" are only possible through such a loud, prophetic mode? The next chapter, which looks at some models of that everyday agent of enlightenment – the intellectual – suggests not.

Chapter 6

Agents of enlightenment: in praise of intellectuals

Enlightenment as a vocation – Intellectual modernity – Truth and time – English intellectualism – Moralists and historians – In praise of empiricism – Judgement – Intellectual enlightenment – Grocers and intellectuals – The University

Foucault and Weber were intellectuals who stylized the relation between truth and criticism in particular ways; such that they can now be said to represent not so much historical figures but proper names to which such styles are irrevocably attached. Obviously other examples could have been chosen, and no great significance should be attached to my choice of those two figures as exemplars of particular kinds of critical attitudes to the question of enlightenment. What I want to get across is not any definitive advocacy for this or that thinker, but rather a sense of the importance just of the *fact* of such activities of stylization; indeed that such activities are central to all forms of intellectual enlightenment, of whatever kind. I think that this realization can serve quite usefully to complicate that question that has proved to be so dear to so many intellectuals: namely, *What is an intellectual?* That is the question that I consider in the reflections that make up this chapter. I shall review some ways of thinking about intellectuals, consider the apparently improbable idea of the English intellectual as a test-case, and then conclude with some brief comments about the functions of intellectuals and their role in the University.

Enlightenment as a vocation

The Enlightenment was, perhaps before anything else, a movement of intellectuals; a movement conditioned by a general secularization of culture across the eighteenth century. At the beginning of the century, the overwhelming majority of writers in France, for example, had been members of the clergy; by the time of the Revolution the figure had dropped to around 20 per cent (only 5 per cent of contributors to the *Encyclopédie* were clergy), and there was a mushrooming of more or less independent writers evidenced in a large increase in the total number of books published. Thus in 1757, around 1000 individuals in France had published at least one book; by the time of the Revolution, this figure had risen to at least 3000 (Darnton 1987: 266; quoted in Heilbron 1995: 60–1).

Such writers saw themselves, no doubt, as agents of enlightenment: voices committed to reason in an unenlightened world. No intellectuals; no enlightenment. But what kind of authority is it that speaks in the name of enlightenment? And what has been the fate of those who since the age of Enlightenment itself have sought to give reason a voice? Contemporary sociologies of the intellectuals have tended to move in rather contrasting directions on these matters. Thus we have Zygmunt Bauman arguing that the enlightenment function of the intellectual – the "legislator" of reason – has, in postmodernity, now suffered a setback. Once the intellectuals were the embodiments of political rationalism: ideologists, legislators (cf. Gella 1976). Now that dream is finished; the intellectuals have little power, no one would dream of turning to them for enlightenment or legislation, and at best their function is one of communication between the diverse orders of discourse that inhabit a pluralized, post-foundational world (Bauman 1987; Bauman 1992a: 1–25). In contrast to this, Alvin Gouldner not so long ago predicted that the Western world would become *dominated* by the intellectuals; that they formed a "new class" ready to come to power. Gouldner's views entailed an impish twist on Marxian orthodoxy: "the slaves did not succeed the masters, the plebians did not vanquish the patricians, the serfs did not overthrow the lords, and the journeyman did not triumph over the guildmasters. *The lowliest class never came to power*. Nor does it seem likely to now" (Gouldner 1979: 93). Instead, a "flawed class" – flawed because divided against itself, in the form of a technical intelligentsia versus the intellectuals *per se* – seemed set to come to power, driven by a normative ideology of rational "elaborated" communication and the will to establish the conditions for its own more or less perpetual reproduction; in fact, the élite of a new form of cultural capital.

These two scenarios are not as contradictory as they might initially appear. The divergence stems from the problem of defining what an intellectual is in the first place; that is, as to whether we take a wide definition or a restricted one. In Gouldner's version, the critical intellectuals are split from the technical intelligentsia (engineers, bureaucrats and others), and besides are more or less permanently alienated from the *status quo*. Such intellectuals hardly conform to their own enlightenment model of what Bauman calls "proselytizing power"; they might form the dominant class, that is, the class whose interests predominate in struggles over various kinds of resources, but they do not rule, and they do not necessarily *legislate*. In other words, we could hold to both Bauman's and Gouldner's theses if we presumed that intellectuals were people with big ideas who sought to legislate and that they were a subordinate fraction in a wider "new class" dominated by a technical, bureaucratic intelligentsia. The bureaucrats might still be in power, but the critical intellectuals would have to be content just to interpret and to criticize.

Perhaps a more adequate response would be to point not to the underlying similarities or dissimilarities but to the limitations in both Bauman's and Gouldner's accounts. Gouldner certainly overstates the ambitions of the intellectual class; indeed, he provides us with no reasons as to why such a class should *want* to seize power or to legislate, instead of just holding to a vaguer cultural hegemony. As for Bauman, he certainly overstates the enlightenment role for the intellectual as if that model ever entailed a "legislative" function as opposed to a critical one. Perhaps we might take a leaf out of Gouldner's own book here. For Gouldner, what is specific to the humanist intellectual, as opposed to the member of the technical intelligentsia, is that they aspire not to a legislative function but to a *critical* function. What drives the intellectuals is their "culture of critical discourse"; a culture "in which there is nothing that speakers will on principle permanently refuse to discuss or make problematic; indeed, they are even willing to talk about the value of talk itself and its possible inferiority to silence or practice" (Gouldner 1979: 28). Even the classical enlightenment model of intellectualism was indebted more to this critical function than to a legislative dream. The intellectuals were not there to legislate but to enlighten – to criticize, to find a way out.

Intellectual modernity

Given this rather negative, critical character of the intellectual vocation – or at least the vocation of the humanist intellectual – it is hardly surprising that the social sciences have had a difficult time working out a "positive" – descriptive, functional – theory of the intellectual. One feature of this difficulty appears to stem from the supposition that the autonomy of the intellectual derives from the fact that, though perhaps a specialist in some field or other, they tend to aspire to an authority that ranges beyond their particular specialism. Indeed, such a "surplus" is precisely what is characteristic, even definitive, of intellectual authority. The intellectual, as Jean-Paul Sartre (1974) once wrote, is a *monster*; which means that we cannot be at ease in defining the intellectual in functional terms or simply in terms of a specified content of what intellectuals actually *do*, for instance, in terms of the content of a particular specialism, or in morphological terms (their function in the "field" and so forth). Rather, not least of the functions of the intellectual is to undermine whatever functions the intellectual might have; which might entail even using the conscience of reason against reason itself – such might be, in any case, the substance of intellectual *enlightenment*.

As a sociological category, the category of intellectuals is strikingly elastic and possibly unworkable. A critique of such categories might serve at least to show that what is required at the end of the day is not so much a formal as an ethical definition of the intellectual. We might contrast, to this end, inclusive theories with more or less exclusive ones. A good example of an inclusive theory would come from the work of Jack Goody. Working for the most part on tribal societies, Goody argues that the category of intellectuals might include magicians, sorcerors, saints and anyone with a specialized access to the divine; "it would be a fundamental human error," says Goody, "to imagine any society without its quota of what we may legitimately call creative intellectual activity, even intellectuals" (Goody 1977: 35). By an "intellectual" he means anyone engaged in "the creative exploration of culture" (ibid: 20). Perhaps there is a clue here even to our current notion of an intellectual. For Goody, intellectuals are creative by definition; they are mediators of the sacred. Goody's point is that in tribal societies, such synthesis does not carry such a visible individual mark as it does in the cultures of the modern West; that all societies do indeed have creative individuals akin to modern intellectuals who invent cultural forms, but because most of these societies are predominantly oral "the individual signature is always getting rubbed out" (ibid: 27). For Goody, the category of the intellectual might be described as being more or less all-inclusive in terms of periodizations in that, for him, just about all societies have intellectuals. Yet it is not all-inclusive in terms of statuses within particular societies. Clearly, for someone like Goody, although we can apply the label of "intellectual" to a wide array of roles in society, the category is still limited by the fact that the intellectual somehow stands apart from the rest of society; that the paradigmatic image of the intellectual is perhaps that of the creative outsider, or even the *fool*.

A different kind of inclusivist approach could be associated with Marxists such as Antonio Gramsci. Should intellectuals be categorized as an independent class or as subordinate to other classes? For on the one hand, there were organic intellectuals; those that were attached to their original class origins. And, on the other hand, there were intellectuals who sought out a vocation as purely objective intellectuals (who usually turned out to be State functionaries). To make matters worse, it is impossible to say where intellectualism begins and ends. "This means that, although one can speak of intellectuals, one cannot speak of non-intellectuals, because non-intellectuals do not exist" (Gramsci 1971: 9). For Gramsci, everyone is an intellectual but some are more intellectual than others. This is a difficulty particularly felt by Marxists not because they are themselves more intellectually limited than anyone else but because the question of the relation between the material infrastructure and the mental superstructure is obviously, by definition of what they do, at the centre of their concerns. For there is clearly a mental or at least non-obviously material, aspect of cultural reproduction that is as basic to the self-renewal of cultures as are material factors themselves (Godelier 1986).

But at what point does the "mental" actually become the "intellectual"? One answer might come from those who take a more exclusivist perspective in arguing that intellectualism, rather than being merely an attitude of mind, is dependent on – albeit hardly reducible to – the availability of particular resources and techniques. But how are we to set the boundaries of this exclusivity? Perhaps the key to what we are looking for comes from the question of *scholarship*. Magicians, priests, shamen and so forth may be intellectuals in Goody's sense, but they do not write things down – hence the rapid eclipse of the memory of their individuality. On the other hand, the scholarly intellectual is dependent above all on the existence of a particular kind of "technology": the written record (Ong 1982). The intellectual, defined along these lines, might be one who practises scholarship in relation to a particular archive of writings. This "technological" definition has its uses precisely because, from a macro-historical viewpoint, only in a few societies in history can we pinpoint anything that amounts to a class of scholars. The most obvious pre-capitalist example, at least from the sociological literature, would be that strata in Imperial China known to Weber as the Confucian *literati* (Weber 1962). The *literati* owed their position not to influence or wealth or ancestry but to the extent of their literary qualification. Indeed, Weber claims that China was unique for twelve hundred years in making literary education the yardstick of social prestige; more so than in either Renaissance Europe or late-nineteenth-century Germany (Weber 1962: 107). Here, then, was a class of intellectuals in accord with something like the modern meaning of scholarship: that is, as committed to something like scholarship for its own sake. Hence Weber's otherwise rather anomalous characterization of the *literati* as "gentlemen"; drawing attention to the fact that, for the *literati*, scholarship was as much a way of life and an end in itself as it was meant for a merely technical form of expertise or bureaucratic ends (ibid: 131–3).

But still, we cannot thereby define the intellectual simply on the basis of an adherence to the values of scholarship. The reason is simply that intellectualism is an inherently relative category. The *literati* were clearly definable as intellectuals in relation to other strata in Chinese society; but transposed to, say, nineteenth-century England (which, after mid-century, also promoted, if in a different way, a model of the official based on the idea of the gentleman scholar), they would seem – in contrast to that other stratum, composed of "men of letters" – less like an independent intellectual formation and more like just common bureaucrats or over-educated officials.

If positive theories of the intellectual necessarily tend not to capture what is uniquely "modern" about the idea of the intellectual, this is because, for the most part, they do not take into account the critical aspect of the ethos of intellectualism since the Enlightenment, a critical status which needs to be built into whatever definition of the intellectual is to be adopted. Students of intellectuals are typically concerned either with the social attachments and interests of particular intellectual strata or with charting the shifting contents of their ideas. Such a perspective is not unimportant. For instance, there is the fact that Western liberal societies have produced more potential candidates for the intellectual life than any other known type of society in history. The growth of mass education, the expansion of university opportunities, the increasing requirements for some degree of an intellectual component in even some of the lowest-paid jobs would all count on this score. As such, societies such as ours will always run the risk of over-producing potential intellectuals. Hence, the predominance in the literature of those kinds of accounts which stress the alienating factors of intellectual life, as, for example, when Bourdieu explains the May events of 1968 largely in terms of the alienation – "downclassing" – of certain sectors of the intellectual community and their students (Collins 1979: 191–5; Bourdieu 1988: 162–72).

Such studies are invaluable. But in taking the entirety of the intellectual field as their concern, they tend to reduce the circumstances of intellectual life straightforwardly to those of individual competition and to a rather mean-minded "politics of credentialism". Such analyses account for the conditions of the intellectual field without always saying a great deal about the rationality of intellectualism as a cultural power. To do that we would have to focus not on the generality of the field but on the rarity of the aristocracy of intellect; at the cultural ethos of those towards which the "masses" of intellectuals are competing, and this would include not just the "academics", those with positions and jobs, but – to recall Sartre's expression – at the "monsters", those who are freelance or working in the arts as well as the important professors; those who stand out from their class and in some ways most embody the ideal of intellectualism as a critical ideal, as well as those who are integrated within it.

The critical, enlightened intellectual is not just somebody who deals in ideas, or somebody who has attained a certain level of scholarship, but somebody who reflects, probes and thinks; who cultivates an entire aesthetic of thought that is unique and that stands as exemplary for others. That at least is part of our everyday grammar concerning what an intellectual is. This exclusivity of "those who think" is implicit even within much of the sociology of intellectuals. Hence the efforts of sociologists to distinguish between, in the modern period, a professional "expert" (someone engaged in a "profession of the intellect') and a *thinker* as such. But is a "thinker" anyone engaged in an "intellectual profession" or does such a person only necessarily belong to that – presumably far smaller – category known as the "high intelligentsia" (Gella 1976; cf. Gouldner 1979; cf. Debray 1981: 22–3, 32; Eyerman 1994)? It is as if the more that the activity of thought becomes an aspect of everybody's daily grind, the more demand there will be to separate off some kind of higher intelligentsia who *really* do the thinking, who cultivate the aesthetics of thought as a demonstration to others.

Perhaps this so far sounds like a rather negative characterization. It makes the intellectuals seem rather pretentious, self-important, types by nature and over-concerned with the status of their own status. But I think that such a judgement would be misleading, not because it is necessarily untrue but because there are good reasons – which should be integral to any defence of the idea of the intellectual – why intellectuals should be so obsessed with the status of their own existence. That is because it may be that intellectuals are people whose own existence is intrinsically and necessarily problematic.

Whereas the scientist adopts a scientific ethos, the expert of conduct helps their constituency towards their own truths; but the intellectual assuredly *agonizes over the truth*. The sense of alienation and detachment intellectuals are often supposed to feel has often led intellectuals to dramatize their plight; even to romanticize it. This is the image of the intellectual as the interpreter of the world, at once disenchanting the sacredness of the world and recasting it in terms of their own self-image. In a fully rationalized world, only the intellectuals themselves – so say the intellectuals – can save us:

> The salvation sought by the intellectual is always based on inner need, and hence it is at once more remote from life, more theoretical and more systematic than salvation from external distress, the quest for which is characteristic of non-privileged strata. The intellectual seeks in various ways, the casuistry of which extends to infinity, to endow his life with a pervasive meaning, and thus to find unity within himself, with his fellow men and with the cosmos. It is the intellectual who conceives of the "world" as a problem of meaning. As intellectualism suppresses belief in magic, the world's processes become disenchanted, lose their magical significance, and henceforth simply "are" and "happen" but no longer signify anything. (Weber 1978, vol. 1: 506)

Weber was not thinking of modern intellectuals here; but the illustration serves to indicate that there is always something akin to an "existential" aspect to the ethics of intellectualism. Weber was not an existentialist in any philosophical sense of that term, but for him – that is, sociologically speaking – existence just *is* a constitutive problem for the intellectual: for intellectuals, the meaning of their own existence tends frequently to pose itself as a "problem"; that is, as a defining ordeal (cf. Brubaker 1984: 100).

Hence, it cannot be surprising that the most renowned intellectual ethos in the modern world – perhaps even the central case of modern intellectualism as such – has been that of a philosophy that actually went by the name of existentialism (see Boschetti 1989; Eyerman 1994: 173–5). There are very straightforward reasons for this. A critical sociology of existentialism, if it posed itself in terms of a critique of enlightenment, would have to be in part a causal analysis focusing on the expansion of the education system and so forth; but it would also have to illustrate the elective affinity between existentialism and ideologies of intellectualism more generally – which would include all those who aspire to the cult of pure intellectualism. And at the heart of all intellectualism there is ambivalence; the fear, no doubt, that intellectualism as a pure force is almost wholly useless, even self-indulgent. Hence, Sartre's whole ethical project: to kill the bourgeois in himself. But existentialism is also absolutely the right philosophy for such an endeavour because – given its motto of existence before essence – it lays so much emphasis on the creative powers of humans. "Man simply is. Not that he is simply what he conceives himself to be, but he is what he wills, and as he conceives himself after already existing – as he wills to be after that leap towards existence. Man is nothing else but that which he makes of himself" (Sartre 1948: 28).

The existentialist intellectual is surely just the epitome of this dream of man as creative project; and the "despair" of man is just the generalization of the despair of the intellectual. Hence it cannot be surprising that Sartre himself was obsessed with working out thought-images of the proper role of the intellectual (Khilnani 1993). One late version makes the intellectual the exemplar of modern responsibility in general. The intellectual is merely a technician of knowledge who has turned upon the ideology that feeds him, and has begun to interfere with things that do not concern him, becoming monstrous, bent on a mission of doing violence to public opinion (Sartre 1974: 231–46). Thus the intellectual is a contradiction; born of ideology yet entirely responsible for his own fate, the emblem of a good faith that feels bad because of the state of the world. Perhaps the main limitation of Sartre's position is that he associates monstrosity too closely with the sphere of politics, quite narrowly conceived. It is as if false intellectuals, for him, are simply those who are not engaged in specific political struggles. Yet there are other ways of making oneself into a monster. Remaining for the moment – and for important reasons – with the French context, we might note that Foucault did so, for instance, specifically by rejecting the kind of ameliorative project that was at the heart of a vision like that of Sartre. Yet the distinction between the two is as much at the level of an aesthetics of truth – the way in which the relation to truth is embodied for oneself and for others – as it is at the level of whether each was engaged or disengaged, political or a-political.

The French model of an intellectual aesthetic has not always been too subtle. Sartre simply *lived* the life of the intellectual, never at home yet never exactly at work either. Everybody knows the cliché. Sartre created an ethos that is inseparable from the proper name, *Sartre*; sitting in cafés, smoking cigarettes, engaging in a rather complex personal life, going on marches and getting arrested – however much such an ethos was actually dictated by circumstance rather than choice. Whereas, for Foucault on the other hand, the role of the intellectual similarly appeared to be to find a critical way of being "in the true" as a way of life. Foucault was, in some rather restricted senses, an existentialist too, if of a kind obviously opposed to the existentialism of Sartre. Perhaps Foucault's merit was that he recognized the existential aspect of intellectualism which, for him, was certainly a question of a certain stylization of existence. That is so at least in his late writings on the subject; writings where he began tentatively to embrace a self-definition of himself as an intellectual: that is, at once to acknowledge the role of the intellectual and its limits (Gordon 1986b). It is true that, for Foucault, the intellectual should not be the Sartrian prophet able to project an entire worldview on the world. But nor really does the rather over-publicized notion of a "specific" intellectual fit Foucault all that well. It suggests narrowness and expertise, and that is not quite right, for Foucault surely wanted to capture an ethos of intellectuality fully as much as Sartre. He wanted to find a way of living critically in the truth that would not be a form of intellectual prophecy, but a kind of ongoing critique of one's circumstances of existence. For such a way of living in the truth is never finalized but is always conditional; one needs an *ethic* of the intellectual, which is the opposite of a sudden, ideological "conversion" (Foucault 1994, vol 4: 675). Hence, what singularized the intellectual attitude for Foucault was not the content of what is said but above all a certain relation to the truth; we might say a constantly questioning "critical attitude to the truth" rather than a positivistic "analytic of truth" (Rajchman 1991: 126). But this relation to truth was not merely "cognitive" or intellectual – it was, as a vocation of enlightenment, as fully existential as was Sartre's celebrated commitment, even if the form of engagement that it took was not always narrowly "political" in Sartre's sense.

Truth and time

It should be clear from these reflections so far that I am arguing that at least the way *not* to think about enlightened intellectualism is according to a rationalist model; that is, in straightforward terms of rationalization or legislation or some such category. In a sense, all intellectuals – even the "irrational" ones – do seek to rationalize the world in so far as their aim is to impose a meaning on the world, and even if that meaning is itself sometimes not so far removed from nihilism. But in each case such rationalization, far from being of a formal sort, is personalized in the very habitus or *ethos* of the intellectual. This means that the idea of the intellectual as a sort of permanent legislator exaggerates the reality even of the *ideal* of the enlightened intellectual.

A better way to think about intellectual enlightenment is in terms of the ways in which intellectuals seek to give voice to different styles of *acting upon time*. In terms of an ethics of time, perhaps. For Nietzsche, the function of the intellectual was precisely to be *untimely*; to act against the current times. For someone like Sartre, on the other hand, operating within the confines of a French model of intellectualism, the purpose of the intellectual is to act in the name of a time to come. The French model relies very heavily on a certain, combative notion of intellectual identity. The intellectual in France – whether it is Foucault, Sartre or whoever – is always speaking out for truth and progress, and against the established powers; it is the Dreyfusard or *j'accuse* model of intellectualism (Sartre 1974: 230; Khilnani 1993: 11; Macey 1995: 6). There is an obvious case for saying that this model owes much to the Catholic heritage in France. The model of the Dreyfusard intellectual is that of the anti-Catholic figure or at least the critical figure who is prepared to speak the truth regardless of reasons of religion or reasons of State (Coser 1965: 215–25). Anti-clericalism is in an obvious sense a decisive force for the promotion of intellectualism in that it both encourages the development of the morals of the ideologue yet also establishes the grounds for the delimitation of the intellectuals' potency, something which intellectuals will tend to resist in seeking to extend the bounds of their vocation. In other words, Catholicism – as a religion of "dogma" – in that it promotes the ideals of scholarship simultaneously promotes the intellectual ideal itself; and in refusing that ideal too much autonomy, simultaneously creates the conditions for the emergence of the critical, anti-clerical intellectual.

The French intellectual is not interested in the Catholic traditionalism towards time, nor simply with easy liberal views of progress. Rather it is a matter of acting on time, even inducing disquietude in the current times, in the name of some future time. As Sartre says, for the intellectual, the human universal exists but is yet to come (Sartre 1974: 253). In France, then, there emerged a particular sort of intellectualism, characterized by a sort of *resistance to the present*, one that even mirrored in reverse the Catholic worldview. Contrast the German perception of the relation between intellectualism and time. The German ethics of time – if we may be allowed to pose these matters in admittedly very crude terms – was not so much a resistance to the present as a rational projection of the future. In Germany, intellectualism was defined far more by its relation to the State than to religion. *The German Ideology* established this point very well. The Germans, not being able to catch up politically, seek to catch up ideologically; in Germany, the intellectual is the man of big ideas, the man not of material reality but of philosophy, merely opposing one set of Hegelian phrases to another set of Hegelian phrases (Marx & Engels 1976: 29–30).

Both the Germans and the French want – "geo-philosophically" speaking – to be fundamentally elsewhere (cf. Deleuze and Guattari 1991: 104–5). The French invented the Enlightenment in order to catch up with the English in matters of thought. The Germans invented what we now call continental philosophy in order to advance themselves in terms of cultural excellence; to compensate for their political insecurities by ideological means. We might add other cases to this crude typology of the ethics of time. The Scottish Enlightenment, for instance, derived from modernizing tendencies in relation to the earlier establishment of English social development. It was Scotland's uneven development in relation to England, coupled with Edinburgh's uneven development in relation to the rest of Scotland, that was so decisive (Phillipson 1974). The ethics of time can be directed against the wider intellectual culture itself; thus certain kinds of intellectualism can be expressive of a contempt for an indigenous intellectual culture held to belong, in effect, to a past or redundant time.

This was the case with the Irish. Here we have a colonized Catholic culture that has perhaps the greatest modern literary tradition in the world. It is not hard to see why. As Samuel Beckett famously said (of the English, about the Irish): "They have buggered us into glory." However, the "us" here is more problematic than the sentiment itself. Beckett, like so many others in the Irish literary pantheon, was Anglo-Irish, a Protestant, who left Ireland because – among other reasons – he could stand Irish, Catholic culture no longer. He was certainly "unevenly developed" in relation to the rest of Ireland. But even the rest of Ireland was an invention. It was invented by people like Matthew Arnold who published his *On the Study of Celtic Literature* in 1867, conjuring up the image of the dreamy Celt "always ready to react against the despotism of fact" (McCormack 1994: 228; cf. Eagleton 1995). As McCormack insists, the celtic Irish tradition was in many ways a Tory myth, and in that sense, people like Beckett might be said actually to constitute a – progressive – *break* in that tradition. But whatever the facts of the matter, it is certainly the case that invented traditions can become, in effect, true. The dislocation of Irish intellectuals in relation to the present breeds, in a kind of self-fulfilling way, ever further forms of creativity and productive escape.

Such rather dramatic critical stylizations of time as can be associated with the Scots, the Irish and the French can make things seem as if the only tone of the voice of intellectual enlightenment is a loud or angry one. But thinking of different kinds of intellectualism in terms of the ethics of time actually brings with it the advantage that we do not have to define intellectualism along the lines of such loud, critical modes alone, thus opening up a space for thinking of intellectual enlightenment in cases that would normally be held to be quite inhospitable to such a form of understanding; and hence furthering one of the aims of the present reflections – to provide a non-rationalist defence of the idea of the intellectual.

English intellectualism

The question of England and the intellectuals has long fascinated historians of culture precisely because it appears to be anomalous. That is why I want to consider that question here; not because there is anything intrinsically important about England or its intellectuals but because the question of the English offers us a kind of test-case, precisely because of its difficulty, of the meanings that our grammar is able to give to the notion of intellectualism.

The English, we are told, are out of joint. They have an ideology (empiricism) but if we think of the twentieth century – which is to exclude a great nineteenth-century tradition of literary and Romantic thought – no intellectuals to speak of (except exiled continentals, plus Bertrand Russell). Indeed if we take the French *j'accuse* model as our paradigm, it is clear that there can be no such thing as intellectual culture in England if only because English intellectuals have been notoriously supine. There are people who call themselves intellectuals in England, but none – bar the odd latter-day, neo-conservative iconoclast and a little band of humanist Marxists – seem to have any proper monstrosity about them.

No doubt, this state of affairs comes down to questions of historical development and the resulting peculiarities of the English cultural heritage. There is a rather inconclusive debate as to whether England did or did not have an Enlightenment. For J.G.A. Pocock, England had an Enlightenment, but one without philosophers, since they were "not much needed" (Pocock 1980: 93). Rather, English anti-clericalism, at least in the seventeenth century, was too sophisticated to require philosophical assistance: "English anti-clericalism had far too many roots in religious and social life, was far too skilled in the combination and permutation of secular and spiritual argument, to require the aid of a philosophic intelligentsia in expressing itself" (Pocock 1980: 96). We can, however, point to evidence of the formation of something like a political intelligentsia arrayed against Walpole in the early eighteenth century, and to the critical ethos of literary intellectuals like Addison and Steele. The Augustan journalists certainly invented a – benign, cosmopolitan – critical culture. But this hardly amounted to a full-scale critical assault, and certainly did not lead to an overriding ideological movement. In any case, its leading form was not anti-clericalism as such. The influence of Deism allowed for a more tolerant attitude to the religious sphere. This does not mean that we cannot speak of an enlightenment. Perhaps the perception of an absence of an English enlightenment is the product of the self-hatred of the Romantics, turning against the inheritance of their own culture (Porter 1981: 3). But perhaps also this perception is down to the fact that because England was the prototype of enlightenment (the French *Encyclopédie*, for instance, derived from a plan to translate Ephraim Chambers" *Cyclopaedia*), so no overt *ideology* of enlightenment was required.

In other words, it would be possible to argue that the question of elaborating a critical ethics of time did not really apply in the English case. England achieved modernity without requiring an Enlightenment to foresee it. England, in the words of Pocock again, was "too modern to need an Enlightenment" (Pocock 1975: 467; cf. Gordon 1986b).

Even so, perhaps the problem in assessing English intellectual culture lies not with the English so much as with the French *j'accuse* model itself. The problem with the French model is that it can be almost *too* paradigmatic; not least in so far as it can generate the ridicule of polemics such as Bourdieu's *Homo Academicus* which, in outlining the limits of the French intellectual star system, seems to damn the very idea of the intellectual along with it (Bourdieu 1988). It can come to seem as if the absence of an intellectual culture such as that in France can be an absence of culture in general. Even were we to grant some kind of a case for the existence of an original English Enlightenment, afterwards everything seemed to go downhill and the nineteenth- and twentieth-century intellectual movements come to seem negligible and nowhere near monstrous enough to qualify as an intelligentsia. This was effectively the argument of one historian when he bemoaned the historical deficit of a coherent critical intelligentsia in Britain and implicitly compared the state of things in England with "other countries" which, at the time, had much more rebellious ideas in circulation (Anderson 1992a; Anderson 1992b).

For Perry Anderson, England did not have an intellectual culture because, barring the colonialist science of anthropology, it did not have a critical intelligentsia dedicated to producing some kind of theory of the totality. In other words, no one was prepared to criticize English society as a whole. Anderson himself was to make good this deficit by showing that, in fact, England suffered from uneven development in terms of the bourgeoisification of society. The lack of a coherent cultural intelligentsia was all down to the complicity of the bourgoisie with the aristocracy, and their acceptance of the existing state of affairs more generally. We might object, in fact, that this was actually only a restatement of the problem; to the effect that England had no critical culture because in England people did not tend to be critical. All that was left of critical culture was in the domain of "culture" itself. "Suppressed in every obvious sector at home, thought of the totality was painlessly exported abroad, producing the paradox of a major anthropology where there was no such sociology. In the general vacuum thus created, literary criticism usurps ethics and insinuates a philosophy of history" (Anderson 1992a: 103).

This is all down to expectations. Because Anderson valorized – rightly or wrongly – a critical intelligentsia in terms of its "thought of the totality" and its capacity for conceptualizing its resistance to the present – that is, effectively along the lines of the French model of intellectualism – he cannot really tell whether England ever actually had any intellectual movements. In fact, the evidence – using Anderson's terms – suggests that, as John Hall has argued, there are some sociological grounds for saying that there was something like an independent British intelligentsia from about 1830 to 1880 (Harvie 1976; Hall 1979: 291). This was a self-conscious critical intelligentsia – even on the lines of the French model – in so far as it took an oppositional stance, fighting not especially for the values of academic freedom and the repeal of the test acts; and as evidenced by the very central place that "freedom of thought" enjoys with regard to freedom in general in Mill's *On Liberty*. Still, this intelligentsia was hardly monstrous in the French sense; Oxbridge dons in favour of an extension of the franchise and the ideal of democratic government hardly seem like French-style fodder for the barricades (ibid: 10–11). And if this was a critical intelligentsia, its ameliorative ideals did tend to be pitched at a level of accommodation with the existing order. But however critical it had been, this intelligentsia became fragmented, Hall argues, as early as the mid-1880s with the achievement of civil service reform, the weakening of church influence in education, franchise reform and the removal of the Test Acts (Hall 1985: 215).

We can still pick out intellectual movements, but none produced truly "critical" intellectuals on the French model. Indeed, everywhere we see worrying signs of an accommodation with the existing political order. There were, for instance, the Fabians with their policy of not upsetting the *status quo*. This was what George Bernard Shaw called "permeation": that is, not taking on the governing powers in oppositionally controversial terms but wheedling the government into doing one's will, primarily on the basis of networking behind the scenes (Coser 1965: 178). Then there was Bloomsbury, typically portrayed as being rather an effete crowd, more interested in raffia work than the political order. Nothing could be further from the truth. Bloomsbury boasted, in Keynes, Britain's foremost economist of the twentieth century, in Leonard Woolf a worthily progressive political activist, and in Clive Bell an admirable proponent of the social point of view. Nevertheless, this is hardly the stuff to inspire those inclined to the French model. Or as Raymond Williams avers in his judicious treatment:

> there were no riots. Because for all its eccentricities, including its valuable eccentricities, Bloomsbury was articulating a position which, if only in carefully diluted instances, was to become a "civilized" norm. In the very power of their demonstration of a private sensibility that must be protected and extended by forms of public concern, they fashioned the effective forms of the contemporary ideological dissociation between "public" and "private" life. (Williams 1980: 168; Eyerman 1994: 133–42)

In other words, Bloomsbury was only politicized to the extent that this was in the interests of their proposed privatization of culture more generally.

But rather than seeking to condemn or rehabilitate the English intellectuals on this or that model of intellectualism, I think it is better to say that, rather than having no intellectuals, the English merely have *another* model of intellectualism. Certainly, this may not be critical in any narrowly political or *j'accusiste* sense; but perhaps there are ways of elaborating an intellectual ethics of time other than merely acting on the present in the interests of some more or less mythical political time to come.

Moralists and historians

As one instance of at least a *different* kind of attitude, take the findings of Stefan Collini's recent work on British intellectualism in the nineteenth century. For Collini, the English intellectual was not a critical oppositionalist on the French model but something like a "public moralist" (Collini 1991). The brilliance of Collini's work consists in showing the extent to which English intellectuals shaped a voice for themselves that was not exactly one of critique, but which amounted more to a particular stylization of conduct in relation to the truth. In contrast to the standard depiction of the Victorian intelligentsia as being marked by a rather selfishly motivated utilitarianism, Collini insists that the real watchword was an almost altruistically inclined principle of "living for others" (ibid: 62–7).

This was an ethical matter as well as a moral one. In other words, this culture of altruism was not simply "other-directed" but directed at the self; it was a way of showing that one was oneself a strong character (ibid: 62). That is why we say that this ethos was "almost" altruistic; for such altruism of intent was really designed ultimately to serve the self. But what, in fact, was at issue was not an opposition between selfishness and generosity, but rather a common concern for the sturdiness of the self. What mattered was to keep at bay the demons of sloth which lead to misery. Hence altruism served to motivate one towards action. Collini writes that:

> The constant, one could say, was the need for purposes – the kind of purposes which, when supported by the appropriate feelings, are sufficient to motivate action. The representative Victorian intellectual, whether believer or sceptic, did not have a constant impulse to serve: he or she had a constant anxiety about apathy and infirmity of the will ... This was *because* altruistic aims were assumed to motivate that Victorian intellectuals found social work an antidote to doubt, and not that, already having the motivation, they "transferred" its direction from God to man. (ibid: 84–5)

No one could say that this was not a social – even a "sociological" – kind of intellectual ethos, even if it was neither a totalizing nor a directly political one. Collini's intellectuals were not exactly "monsters" in the Sartrian sense of that term. But they did, nonetheless, embody a certain critical attitude to time. For them, time was empty of meaning until given shape by our commitment – again, it is not dissimilar, in its own way, from an existentialist ethos. Time was empty until filled with human innovation; it was up to the individual to give meaning to time, through action, conviction and work.

It does not take too much breadth of insight to see the compatibility of this critical attitude to the question of time with the generically historicizing tendencies of English thought. The English ethics of time, one might say, entails a kind of immanent critique of time itself. For the English, it might be said that the lesson of history was that things are contingent, that people act, that people will govern each other in certain ways, and that some things will go wrong, and others may never be understood. Here enlightenment consists of a kind of contextualist, even ethnographic, attitude to time: to follow its episodes, interruptions and flows, to bring to bear a painstaking erudition on its circumstances.

The notion of an "English" thought is used only advisedly. Perhaps its paradigmatic exponent was the Scotsman, David Hume; and it should not be surprising that it should take a critical outsider to develop the most rounded statement of the approach. Nicholas Phillipson has written movingly about the difference between the Humean historical sensibility and that of the Germans. The object was not to create a science of the past as it actually was, "believing in an authoritative history and in historians who are able to legislate for their readers". Rather, "Hume's discursive philosophical history is not in the least authoritative. It is written for those who are curious about their past, and want to rethink the stories they have been told about the worlds they have lost" (Phillipson 1989: 140). The purpose of history is to open up a space for judgement, to construct a terrain of evidence such that humans might come to understand for themselves "how the culture into which they had been inducted had been formed". This might seem like the sort of Whiggism of approach for which the English have occasionally berated themselves. But Hume is really the prototype of a sceptical approach to human affairs, one which is peculiarly sensitive to the uniqueness of each particular epoch (cf. Phillipson 1989: 109). This is not to say that subsequent English historiography derives from Hume in a derivative way. On the contrary. Hume was the bugbear of historical writing for at least half a century after the publication of his *History* (Burrow 1981: 26). But we might say that if this was the case, it was because Hume embodied both sides of the debate; rather as Marx says of Hegel, that his enemies just used the one part of his thought – either the Whig emphasis on the modernity of liberty, or the Tory emphasis on a certain relativism of approach in matters of power – to attack the other.

Obviously there is nothing particularly novel in describing English thought as being characterized by a certain kind of historicism. The Marxist tradition has celebrated the talent for history of the English; and this can be related quite specifically to the history of English institutions and forms of government themselves. The English think history through convention; their common law is based on precedent, their institutions are in permanent evolution – and so forth. We might say that for the English intellectual personality, it is history rather than metaphysics or ideology that forms the ultimate horizon of cognitive legitimation. That can be a reactionary tendency; often it has been – but that this is not necessarily or logically the case can be seen from a cursory look at the great ideology that is at the centre of the very idea of English thought.

In praise of empiricism

English empiricism, if indeed it can be described as an ideology, has been the despair of metaphysicians the world over. But empiricism was always far more than just a common-sensical view of the world. Empiricism represents, not least, a very English – or rather "English" – way of stylizing our responsibility towards the truth; basing itself on a form of history that is not related to ideologies of progress or of dogma. But this is not to say that empiricism is not likewise a *creative* form of thought. Empiricism analyses "the states of things, in such a way that non-pre-existent concepts can be extracted from them ... The essential thing, from the point of view of empiricism, is the noun *multiplicity*, which designates a set of lines or dimensions which are irreducible to one another" (Deleuze and Parnet 1987: vii). Empiricism is also an *ethic* of cognition in that it implies precisely a particular kind of work on the self: that is, on the agent of cognition. The empiricist has to remain as close as possible to the facts, to recover every instance of possibility inhering in the past and to curb whatever will resides within themselves to go beyond the data or what is there. In that sense, empiricism is not a dogma or a method. It is more a kind of asceticism, a restricted, ethical way of relating to the telling of the truth; one that resides – we imagine – paradigmatically in the English model of personality. By talking about "Englishness" here we do not mean to refer ourselves to a kind of realism of actual attributes. What is at stake is not real people, English or otherwise, but the construction of a model of intellectual personality understood as being appropriate to the "English" way of doing things.

No doubt, some awful acts and prejudices have been legitimated through this ethic of empiricism. For the empiricist it can be all too tempting to see the existing state of affairs as being all too self-evident; thus running the danger of naturalizing, hence legitimating, the present, whatever its characteristics. But empiricism also breeds counter-attacks; for instance, in the great tradition of Marxist historical writing in Britain, a tradition which could come about only through a close encounter with empiricism and, we might add, through the generation of a novel – and non-reductive; we might even say "ethical" – approach to Marxism itself. There are some who would seek to attack empiricist historiography as being naïve, reactionary, out of date and too full of unacknowledged assumptions (Stedman Jones 1972). That is all very well, so long as one keeps in mind that historical thought, even in its most empiricist modes, is not just a common-sense, hence naïve, view of "the facts" but also something akin to a laboured, ethical commitment that one makes; a veritable style of reasoning that produces its own kind of relation to the truth.

And if one wishes to seek out the English intellectuals who have been responsible for dramatizing these relations to truth one would, indeed, have to look precisely to the historians; or, at least, to those somewhat rarer kinds of historian – English "monsters" perhaps – who, for various reasons, have been at the margins or on the outside of this otherwise rather organic tradition of historiographical empiricism (see the references in Collini 1991: 217, and 216–24 more generally). And one would look, for sure, at the great nineteenth-century ideologues of English historical consciousness; at Acton, at Freeman, at Stubbs, at Dicey. It is certainly the case that the rather worn-out category of "professionalization" is hardly adequate to describe the character of late-Victorian history-writing (ibid: 216). It was rather that, in their writings these authors – in very different ways – were attempting to elaborate an ethic of investigation proper to their calling as historians. What was at stake was not merely the establishment of the "methods" appropriate to history as a discipline but, in Collini's terms, a coherent critical "voice" from which one could speak as an historical authority. Primary here was the cognitive ethic of "disinterestedness" which "implied that one's judgement deserved a special respect which could be eroded or forfeited if it descended too readily from its pedestal" (ibid: 224).

Judgement

Such disinterestedness was not, then, such a thing as a "method" so much as the *result* of the hard labours of careful empiricism itself. The historian was the one who had been to the archives and back and learned ethical lessons for the trouble. For the late nineteenth-century ideologues of historical consciousness, history was not exactly a professional – that is to say, "scientific" – discipline. Rather, history was to be the successor to Greats as a training in good judgement; the purpose of knowledge being not so much to produce positive knowledge as to cultivate appropriate people. Hard facts were a means to this training in judgement and not really an end in themselves except in so far as being ends in themselves contributed to the training of that judgement. But whereas Greats related to the static past of the Ancient World, history showed that the analysis of the truth required a dynamic kind of judgement, oriented to the question of time (Soffer 1994: 67–8, 71). When compared with Ancient History, said Stubbs in 1887, the study of modern history "is like the study of life compared with that of death, the view of the living body compared with that of the skeleton" (Stubbs 1887:15). As a result of studying such living history, the student will be able to cultivate sober and realistic principles of judgement; "he finds, if his study has taught him facts as well as maxims, that the great necessity of practical judgement is patience and tolerance, and that the highest justice must rest content for a time to see many things continue wrong that cannot be righted without a greater wrong" (ibid: 21).

Even if it is hardly a "critical" tradition in the strong sense, it would be wrong to say that this vision had nothing to do with politics. On the contrary, the historian learns that politics is the ultimate field of reality: the very stuff of everyday life, the most obviously "real" aspect of existence. And history helps us to act within politics in ways that are denied the more ideologically motivated student of politics. Modern politics, says Stubbs, furnishes not specific ideologies but training only, and, at that, incomplete training. But modern historical sensibility is a training in modesty; it charts the unintended consequences of our actions, and the limits of our actions; indeed something like "despair" – the necessity of action, the necessity of responsibility for our actions, yet the tragedy of never seeing our actions fulfilled:

We learn patience, tolerance, respect for conflicting views, equitable consideration for conscientious opposition; we see how differently the men of the particular time seem to have read the course of events, which seem to us to have only one reasonable bearing; we see how good and evil mingle in the best of men and in the best of causes; we learn to see with patience the men whom we like best often in the wrong, and the repulsive men often in the right; we learn to bear with patience the knowledge that the cause which we love best has suffered, from the awkwardness of its defenders, so great disparagement as in strictly to justify the men who were assaulting it; we learn too, and this is not the last of the lessons, that there are many points on which no decision as to right or wrong, good or evil, acquittal or condemnation, is to be looked for; and on which we may say that, as often the height of courage is to say I dare not, and the height of love is to say I will not, so the height of wisdom is to have learned to say, I do not know. (Stubbs 1887: 109–10)

Stubbs took a specific perspective on these matters, and it would be well not to generalize on the basis of a single case. Yet the late Victorian historians, though differing hugely among themselves, remained similarly concerned with the need for locating the specific cognitive ethic appropriate to history. For, in each case, their actual historical writings are as much a methodical reflection on history as simply the writing *of* history. And this ethic embraces simultaneously a reflection on the conditions of freedom; for that is what is always at stake – whether for or against – when writing history from an English point of view and whether it is a case of considering the Norman Yoke, the ancient constitution, modern constitutional development, or whatever. This ethical perspective can seem like a present-centred one; that is, Whiggish in Herbert Butterfield's – negative – sense (Butterfield 1950). But if such history is seen as a reflection on the circumstances of the present, then the Whiggish label can be generalized well beyond the confines of those who took a simplistic, meliorist, even teleological view of the relation between past and present. Rather, the "Whig interpretation of history" is but one, simplified variant of the general tendency, from just about whatever perspective, of the general task of English historiography; to reflect on the present status of freedoms in relation to the constitution of freedoms in the past (cf. Burrow 1981: 294).

Today there are some who seek to overturn the tradition of English historiography; to resist the legacy of those who have reflected on history in an empirical way; to oppose the legacy of philosophers such as R.G. Collingwood or Michael Oakshott, or historians such as Lewis Namier, as well as the tradition of Marxist history-writing that formed in the wake of, and as an internal reaction to, this tradition. But those who advocate either a more "theoretical" approach in English history, or even a postmodernist one are, perhaps, setting themselves up less as the advocates of a belated spirit of reflection on the nature of historical discourse but only as advocates of *other* kinds of historical discourse. There is certainly nothing in postmodern thought capable of a definitive – that is, epistemological – subversion of English historical consciousness (Kirk 1994; Vernon 1994; Eley & Nield 1995). Postmodernism cannot subvert the presuppositions of traditional historical consciousness, because those assumptions themselves are as fully ethical as they are rational. The best that the postmodernists can do is provide alternative models of historical consciousness; at best revealing what has been missed by more traditional conceptions of history and at worst, succumbing themselves to a form of self-congratulation that only mirrors some of the more regrettable tendencies of some of their opponents.

Just as there are honourable things about empiricism, so are there justifiable things about the English tendency in historiography, and – by extension – about the English model of intellectual personality based on the figure of the historian. A critique of historiographical enlightenment would not consist of the bringing in of a "better theory" of history, or a superior or more urbane methodology or epistemology, but in the analysis of the limits of such models themselves, for instance by bringing in the tools of historicist thought against the norms of history – which, incidentally, is one reason why the work of people like Foucault might still have some strategic, that is pro- vocative, uses in relation to this empirical tradition, although any more positive, "theoretical" uses would be quite another matter.

Intellectual enlightenment

In any case, the English do have norms of intellectual personality, even if these can seem like rather shallow probes from the perspective of a continental tradi- tion that likes to use theories with a view to digging major earthworks. Endowed with what we might suppose to be a form of historical consciousness at radical odds to the English point of view, the Nietzsche of the *Genealogy of Morals* castigated the purveyors of a certain kind of history:

> does modern historiography perhaps display an attitude more assured of life and ideals? Its noblest claim nowadays is that it is a mirror; it rejects all tele- ology; it no longer wishes to "prove" anything; it disdains to play the judge and considers this a sign of good taste – it affirms as little as it denies; it ascertains, it "describes" ... All this is to a high degree ascetic; but at the same time it is to an even higher degree *nihilistic*, let us not deceive ourselves about that! ... Here is snow; here life has grown silent; the last crows whose cries are audible here are called "wherefore!", "in vain!", "*nada!*" (Nietzsche 1969: 157)

In the context at least of English intellectualism, we might agree with the first claim made in this quotation – that history is ascetic – but disagree with the second – that it is nihilistic. Or rather, we might disagree about the implications of the second claim; that such nihilism is somehow a denial of life but may be – if nihilism it is – a deliberately critical attitude to time. It may be that the English *are* too normal; they tend to stuffiness, to be critical of imagination; but that is not to say that English thought does not purvey its own traditions of enlightenment. It all depends on the model of intellectualism we use. If we think in terms of the *j'accuse* model, we will see few intellectuals in Britain; but that may be only because British intellectuals, being typically historians, are more often than not hidden away in the archives.

If there is a lesson in any of this it is only that getting our model of intellectual enlightenment straight may itself be an aspect of enlightenment. We cannot, for instance, simply overturn practices of critical reflection based on one kind of ethic of time, and impose another overnight. We cannot just impose continental models of intellectualism on inhospitable soil; and the inhospitability is not necessarily a sign of vulgarity or anti-intellectualism.

Nevertheless, the fact that there may be different models of intellectualism does not itself serve to secure a defence of the very idea of the intellectual. For all models may be equally damned. Rather, if we are to show that the idea of the intellectual is something that is needful, we need to connect intellectual responsibility up to wider responsibilities and usages. And this is to ask: of what general kind of responsibility is intellectual responsibility itself only exemplary?

Grocers and intellectuals

I suggest that Gramsci was right: there is an intellectualism in everybody and the intellectuals are difficult to define sociologically without some or other recourse to more or less arbitrary demarcations. Let us only say that the intellectual is someone who enacts in the form of a *vocation* the demand that we must attempt to be ethically responsible before the truth; in the terms of a famous and much-referenced essay by Vaclav Havel, *to live in truth* (Havel 1986). It is not just a question of finding out what is the truth about this or that subject, but about living a life that is existentially devoted to the truth. But Havel's example of the person who lives in the truth by cultivating a respect for self through a respect for truth is not some high-minded intellectual but a grocer who one day wakes up and refuses to put up a sign in his shop supporting the authoritarian-socialist regime. This grocer begins to live in the truth precisely because it would be so easy to carry on living the quiet life and still put up such signs, yet living a lie. In other words, it is the very triviality of the example that is important. The grocer is not an intellectual; but the grocer merely by putting up a sign, does begin to live in the truth because oriented to the truth, valorizing the truth as a condition of life itself.

This kind of responsibility before the truth is, Havel thinks, an aspect of human responsibility in general. The intellectual, we might add, is only the dramatization or incarnation of such responsibility. So the point is not in fact just that – as Gramsci and Montefiore point out – everyone is, at least to an extent, an intellectual (Montefiore 1990: 223). It is also that intellectuals are, in a sense, only an extreme case or dramatization of a responsibility that all of us owe to thought. For everyone, as an aspect of daily life, is confronted with a certain responsibility – the challenge of which may or may not be taken up – to relate oneself to the truth; and what we call *an* intellectual as such is only somebody who takes such a responsibility as a calling. Intellectuals are only exemplars of a responsibility that lies potentially within all of us. Montefiore gets the tone of this exactly right:

> This fundamental responsibility for truthfulness and respect for truth, to respond truthfully and thus to provide reliable checks on each other's understanding and use is, then, one that we all carry with us everywhere. It is not possible to abandon it altogether without abandoning the realm of human discourse as such, the only realm within which we have potentially self-aware access to our own essential humanity. But if this responsibility is indeed partly constitutive of our very background to ourselves, that does not mean that it must form the main explicit focus of interest for everyone in the main preoccupations of their lives ... [I]ntellectuals, however, are bound always to find themselves among the first to confront the implications of this responsibility by virtue of their central commitment to an interest in validity and truth for their own sake. (Montefiore 1990: 227)

To say that there is a political responsibility inherent in the vocation of all intellectuals is perhaps to put the matter too narrowly. It just depends on what we mean by politics; but perhaps a better term would just be ethical responsibility. Along these lines, the intellectual would just be someone who exemplifies a particular ethical style of being responsible for the truth. We cannot, however, say – that is, outside of any particular style – which particular style is constitutive of true intellectualism. Above all, we should not make the mistake of assuming that what we need is a thought of the totality, or worse – an indigenous *philosophy*. For philosophy is not the only way to ground thought. The intellectual is the paragon of creativity in thought, but that does not mean that the intellectual is always a philosopher in the narrow sense.

One might object at this point that this is just to embrace a regrettable relativism when referring to such things as styles of responsibility towards the truth. But, if that is the case, this is a relativism that relates only to styles of *responsibility*; putting it glibly, styles of *irresponsibility* would be entirely another matter. In other words, this is not to be a relativist about irresponsibility – for intellectual irresponsibility is just wrong, that is, unamenable to considerations of an ethical kind. But that does not mean that responsibility in matters of truth is not a difficult and far from self-evident business. In this sense, absolutism in terms of intellectual responsibility is perhaps only the highest form of irresponsibility.

The question then becomes how to *cultivate* such forms of responsibility. To do so, a site is required in which it is possible that truth might not be assumed but where truth is explored, put up for grabs, made the object of an enquiry. Such a site would have to be, in effect, sequestrated from the outside world; it would be a place not just of enlightenment but where enlightenment itself would be systematically *called into question*.

The University

Such a place is – or should be – the modern University. It is commonly observed that the rationale of the University is that it is supposed to be a place of learning and experience as opposed to instruction. That ideal is integral to the very possibility of such a thing as the University. Such an ideal has often been defended in what can commonly be seen as terms that are ideologically backward. The aim of the nineteenth-century University was, in Newman's words, the teaching of "gentleman's knowledge" (Heyck 1982: 69). T.H. Huxley told the Cowper Commission of 1892 that "the primary business of the universities is with pure knowledge and pure art – independent of all application to practice, with progress in culture not with increase in wealth" (quoted in Halsey 1965: 48). The theme is a familiar one. J.S. Mill claimed in 1867 that there was some agreement that a university was not a place of professional education, and that the object of universities was "not to make skilful lawyers, or physicians, or engineers, but capable and cultivated human beings" (quoted in Rothblatt 1968: 248). Such an ideal is not necessarily compromised by the notion of the Unviersity as a place of research, an idea that dates from at least 1943 in Britain, when Bruce Truscot published his book, *Redbrick University*. Reacting against the more functionalist ideas of the University proposed early in the century by the Asquith Royal Commission on Oxford and Cambridge, Truscot argued that research itself was a broadening experience, and an aspect of educational cultivation rather than entailing just the increment of positive knowledge (see Heyck 1987: 207). In other words, Truscot's research model was as much as anything else an *ethical* model of University learning in that it was supposed to apply to the student too. For the student was supposed to succumb to the wiles of an ethic of discovery fully as much as the researcher: thus liberal education was to be inclusive rather than exclusive of a professionalized research ethic.

If, then, the University is a place of enlightenment, it is not so on the basis of anything like a rationalist model of instruction. Even where the primary aim is research as opposed to traditional kinds of "liberal education", the notion of research itself takes on an ethical import; for research can itself be an aspect of cultivation. And those who teach in universities should not be regarded as researchers or teachers but as intellectuals, those who embody particular ethics of truth. This will seem like a rather naïve, wide-eyed and outdated model of the University. For some – indeed for most – it seems that such an ideal is now more or less dead; that the University has become subject to the will of government or the performativity of the economy, and thus reduced to the demands of a technocratic civilization (cf. Halsey 1965). But such a view, opposing the principles of cultivation and government, is really erroneous. For in fact, the University – even in the golden age of liberal education – was always linked up to various ideals of government; for instance, as Hunter shows, the ideal of a liberal education itself – cultivating knowledge "for its own sake" – fitted perfectly well a certain pastoral model of statecraft (Hunter 1990).

I want to insist that it is not that the ideals of liberal education cannot stand up to the demands of government in a neo-liberal age, but that the advent of new emphases of government lead to new – or renewable – demands on education. Referring back to paternalist ideals is not the answer to the current crisis of the University; but that is not to say that the spirit of university education is necessarily dead. Rather, a "technocratic" argument can be made even for the principle of ideas for their own sake. Thus Paul Hirst argues that precisely because of the technological complexities of modern economies, there is a need for forms of education that embody the cultivation of intellectual "craft" in a general sense rather than a specialized, narrowly vocational one:

> Modern societies are too complex, too enmeshed in elaborate divisions of labour and too subject to technological change for traditions (that is, existing ways of doing things sanctioned by long usage) to provide their ideals or their ways of coping with the future. For the same reasons, because they are complex and subject to rapid technological change, societies cannot rely for their guidance on technical knowledges. Technologies are at once the products of highly specialised knowledges and at the same time are capable of producing wide-ranging social effects, effects which are usually unanticipated at the technical level. Technicians – and politicians and managers can be included in this category – thus have little capacity to imagine or anticipate the future. They are poor guides for modern societies because, as part of an elaborate division of labour, they find it difficult to rise above their specialized role. (Hirst 1995: 3)

In order to educate those capable of imagining or anticipating the future, at least the elements of a different form of education would be required. This would not necessarily amount to the same thing as that rather discredited ideology of a liberal cultivation of a totality of capacities. It is not necessarily the well-rounded individual that needs to become the object of cultivation; indeed, we might envisage a form of education that was rather *specialist* with regard to the cultivation of human capacities. We can cultivate human capacities without seeking out, or assuming, some teleological *totality* of such capacities as a norm.

A critical attitude to enlightenment – for such a thing might be at least one aspect of such an educational ideal – would entail not the romantic ideal of the cultivation of whole persons, oriented towards well-rounded ideological or moral norms, but only persons capable of subjecting themselves to the discipline of judgement, and especially of judgement in relation to the truth; persons, in other words, able to adopt the question of enlightenment *as* a question in the context of our age of enlightenment. Perhaps this view accords quite well with Alasdair MacIntyre's vision of the University as a place of constrained disagreement; the point being to initiate students into conflict; in other words, to make things difficult, to produce persons acclimatized to the difficulties entailed in any engagement with truth (MacIntyre 1990: 230–1). Such persons are "required" for quite good sociological reasons; specifically, that our societies are such that citizens and subjects are inherently governed *through* claims to the truth; hence such judgement is required strategically, on the basis of certain characteristics of government in our age of enlightenment (cf. Chapter 1, above). This does not mean that it is the purpose of the University to *dictate* as to the kinds or contents of judgement – the "ultimate values", in Weber's sense – that are employed; and, in that sense, MacIntyre's worries about the subversive effects of what he calls genealogical thought seem misplaced, as does his dissocation of such forms of thought from their place in the University, an association which he appears to regard wrongly as intrinsically anomalous (ibid: 218, 233). The educational aim would be really only to open up a space for the workings of judgement itself. And the only recurrent lesson would be that judgement is difficult, requiring the experience of involvement with the problems of truth in order to come into existence.

This does not imply that University teachers should all be subversive genealogists or Nietzschean iconoclasts. On the contrary, the quest for the truth would be about the inherent difficulty of a task to which, however theoretically intransigent it proves to be, all intellectuals *qua* intellectuals are condemned to address in their teaching and their work; the separation of facts and values. As Weber observed:

> Universities ... are not institutions for the inculcation of absolute or ultimate moral values. They analyse facts, their conditions, laws and inter-relations; they analyse concepts, their logical presuppositions and content. They do not and cannot teach what should happen – since this is a matter of ultimate personal values and beliefs, of fundamental outlook, which cannot be "demonstrated" like a scientific proposition ... The one element of any "genuine" ultimate outlook which they can legitimately offer their students to aid them in the path through life is the habit of accepting the obligation of intellectual integrity; this entails a relentless clarity about

themselves. Everything else – the entire substance of his aspirations and goals – the individual must achieve for himself in confronting the tasks and problems of life. (Weber 1973: 21)

What this means is not least that the drawing of a line between facts and values is not something that is written in stone, or even straightforwardly within the world itself. In that sense, the world is indeed, as Rorty has it, well lost. For, the fact-value distinction of which Weber speaks is something that, for Weber at least, has to be worked at, and struggled for, more in the manner of an ethical ordeal than as a fixed and easy doctrine. It is not that the University intellectual finds it easy to separate them; rather that it is an aspect of the duty of such people that, at least in the lecture-hall, they should seek to do so. In other words, this is not a straightforwardly liberal model of educational values, but it may be a strange or peculiarly liberal one.

Perhaps, in the final analysis, the intellectual is not a special kind of person but only somebody who is deemed to be well-practised, however succesful or not, in these arts of judgement, in this ongoing game of separating facts and values. And this, in turn, would mean that it is absolutely worth the candle to defend the notion of the intellectual, even if it is true, finally, that contained within this very notion is something that is often rather unpopular: the idea of an *aristocracy* of intellect. That is in fact because the requirement for the exercise of intellectual forms of judgement is an absolute academic freedom; for, after all, it makes no sense to talk about the ethics of truth if there is no such thing as complete freedom to shape our relation to truth in the manner in which we think best fit. And freedom in academic matters dictates that Universities, and all centres of intellect, should be governed along democratic lines by those who think and work there themselves, even if the natural upshot of such forms of democracy is a tendency towards aristocratism in matters of intellect. In the context of the University, a certain aristocracy of the talents is, as Weber observed, a consequence of democracy itself (Weber 1978, vol. 2: 948–52). This is because any intellectual institution devoted to the emergence of truth will have to establish itself on the basis of an equality of talents; and an equality of rights to the truth tends to lead inevitably to a kind of "rule by notables" in matters of truth. But, as Hirst insists, there are senses in which it might be as well to defend the idea of an aristocracy – precisely in the interests of the democracy of intellect, and even just in the interests of democracy itself; for the interests of "craft" are always best served by those who have gained an acknowledged "excellence" in what they do (Hirst 1995: 11).

We might push this point further and claim that the existence of intellectuals of a critical sort, those capable of questioning enlightenment itself, is actually an *indicator* of the existence of such a democracy and that to be such indicators, if anything, is their *function* – which, in the very widest sense, is therefore political. For given that we are all agents of intellect and hence, in Havel's sense, required to fashion our responsibility towards the truth, the intellectuals are only those who are required to make a specialized, if occasionally monstrous, ethic out of the very requirement for such responsibility; that is, not necessarily to conserve particular traditions of responsibility but to take such responsibility to its limits. Hence, if we value democracy, we would do well to value the existence of intellectuals, which is, as we have seen, likewise to find ourselves valorizing the very idea of an aristocracy of intellect, albeit one wholly open to all talents. Even though the best home for such an aristocracy may not be the University, the fact that, as classically conceived by its modern founders, it was an intrinsically aristocratic institution is not one of the major things which told against it.

Conclusion

Social theory, sociology and the ethics of criticism

Social theory – Learning and politics – Sociology and enlightenment – In praise of reductionism – Ethics and enlightenment – Social theory again

I have made out a case in this book for the general viability of the idea of a critical attitude to enlightenment; a form of critique that would not be just a kneejerk anti-foundationalism but an adjunct to a commitment to enlightenment itself. Anti-foundationalism might have a place here but it would not be of an irrationalist kind; rather it would even be quite sensibly realist in outlook. Now, tied to these matters, I have also been concerned to show that this notion of a critical analytics of enlightenment might be tied quite specifically to the fate of social theory as a discipline. This latter theme, however, has not as yet involved much comment of a theoretical order, and for good reason. This book has not been one of those immodest attempts to rebuild a discipline from the ground up. Rather I have attempted to show how social theory might be reconfigured – regarded in a particular aspect – out of elements that already exist. I have done this more by example than by theoretical articulation; by picturing the kind of terrain a discipline concerned with the question of enlightenment might occupy in relation, for example, to the fields of scientific, therapeutic or aesthetic reason or in relation to particular thinkers like Foucault or Weber and particular constituencies such as French or English schools of intellectuals. This is not to say, however, that it is not possible to say some more general things about this question of social theory as a discipline. In any case, I now want to address this question just a little more directly than hitherto, and this will involve outlining – hopefully in not too polemical a way – some of the limits and specificities of the idea of a critique of enlightenment in relation to other kinds of commitments – whether critical, epistemological, political or ethical – in sociology and the social sciences.

Social theory

There are two important senses in which it is rather misguided to claim any special rights for social theory with regard to the idea of a critique of enlightenment. First, no discipline can in fact claim such exclusive rights; rather, we have seen how principles of enlightenment are inscribed within various practices, and even that various forms of critique are internal to many such practices. Second, it might seem rather incongruous to claim special rights for social theory, having spent so much of this book attempting to dissociate questions of enlightenment from more traditional sociological questions such as those which focus on the category of modernity.

I do not want to question these two suspicions, but rather to counter their effects through two sets of observations. First, it follows from what I have said about the restricted character of the idea of a critique of enlightenment that indeed it does not make much sense to think of a critique of enlightenment as an exclusive kind of vocation. The idea of a professional "critic of enlightenment" seems rather absurd in that context. Such criticism is a restricted exercise, a separation of ourselves from our existing relations to truth; it is not a cognitive morality directed at the whole of life. Such forms of separation amount to another reason why the University might be a suitable place to practise such forms of critique, for the University is itself often regarded as a kind of separated space, a space of passage or "time out" rather than of settlement and rest. And in the University there may be people who specialize in the teaching of forms of the critique of enlightenment on a full-time basis but who, nonetheless, would not necessarily be iconoclasts in everything to do with truth; people, that is, who would not necessarily be committed to the subversion of truth as a whole way of life. But then specialization is not the same thing as wholesale commitment, just as a spiritual exercise is not the same thing as a complete moral code.

The second observation is that social theory is indeed – or should be – different from realist, critical and radical forms of sociology. I shall discuss some such differences and their character further below. However, a quick and preliminary way to isolate one key difference is to note that what most forms of social theory have in common is not some or other commitment to a "social" analysis of this or that phenomena, but the aspiration to produce critical diagnoses of various aspects of the spirit of the present. Increasingly within social theory the term "social" has come to seem rather redundant, for much social theory does not seem to work with any determinate category of society. To accept this state of affairs is not to dismiss sociological analysis or the category of society, only to emphasize the differences between such forms of analysis and social theory itself.

But what, then, is social theory? For quite a long time, in so far as it has sought to be an autonomous discipline, it has in fact been something of a "discipline without discipline". Although it has sought to autonomize itself from lateral areas of enquiry like empirical sociology or sociological theory (methodology), today it seems as if it occupies no particular field of investigation at all, preferring to establish itself just as a general theoretical enterprise, at times indistinguishable from certain kinds of philosophical speculation. Especially in the Anglo-American intellectual world, the emergence of such an autonomous social theory can seem something of an anomaly. The discipline, if discipline it is, often seems to hover somewhat awkwardly between *sociological* theory, epistemology and continental philosophy. Autonomous social theory of this kind has been very strong on generating neologisms and multiplying distinctions, but less good at generating *concepts*. The effect has been one of an endless proliferation rather than a contribution to the furtherance of specific problematics and research programmes in knowledge.

It is fundamental to the argument of this book that such "autonomous" social theory is really a misguided enterprise. Social theory, to be an autonomous discipline, has to have an "object" of its own, or at least a problematic that is somehow central to its concerns. Hitherto, the central category of this kind of theory has been that of modernity or, what amounts to much the same thing in this context, postmodernity. As I noted in Chapter 1 of this book, it can sometimes seem uncertain as to whether modernity is a period of time, a structural ideal or an ongoing process. In any case, the fact is that modernity is ill-suited as the central concept of social theory simply because, if it is to make any sense – that is, as the epochal category that it aspires to be – it would have to be a sociological concept: it would have to have a determinate empirical content – something which it manifestly does not have in most studies of modernity, where it is usually discussed in terms of a set of worldviews, vague processes or tendencies, or as an indeterminate *Weltanschauung*. But my purpose has not been to dismiss the category of modernity out of hand; no doubt many well-worked out sociologies of it do exist. It is only to suggest that, were it addressed as it demands to be addressed, there would be no difference between social theory and sociology as ordinarily conceived, and it is just such a difference that I want to defend.

In place of the category of modernity, I have suggested that social theory should limit its epochal ambitions and embrace a deliberate restriction of its problematic to the concept of enlightenment. I stress the *concept* of enlightenment, and not necessarily the word. This is not one of those proposals that is designed to change everybody's habits overnight. In fact, as I have insisted, much of social theory – even that focused on the category of modernity – is *already* concerned with the concept of enlightenment in this sense, so my argument entails at most a reconfiguration rather than a plea for a wholesale revolution; a plea for a reconfiguration of social theory itself under a new aspect rather than a revisualization of it altogether.

But what kind of a concept is enlightenment? Aside from the important consideration that it is already a key concept in social and critical theory, its merit is, in a nutshell, that it holds itself hostage neither to a determinate content (rationalization, alienation or whatever) nor a periodization (modernity). The spirit of enlightenment is rather that spirit that would seek to connect truth to freedom; that would seek to govern in the name of a truth that was also a truth of freedom. This is an aspiration or a kind of *spirit* rather than a reality as such; and we saw that to be realist about enlightenment entailed being realist about that spirit. When given a determinate content, that is, as *knowledge* or *rationalization*, critical scope is given in advance on an either/or basis. The result is the kind of pointless dichotomous thinking that we see in the modernity versus postmodernity debate, which overdramatizes social change and converts what should be a reflection on the specificity of the present into the deductive phenomenology of an epoch.

Care needs to be taken with this concept of enlightenment. I think that too much of the literature associates enlightenment with a sociological *process*, somewhat akin to the idea of the rationalization of the world. The category of rationalization is, as I argued in Chapter 1, intrinsically problematic when utilized at the level of a general theory, as opposed to particular contexts or perspectives. One cannot speak meaningfully of a general rationalization of society, just as one cannot speak of an enlightened age but only an age of enlightenment. When considered in such substantive rather than attitudinal terms, such views of enlightenment only lead to a rather facile association of enlightenment itself with rationalism. Quite often the association is directly with *political* rationalism, which can be quite misleading. In such instances, we typically find enlightenment blamed for all the travails of recent history in quite a direct and literal way. Thus, for instance, the collapse of the Soviet Union can be seen as the collapse of enlightenment itself; hence to be anti-enlightenment can mean to be something like a liberal and – pushing things to rather absurd extremes – quite respectable forms of pluralism – such as in the work of Isaiah Berlin – can come to be associated with postmodern irrationalisms and post-enlightenment mentalities themselves (Gray 1995, Gray 1997). Hence a double assimilation; not only is the baby of enlightenment thrown out with the bathwater of political rationalism, but the baby of political liberalism, which really did not need a wash, has been thrown into the bathwater of postmodernism – which can be a very murky place indeed.

The problem with these assimilations is simply that they do not respect the autonomy of the question of enlightenment. Such a respect requires that we hold that question deliberately open. Hence the object of a social theory concerned with this question should not be with the direct equation of enlightenment with this or that kind of politics nor with theorizing it from the ground up, but with following the actual fortunes of enlightenment and in the process conducting a kind of permanent critique of it. Regarded this way, the dichotomies of modernity versus postmodernity and their equivalents lose their sense, and what is at stake is not a question of either the defence of the enlightenment or the death of the enlightenment but an *ethical* commitment to the ideal of an ongoing critique of enlightenment.

Actually this might make social theory quite deliberately a rather strange or peculiar discipline; for it would have to be inherently parasitic. It would amount to a form of rationality of which the purpose was to reflect critically on other forms of existing rationality rather than to legislate on reason in its own right (for instance, in the manner of many kinds of philosophy). This would make social theory less an autonomous discipline in an orthodox sense so much as a kind of intellectual habit; one that draws in not just people who call themselves social theorists but many of those working in the humanities and the social sciences in all sorts of different ways. Those who called themselves social theorists would only aspire to the status of generalists in such matters.

Were we to understand social theory as the discipline that reflects on the character of enlightenment in this way, then we can see that social theory might have an important – if peculiar – place not just as a scholarly enterprise but as an instrument in education.

Learning and politics

Although it might be concerned, as with any academic discipline, with research into particular subject areas, the specificity of social theory – in so far as it might be a form of reflection on the status of enlightenment – actually resides in the fact that it is not really just a domain of research in the normal sense.

I have claimed that enlightenment is, in its own way, capable of treatment from a realist perspective. And I have insisted that such a treatment would take us quite some way from either a rationalist fideism or a postmodern irrationalism; a third way, perhaps, but not a reconciliation of alternatives, nor even, as Ernest Gellner has it in a polemical text, the living of a "double life" – being sceptical yet loyal to truth – in what he describes as a constitutional monarchy ruled by truth, but perhaps something like a commitment to finding an ethics appropriate to living in a republican federation of truth (cf. Gellner 1992b: 94–6). It might be true that what is, on occasion, the sceptical character of a critical attitude to enlightenment can give it the look of an antifoundationalist postmodernism; especially in so far as it leads to what could be called "contingency effects": its ethical foregrounding of contingency. But this is no more one of those pretentious post-structuralist moralities than it is a celebration of postmodern, pluralist liberalism. Contrast the position of someone like Richard Rorty for whom the philosophy of contingency should be understood in the language of irony, an ironist being, not a cynic, but "the sort of person who faces up to the contingency of his or her own most central beliefs and desires – someone sufficiently historicist and nominalist to have abandoned the idea that those central beliefs and desires refer back to something beyond the reach of time and chance" (Rorty 1989: xv). Such a project can be interpreted in one of two ways. Either it is trivial: that we are all creatures of time, chance and evolution – which, in turn, raises the problem of what in Chapter 2 I called the "relative" aspects of relativism, which is to say, that some of our attributes (for instance, species characteristics as opposed to psychological characteristics) are clearly "more relative" than others. Or otherwise, it can be interpreted as a kind of moral philosophy of contingency, with determinate consequences in all departments of life. Either way, it is not – to adopt Rorty's own pragmatic criteria of judgement – a terribly *useful* doctrine. Such an idea is not, anyway, to be confused with a critique of enlightenment, even though such a critique may appear generically concerned with the illumination of contingency. The difference lies, above all, in the implications of such an attitude. For the attitude of a critical analytics of enlightenment is not of necessity obsessed with language, is not of necessity a philosophy of identity (or of non-identity), and, most importantly, does not of necessity presuppose a general philosophy, ontology or epistemology of contingency, or require us to embrace contingency as a worldview with direct consequences for politics. In short, it is not an all-embracing scepticism, but an ethical, or perhaps an ascetic, restricted one.

Hence I have claimed that the attitude of a critique of enlightenment is best seen not as a worldview but as a kind of *ethical* discourse, which is to say, simultaneously, a *strategic* discourse; to be understood more as a restricted "discipline" in the literal sense of the term: that is, as an educational "exercise" rather than as a world-embracing morality. Such exercises will tend to be directed only at particular problems; above all, where freedom seeks to realize itself, or wherever freedom is most in question. And because the critique of enlightenment has this "educational" character, I have argued that the University is as good a place as any to exercise it.

Social theory might serve a function in the University as the epitome of a discipline of *learning*. Enlightenment through learning is not the same as being taught something. Learning, according to Michael Oakeshott, is:

> an activity possible only to an intelligence capable of choice and self-direction in relation to its own impulses and to the world around him. These, of course, are pre-eminently human characteristics, and ... only human beings are capable of learning. A learner is not a passive recipient of impressions, nor one whose accomplishments spring from mere reactions to circumstances, nor one who attempts nothing he does not know how to accomplish. He is a creature of wants rather than of needs, of recollection as well as memory; he wants to know what to think and what to believe and not merely what to do. Learning concerns conduct, not behaviour. In short, these analogies of clay and wax, of receptacles to be filled and empty rooms to be furnished, have nothing to do with learning and learners. (Oakeshott 1989: 43–4)

This notion of learning might be contrasted with that of what is often called "research", which means the results of knowledge. Now, properly speaking, research in this sense, should – from the perspective of a liberal education – be a mere adjunct to learning:

> A university will have ceased to exist when its learning has degenerated into what is now called research, when its teaching has become mere instruction and occupies the whole of an undergraduate's time, and when those who came to be taught come, not in search of their intellectual fortune but with a vitality so unroused or so exhausted that they wish only to be provided with a serviceable moral and intellectual outfit; when they come with no understanding of the manners of conversation but desire only a qualification for earning a living or a certificate to let them in on the exploitation of the world. (ibid: 104)

Learning in this sense can be tied to the ideal of maturity; the ideal of being an autonomous being, freed from the necessity of simply being "taught" or from received forms of dogma. That is the idea that Kant associated with enlightenment itself; defining immaturity as "the inability to use one's own understanding without the guidance of another" (Kant 1970: 54). A critical attitude to enlightenment would be oriented to the ideal of maturity in precisely that, rather literal, way. It is an exercise directed at making sure that we are *not* immature, that is, over-dependent upon our prejudices or received ideas even when these can be enlightened prejudices or ideas. To put matters bluntly, there is a lot of "growing up" to be done in the domain of "theory".

Perhaps what is required most of all is to end the childish associations that are often insisted on between theories and politics. That anyway is where much of the growing up should be done. As I mentioned in the Introduction, it is striking the extent to which "modern" realists and their ilk like to debunk postmodernism not – as one might expect – on rational or epistemological grounds but on grounds of political expediency. For such critics, what is wrong with postmodernism tends less to be that postmodernism itself is wrong but that its consequences are fatal for political activity; that if we embrace postmodernism, then – politically speaking – the sky will fall on our heads.

There are many grounds for not embracing postmodernism but that is not one of them. A better reason again follows from the spurious linkages that tend to be made between theories and politics within postmodernism itself. Postmodernists often claim that postmodernism, in the form of the decentering of everything, is somehow more "radical" in its implications than stuffy old realist modernism with its subjects, its truths and so on. But actually there is no reason to think that any determinate consequences whatsoever follow from the so-called decentering of the subject and whatever else it is that postmodernists like to do. As if an epistemological posture could not lead to a multitude of widely differing politics. Such claims as those of the postmodernists – and equally, if more obviously, those of their fideist opponents – are really just symptomatic of the grossly inflated intellectualist discourse that postmodernism really is. Hypersolipsistic about the power of concepts, postmodernism would seek to bring about a pluralist republic of concepts where all concepts would ultimately carry – because "contingent", relative or whatever – the same status.

But such a view is to misunderstand what is meant by a concept in the first place. Concepts impose restrictions; they are instruments of discipline. Indeed, the very idea of a concept presupposes the idea of discipline. Hence it is no use postmodernists and other relativists complaining or proclaiming that all concepts are the same under the sun; for disciplines do impose powers on concepts, which means that some concepts are able to do more work than others. Those who work in the domain of "theory" should indeed grow up; what is required is not a pluralism of ontologies or epistemologies but a recognition only of the plurality of modes of critique. There may be only one world, but there are many different things to criticize and many different ways to conduct criticism.

Does this mean that the idea of a critique of enlightenment is strictly neutral with regard to the political sphere? And is that to say, as some may undoubtedly suspect, that it is, *de facto*, conservative (cf. Kant 1970: 103)? In fact, its political credentials are likely to be necessarily – even deliberately – indeterminate. Not least of its functions would surely have to be to break down any easy assimilation between types of knowledge and types of politics, for the very assumption that such an assimilation is possible would be to go against our regulative ideal of negative enlightenment: that it is an aspect of enlightenment that we can never finally know what enlightenment is.

But does that mean that the idea of a critique of enlightenment would be necessarily gestural in relation to politics? Even that it might function as a model for a liberal form of enquiry; one inclined to sit on the fence in political terms? I think not. It may function, for example, among many other things, to create an *attitude* for politics and for the kinds of judgement that might be applicable to a properly political sensibility. And perhaps it would indeed be liberal, if only in so far that a key liberal tenet is that there should be some kind of autonomy for the sphere of politics; that politics is not simply reducible to anything else be that society, class, the economy or whatever. But the very idea of a critical attitude to enlightenment is also generically anti-liberal – or perhaps strangely or peculiarly liberal – in as much as its aim should be, not as with Oakeshott or Rorty in their not so entirely different ways simply the pursuit of "conversation" but rather to create a disturbance. Its aim is to stimulate both the need and the capacity for judgement. And judgement is activated not least through perplexity; judgement needs if it is to be "exercised" to be *provoked*, not least through the activity of making things difficult to think as much as through any specific "pedagogy" of judgement. Hence, the idea of a critical attitude to enlightenment in fact points in two ways at once. It calms us down with regard to knowledge and epistemology, but it is not doing its job unless it unsettles us with regard to ourselves.

Perhaps, then, maturity consists simply in a recognition of the *difficulty* of enlightenment, the difficulty of truth, that truth is both an obligation and a labour (Chapter 7, above; cf. Malpas 1996). Rational fideists and postmodern relativists have a tendency to unite in believing that the connections between beliefs and action, epistemology and politics, are direct, unmediated and un-problematic (once, that is, we have got our beliefs or epistemologies right) – a good example of simplicism if one were needed. The idea of a critical attitude to enlightenment is not least a strategic response to such simplicism. There is room more than ever for the cultivation of a Socratic maturity that acknowledges the difficulty of telling the truth and polemices not against its serious epistemological opponents but only those who would reduce the problem of truth to the matter of certainty, and as a consequence, easy polemic.

Sociology and enlightenment

So where does this leave "sociology", in the sense of all those disciplines that seek the truth of ourselves – sociology, anthropology, social history, certain kinds of philosophy and so forth – on the basis of the truth of society? My argument might seem to lead us into a dualist position; on the one hand, we would have the positive, nomological sciences of society, and on the other the more sceptical pursuit of a social theory concerned with enlightenment.

But such a view would be, in fact, to make a category mistake about the kind of autonomy that might be envisaged for social theory in this context. I do not claim, in any case, that a critical analytics of enlightenment could be quite autonomous in that sense. Or rather on the one hand, this would have to be a peculiarly "parasitic" autonomy; for, as we have seen, the idea of a critique of enlightenment appears to presuppose an attitude of enquiry that precisely in sticking to the discipline of the concept of enlightenment necessarily seeks it out in the field and in all sorts of places. In other words, it is an autonomy that in itself presupposes not that such a critique is independent of other fields – embodying, for instance, a particular "theoretical attitude" proper to itself – but that, on the contrary, it only exists in relation to such fields, and leans on them, interrogates them, is provoked by them and provokes them.

On the other hand, the kind of unsettling effect that a critique of enlighten-ment – especially in its more negative forms – can be designed to achieve is not unique to it; it is rather that it dramatizes that kind of effect, and makes of it something of a specialty. The idea of a critique of enlightenment, indeed, makes a *reduction* of a principle that all those who have ever taught the social sciences will have experienced. For it is very common to feel that one's primary purpose in these disciplines is to produce controlled affects in people at the level of experience. That is true even of the most "explanatory" ends of the social sciences. These disciplines all specialize in illocutionary effects; they change the position of both speaker and hearer in their very enactment. In critical sociology, the holy trinity of class, race and gender belongs to an ethical problematic as much as anything else. A mature student, of whatever gender, on a course in the sociology of gender is not just going to be enlightened as to forms of oppression that have already been experienced. It is both more and less than that, because here enlightenment takes fully as much the form of a stripping away or a subversion of capacities as it does a reconstruction of them.

The difference between sociology and social theory might be, then, only that the latter takes the difficulty of critique as its very object; it is not a meta-discipline or even really a separate discipline but a disciplinary testimony to that difficulty, a kind of critique of critiques. I think that the mere *existence* of such a discipline could be said to have a positive value in relation to sociology and the social sciences. For such an existence serves as a constant reminder that the link between knowledge and criticism is not as fixed or obvious as, in some contexts, it can be tempting to think. Social theory would not, then, be an autonomous discipline in the sense that it would have its own empirical field, or even necessarily its own "professional" and full-time practitioners, but it might have a certain autonomy as the place where sociology and the social sciences would be constantly reminded of their obligations – to criticize – and of their difficulties – to link up evidence and criticism, facts and values.

For facts and values are not separable on a nomological basis; rather, such separation requires work. Few would disagree that social science can never be just a question of an automatic value-freedom; but it is assuredly always – even for those who want to make the most directly political points in their work or in the lecture-hall – an exercise in striving for value-neutrality, of attempting to separate one's criticisms and one's politics from the content of instruction. Perhaps a social theory oriented to a critique of enlightenment could act as the conscience of such a will to value-neutrality, testimony to the fact that such a will is difficult, endless and the product of an ethical labour. In this sense, social theory would not be a "scientific" discipline that would expect concrete or cumulative "results". Rather it would be a place where one went to exercise one's judgement in reminding oneself of the ordeal that truth places on the social sciences in the form of the simultaneous impossibility of separating facts and values in any definitive, final, "scientific" way and the constant ethical compulsion to attempt to do so.

Note that this perspective leaves things much as they are within sociology itself. The idea of a critical attitude to enlightenment may indeed lead us to be critical of projects, of unities and of good intentions. But in so far as it would amount to an attitude rather than a doctrine, such scepticism would not be an anti-enlightenment position; it would not be – as with the postmodernists – to deny that projects, unities of explanation and good intentions are part of the actual duties of the social sciences. The projection of ideals, the envisioning of future worlds, is precisely what the social sciences *do*. To abdicate such ideals in the name of a spuriously enlightened postmodernism is actually to abdicate the very ideals that are *intrinsic* to such disciplines themselves. Perhaps such schemas are, as Weber said of Marx, always if not exactly necessary fictions then ideal-types that are imposed upon the world. The ideal of progress is internal to the very idea of the social sciences as a project, even to the latter-day postmodernized versions of such sciences. And as for those who would regard such a notion as an attempt to smuggle in a certain élitism – after all, who is to say how we should be enlightened? – then we can only respond by saying that there is a gulf between acting in the name of somebody and attempting to speak in their name. So when, for example, feminists speak in the name of all women, it is strictly an act of immaturity to complain with the postmodernists that, after all, no one can speak *for* anyone else. On the contrary, to speak for others is simply an intrinsic feature of what it is to study social worlds or to do criticism or, come to that, to live in the world. Which does not mean that such speech acts will be successful; for, after all, others, including postmodern feminists and male chauvinists, can always fight back, argue to the contrary, or simply refuse to listen.

To be enlightened is not, then, to abandon any attempt to speak but is to learn to live, perhaps, with that tension that exists between enlightenment and a certain élitist impulse; the assumption that some people, those who are speaking, are "in the know". In fact, it is to subject that intrinsic élitism to a sort of permanent critique, which involves a recognition that such a stance is ultimately ethical and cannot be "grounded" in any ultimate claim to truth, even though a commitment to the truth would indeed have to be a necessary component of it. Maturity here implies, then, a certain humility, a certain consciousness of the ordeal that truth places on us, not the insistence that either what we say is always right for everybody or, conversely, that nobody ever has the right to speak on any one else's behalf.

In any case, this latter kind of alternative is not very helpful. Instead of immature debates over who does or who does not have the "right to speak" or to criticize, attention might better be devoted to the creation of concepts with an end to criticism. For that, in the end, is all that legitimates one form of discourse against another. The only rule in assessing different approaches should be – not anything to do with materialism or idealism, realism or relativism or whatever – that the purpose of any discipline is to create a discipline of concepts. The Marxist philospher Louis Althusser's by now rather notorious Bachelardian view of science – that there is a fundamental difference between science and ideology, that science is inaugurated at the moment of a "break" from everyday ideologies – may be wrong as a view of science, but it is correct if we think in terms of disciplines. The distinction should not be between science and non-science, but disciplines and pseudo-disciplines or systems of morality. A discipline worthy of the name begins to generate its own concepts, however feeble; it is like a little island of thought where entropy is put, however temporarily, on hold. In that sense disciplines tend to be reductive in character; and such reductionism is surely to be praised not bemoaned from the perspective of a romantic humanism that is all too common in the social and human sciences. For typically the creation of concepts comes at a certain cost: that of the concentration of concepts. Reductionism is not the same thing as determinism. Instead of raging against reductionism, we should do better to ask of it – as Amartya Sen asks of equality – reductionism of *what*? Perhaps, in the interests of the plurality of criticism that was advocated earlier, we can say that the social sciences require not a single form of determination (the economy in the last instance and so forth) nor an empty postmodern epistemological pluralism (which is to say the denial of epistemology) but a *pluralism of reductions*. To reduce, to conceptualize is the condition of a succesful – which is to say, serious, "mature" – sociological discipline.

In praise of reductionism

So, for example, to make a sociological theory out of the category of modernity, we should have to reduce that notion to further concepts, which also means autonomizing it through concepts. What, for example, is the central category of the sociological disciplines if not the category of *domination*? This is already an abstraction or a reduction, since not every form of social action is properly reducible to domination (Weber 1978, vol. 2: 941). And following Weber we might further reduce domination to two basic orders: domination "by virtue of a constellation of interests" and "domination by virtue of authority, i.e. power to command and duty to obey" (ibid: 943).

For instance, if the sociology of modernity is to take the first road in the study of domination, then one of the best conceptual candidates would still be not endlessly proliferating neologisms and cultural categories but specifically *economic* concepts. The sociological theory of modernity might be able even to redeem itself were it to embrace the economic paradigm rather than constantly reverting to vague talk about identity, subjectivity and so forth. That assumes that there could be such a thing as a sociological economics; that is, a form of economics that is concerned with questions of culture, trust and social relations. Weber himself held the view that modernity could be analyzed economically not least in so far as agents increasingly came to fit the economic picture of individual rationality; in other words, the economic model of "man" was becoming increasingly close to the facts. Who would be surprised, then, that economic paradigms of explanation have been of such import in the social sciences in recent decades? Instead of bemoaning the failure of rational choice theories, social choice and game theory – not to mention Marxist economism – to live up to the complicated realities of the world, those who work in the social sciences should recognize that such reductionism is simply the price we pay for explanation worthy of the name.

As for domination which takes the form of "power of command and duty to obey", this field has been rather over-colonized by the more restrictive tradition of radical or *critical* sociology. Such sociology has traditionally regarded any form of domination as being ripe for critique, instead of investigating the social fabrication of different forms and styles of authority which require other methods than just a dismissive critique. So what of sociological reductionism? Critical sociology typically argues – against the alternative reductions of biology, science, psychology and so forth – that it is society that determines all differences. This problematic can be criticized not least for its indeterminacy on the question of relativism; for such sociologists tend to be vigorously anti-relativist even though the logic of their position is, ironically enough, itself often relativist with regard to the question of social determination itself. But if critical sociology tends to regard societies in relative terms, the category of *solidarity* - whether of class, race, gender or whatever – does tend to be a constant in their analyses. Critical sociology typically *assumes* solidarity as both the condition and the goal of human association. Given that such an assumption is strictly speaking teleological, we have to grant it an *ethical* status. Solidarity is something that people want; it is a value. Hence the critique of enlightenment does not rule such a project as critical sociology out of hand. If there is a problem with critical sociology it is not that it is "untrue" (as the rather more self-congratulatory elements in postmodernism would like to think) but, more often than not, that it does not tend to recognize its own status as primarily an ethical discourse, which often means that it has a tendency to become a *moral* or moralizing and sententious one. But we cannot *prove*, for example, that the working class is the subject of history or that all women enjoy a particular kind of solidarity. We can embrace such things on an ethical level, however; and, indeed, critical sociology might be regarded as a venerable tradition of thought that is really conditional in orientation; it takes the form of saying, in a rather utopian, counter-factual fashion: "What would be the case were this situation to be so?" Or for instance: "How might we read the course of history given the assumption that one day the working class will indeed receive justice?" Such sociology is itself utopian and ethical before it is "scientific" or truly nomological, but the recognition of this state of affairs is more, perhaps, to defend the tradition of critical sociology that to damn it out of hand.

This is not to say that we cannot be critical of critical sociology. Critical sociology has to guard more than anything else against its own tendencies to a certain kind of complacency. All too often it just sinks into the reiteration of what has already been said, without any regard to the production of the new by way of concepts; and all too often it indulges in a sort of complacency with regard to time, for it assumes that justice inheres within time; that *within time*, there will be justice. All critical sociology is really a bet played with time, invoking a future free of domination less as a regulatory ideal than as an implicit norm. The critique of enlightenment, on the other hand, is really a moral education in the *ethics* of time; less a putative science of society than a mode of reflecting on the circumstances of our present (Bell 1994). Here one does not take time so much for granted; the aim is to diagnose the present not to denounce it out of hand. Which is not in turn to suggest a postmodern attitude to time.

The postmodern perspective seems often to do little more than to reverse the redemptive view of time, and replace it with a cynical reaction to time. Perhaps one mistake of this postmodernism was, not least, that it failed to characterize the older sociology correctly, dismissing it for its narrowness and what it taught; and substituting a sort of macro-understanding of the present as an epochal historical bloc, labelled postmodern or whatever, fails to think through issues of the present. We need to replace both the progressivist and the epochal views of time with a critical atttitude to the present; one which is concerned, above all, with the particular circumstances of our present, without being tied to the present as mere actuality. The critique of enlightenment would be an aspect of just such an enterprise, but in being so, it only dramatizes the current reality of much critical sociology. In other words, the proper effect of a critique of enlightenment in relation to critical sociology is not to denounce it as falsehood or ideology but to request that it adjusts its view of itself to fit more closely the reality of its own practices.

Take again, in this context, the example of the academic politics of gender. The sphere of gender studies is in something of a ferment because a predominantly older generation of feminists – those who espouse all the old traditions of "critique" – are under threat from a younger generation who would claim that there is no such thing as a specific, gendered identity; hence, some would say, rendering the very idea of a feminist politics an impossibility. A strictly neutral sociology of this state of affairs would itself be interesting. What such a study would no doubt show would be that what comes first with regard to such feminist politics is neither politics nor epistemology but ethics. As a condition for the "debate" between radical and postmodern feminists there has to be the conception of some kind of a feminist *project*. But this is an ethical commitment not a political or epistemological one. Put crudely, the difference might be that the radical feminists believe they can still base a feminist politics on epistemological grounds (the fact that there exists a class of women that are oppressed) whereas for the postmodernists, the political existence of feminism comes first; it is local struggles that have to be given priority (see for instance Yeatman 1994). But in fact this is a false opposition; each is just a different way of problematizing the ethical status of feminism. And the point here is that either ethical problematization can lead to both different or the same political orientations; *both* positions are less determinate, in terms of politics, than tends to be thought. While postmodern feminists certainly completely overstate the epistemological problems of critical feminism, the critical feminists overstate the political problems of the postmodern feminists; whereas in fact no determinate political positions can be straightforwardly deduced from either position.

What comes first, then, is the fact that it is our ethics that inform the very grammar of our conduct in relation to these questions; a position which perhaps leads us in the direction of moral realism or, as we might prefer to call it, an ethical realism (cf. Lovibond 1983). Feminism, to continue with this example, is neither initially a politics nor an epistemology but a form of ethical authority which means simultaneously that it is a site of ethical argumentation, a place where certain people seek out certain kinds of truth in the realm of ethics, using certain forms of knowledge to do so – a view which neither makes any particular feminism universally "true" nor which does anything to dismiss the feminist project altogether.

Ethics and enlightenment

Such an ethical realism – if it is not too misleading or question-begging to call it that – has another advantage which is that it leads us away from the dichotomizing options that hold there is an ethical life-world on the one hand and a world of system and expertise on the other (cf. Habermas 1987b). The outcome of such stories are always much the same; that ethics is colonized by science, expertise, even by enlightenment itself. Many influential thinkers in contemporary social theory hold to this line; instead of seeking out a limited reductionism of concepts, such theory pursues dichotomies in an endless tautology.

Such philosophical sociologies of modernity typically start with a kind of baseline philosophical anthropology – that humans are made up of this, that or the other set of attributes – and then go on to recount a narrative of the loss of the integrity of the ethical experience in question. Even Alasdair MacIntyre's influential work would be a case in point; for it shows the extent to which these philosophies of loss can be both sophisticated, even brilliant in their execution, and yet still rather too predictable in their outcome. For MacIntyre, the modern world has retained only the vestiges of the pre-modern vocabularies of virtue; and now even the conditions of use of such a vocabulary have faded away (MacIntyre 1981). The human sciences and the enlightenment project have had some part to play in this state of affairs; indeed, MacIntyre assimilates the enlightened social sciences and "managerial discourse" in his analysis, albeit with the ironic proviso that the effects of enlightenment "have been to produce *not* scientifically managed social control, but a skilful dramatic imitation of such control. It is histrionic success which gives power and authority in our culture. The most effective bureaucrat is the best actor" (ibid: 107).

Such philosophical sociologies find themselves forced into an unequivocal, and ulimately romantic, denunciation of the present times. They force us to *deduce* our judgements from a particular philosophical history. But they do not and cannot provoke us to *exercise* our judgement. Against such philosophical sociologies, we need to insist that there is not one modern moral world-order, and there is not but one form of rationalization, just as there is little distinction between a totally administered world and MacIntyre's more subtle vision of a world inhabited by social scientists who act as if it were totally administered. Neither hope nor despair should necessarily – that is, *deductively* – be the order of the day. That is why we need to develop an alternative view of both the social sciences themselves – perhaps one based, at least in part, on the *actual* history and structuration of those sciences, which includes the internal forms of normativity presupposed by those sciences, as opposed to a history of some of the ideologies that have been attached to them – *and* an alternative view of the very idea of enlightenment. This would have to take account of the ethical character of such sciences, as well as of enlightenment itself. In doing so, we would hopefully find ourselves as distant from postmodern reconceptualizations of ethics as it would be from communitarian moral fantasies; that is, from either the view that the present has witnessed a demise or, on the contrary, a radical reinvigoration of the very possibility of ethics.

Take, as an instance of the latter view, and as a contrast to MacIntyre, recent postmodern writings on the subject of morality. Zygmunt Bauman, for example, regrets that:

> What has come to be associated with the notion of the postmodern approach to morality is all too often the celebration of the "demise of the ethical", of the substitution of aesthetics for ethics, and of the "ultimate emancipation" that follows. Ethics itself is denigrated or derided as one of the typically modern constraints now broken and destined for the dustbin of history; fetters once deemed necessary, now clearly superfluous: another illusion the postmodern men and women can well do without. (Bauman 1992b: 2)

In place of such nihilism, Bauman would seek to impose an alternative – properly postmodern – sense of ethical obligation on us, one based on a particular theory of what is *given* to us ethically, in fact, an intensified Kantian conception based on "a posture guided solely by the concern for the Other *for the Other's sake*, and the respect for the Other as a 'free subject' and the 'end in itself'" (ibid: 49). It seems that the postmodern re-evaluation of all values involves an intensification of our values to ourselves and others; that ethics is reborn under postmodernity precisely in so far as overarching moralities and vocabularies of virtue have been left behind.

The problem is that both these kinds of account – whether that of MacIntyre or Bauman – seem to over-dramatize the present situation. Instead of seeking to locate the specificity of the present they turn modernity into an either/or situation; either today's world presents the possibility of ethics, or it does not. But perhaps all that is different is not so much the rise or decline of the possibility of ethics, but rather the growth in importance of discourses about ethics; in other words, discourses that problematize the very characteristics of freedom, contingency and choice. In fact, it is difficult to resist the conclusion that the current obsession with everything ethical is itself what has produced the demand for philosophical sociologies which bemoan the fact of our moral decline. Perhaps it is even our ethical obsession that makes us feel we are no longer moral.

A properly critical attitude to enlightenment would be somewhat different again; which is a good thing if only in that it helps us to bypass this impasse, to find a way of escape from it. It does so in part because of what it avoids rather than what it embraces. For my intention in using the vocabulary of ethics here has not been so as to join the decisionist bandwaggon by saying that ethics is all, in effect, that we have left. It is rather to isolate the ethical dimension that is the background to all our coherent human activities, including those associated with the pursuit of truth. That means that a critique of enlightenment would be completely useless in formulating any kind of ethical *theory*. It is more deliberately artificial than the grandiose projects of a MacIntyre or a Bauman in that it is concerned not with a general diagnosis of the possibility of ethics in the present; but with, so to speak, acting directly on our ethical propensities. This is not a discourse *about* ethics, but an ethical form of discourse in its own right; one which takes its task to be to stretch the limits of what it is possible to think, not in the interest of this or that project of enlightenment or reform, but in the interests of an exercise in judgement itself.

Above all, a critical analytics of enlightenment attempts to open up a space for thinking of something even as important as truth in an ethical way. What such an enterprise involves cannot be stated in advance of actual studies; that no doubt is why doyens of the critique of enlightenment, such as Weber or Foucault, preferred to work with empirical material rather than in abstract reconstructions or reflections, or through philosophy in any orthodox sense. This concern obviously has nothing to do with rationalist understandings of truth, but nor is it a postmodern critique of the very idea of truth. We cannot just step outside of truth, and postmodernism really is ridiculous in so far as it attempts to do just that. As Malpas insists: "to reject talk of *truth* in favour of talk of a multiplicity of competing *truths* is already to have misunderstood the very demand that truth places upon us that makes it such a powerful notion to begin with" (Malpas 1996: 161). Truth would not be worthwhile if it were not something of an ordeal; and it is the fact that truth is an ordeal that leads to the requirement that we should bring the question of ethics to bear on something so precious as truth.

Social theory again

Finally, I want to reiterate that the idea of a critical attitude to enlightenment is not something that has been invented recently. It has not required any "last men" or the revaluation of all values to bring it into glittering existence. Nor is it intrinsically subversive in relation to its neighbouring disciplines. The whole point is rather that much of what we do in the social sciences and sociology is quite worthwhile, and people should be far less ashamed of those disciplines than the reflections of "theory" often make them feel. In an equally deflationary spirit my contention is that the critique of enlightenment is something that people in all sorts of different fields have been doing all along; even that it is a practice that is internal to practices of enlightenment themselves. Social theory, then, should not be regarded as the only place where the critique of enlightenment is possible; but it might be the place where it is conducted as a generalism: where a critical attitude to enlightenment attempts to take most thoroughgoing cognisance of itself.

Such a social theory would be like a "third way" between realist or rationalist fideism and postmodernism. A plague on both their houses. We are repeatedly told by both traditions of thought that there is a crisis in Western reason; that reason itself has collapsed in ruins. The problem is that all too often the progress of reason has been assimilated – by both strands of thought – to something quite different: the model of rationalism. It is certainly the case that as an ethic of reason, rationalism has no future; but then the influence of rationalism since the enlightenment has been vastly overstated. Rationalism was really a pre-Enlightenment and then a post-Enlightenment discourse, and we owe to the Enlightenment itself a very different model of reason, even on something like an ethical model. In this context, the fury of our current debates over truth is only testimony to the *persistence* of enlightenment, not to its demise. So perhaps our practices of reason are not so out of order as we might think; maybe it is only our practices of interpretation with regard to those practices that still leave something to be desired.

Bibliography

Abbott, A. 1988. *The system of professions*. Chicago: Chicago University Press.

Abercrombie, N. & J. Urry 1983. *Capital, labour and the middle classes*. London: Allen & Unwin.

Adams, P. 1996. The violence of paint. In *The emptiness of the image: psychoanalysis and sexual differences*. London: Routledge.

Adorno, T. 1984. *Aesthetic theory*. Oxford: Blackwell.

Adorno, T. & M. Horkheimer 1986. *Dialectic of enlightenment* (1947). London: Verso.

Aglietta, M. 1987. *A theory of capitalist regulation: the US experience*, trans. D. Fernbach. London: Verso.

Airaksinen, T. 1994. Service and science in professional life. In *Ethics and professions*. R. Chadwick (ed.) Aldershot: Avebury Press.

Althusser, L. 1984. A letter on art in reply to André Daspré (1966). In *Essays on ideology*. London: Verso.

Anderson, P. 1992a. Components of the national culture (1968). In *English questions*. London: Verso.

Anderson, P. 1992b. A culture in contraflow. In *English questions*. London: Verso.

Anscombe, G. 1966. *Intention*. New York: Cornell University Press.

Bachelard, G. 1984. *The new scientific spirit* (1934), trans. A. Goldhammer. Boston: Beacon Press.

Bacon, F. 1870. On the dignity and advancement of learning, Books II–VI (1640). In *The Works of Sir Francis Bacon*. vol. IV, J. Spedding, R.L. Ellis & D.D. Heath (eds). London: Longman.

Baker, K. 1975. *Condorcet: from natural philosophy to social mathematics*. Chicago: Chicago University Press.

Bakhtin, M. 1986. The problem of speech genres (1952–3). In *Speech genres and other late essays*, trans. V.W. McGee. Texas: University of Texas Press.

Barry, A. 1993. Television, truth and democracy. *Media, Culture and Society* **15**, 487–96.

Baudelaire, 1992. The painter of modern life (1863), trans. P.E. Charvet. In *Selected writings on art and literature*. Harmondsworth: Penguin Books.

Bauman, Z. 1976. *Socialism: the active utopia*. London: Allen & Unwin.

Bauman, Z. 1986. *Modernity and the holocaust*. Oxford: Blackwell.

Bauman, Z. 1987. *Legislators and interpreters; on modernity, post-modernity and intellectuals*. Cambridge: Polity Press.

Bauman, Z. 1991. *Modernity and ambivalence*. Cambridge: Polity Press.

Bauman, Z. 1992a. *Intimations of postmodernity*. London: Routledge.

Bauman, Z. 1992b. *Postmodern ethics*. Oxford: Blackwell.

Baxandall, M. 1972. *Painting and experience in fifteenth-century Italy*. Oxford: Oxford University Press.

Baxandall, M. 1985. *Patterns of intention: on the historical explanation of pictures*. New Haven: Yale University Press.

Bell, D. 1973. *The coming of the post-industrial society*. New York: Basic Books.

Bell, D. 1980. The social framework of the information society. In *The microelectronics revolution*. T. Forester (ed.). Oxford: Blackwell.

Bell, V. 1994. Dreaming and time in Foucault's philosophy. *Theory, Culture and Society* **11**. 151–63.

Bell, V. 1996. Bio-politics and the spectre of incest. In *Global modernities*. M. Featherstone & S. Lash (eds). London: Sage.

Berger, J. 1972. *Ways of seeing*. London: BBC Books.

Berger, P. 1965. Towards a sociological understanding of psychoanalysis. *Social research* **32** (1), 26–41.

Blumenberg, H. 1983. *The legitimacy of the modern age* (1966), trans. R.M. Wallace. Cambridge, Mass.: MIT Press.

Born, G. 1995. *Rationalising culture: IRCAM, Boulez and the musical avant-garde*. California: University of California Press.

Boschetti, A. 1989. *The intellectual enterprise: Sartre and "Les Temps Modernes"*, trans. R. McCleary. Evanston: Northwestern University Press.

Bourdieu, P. 1971. Intellectual field and creative project. In *Knowledge and control: new directions in the sociology of education*. M.F.D. Young (ed.). London: Collier-Macmillan.

Bourdieu, P. 1986. *Distinction: a social critique of the judgement of taste*, trans. R. Nice. London: RKP.

Bourdieu, P. 1988. *Homo academicus*, trans. P. Collier. Cambridge: Polity Press.

Bourdieu, P. 1991. *The love of art*, trans. C. Beattie and N. Merriman. Cambridge: Polity Press.

Bourdieu, P. 1993. *The field of cultural reproduction*, trans. R. Johnson. Cambridge: Polity Press.

Bourdieu, P. 1995. *The rules of art: genesis and structure of the literary field*, trans. S. Emanuel. Cambridge: Polity Press.

Bourdieu, P. & H. Haacke 1995. *Free exchange*. Cambridge: Polity Press.

Bowness, A. 1971. Conversations with Barbara Hepworth. In *The complete sculpture of Barbara Hepworth 1960–1969*. A. Bowness (ed.). London: Lund Humphries.

Boyle, R. 1772. A free enquiry into the received notion of nature (1686). In *The works of the honourable Robert Boyle in six volumes*. T. Birch (ed.). London.

Breuer, J. & S. Freud 1953. Studies in hysteria. In *Standard edition of the collected works of Sigmund Freud*. London: Hogarth Press, vol. 2.

Brubaker, R. 1984. *The limits of rationality: an essay on the social and moral thought of Max Weber*. London: Allen & Unwin.

Burchell, G. 1993. Liberal government and techniques of the self. *Economy and Society* **22** (3), 267–82.

Burchell, G., C. Gordon, & P. Miller (eds) 1991. *The Foucault effect*. Hemel Hempstead: Harverster-Wheatsheaf.

Bürger, P. 1984. *The theory of the avant-garde*. Manchester: Manchester University Press.

Burrow, J. 1981. *A liberal descent: Victorian historians and the English past*. Cambridge, Cambridge University Press.

Butterfield, H. 1950. *The Whig interpretation of history* (1931). London: Bell.

Callon, M. 1986. Some elements of a sociology of translation: domestication of the scallops and the fishermen of St. Brieuc bay. In *Power, action and belief*. J. Law (ed.). London: Routledge.

Callon, M. & B. Latour 1981. Unscrewing the big Leviathan: how actors macro-structure social reality and how sociologists help them. In *Advances in social theory and methodology: toward an integration of micro- and macro-sociologies*. K. Knorr-Cetina & A. Cicourel (eds). London: Routledge.

Campbell, C. 1987 *The Protestant ethic and the spirit of modern consumerism*. Oxford: Blackwell.

Canguilhem, G. 1968. *Etudes d'histoire et de philosophie des sciences*. Paris: Vrin.

Canguilhem, G. 1980. What is psychology? trans. H. Davies. *I&C*, 7. 37–50.

Canguilhem, G. 1988. *Ideology and rationality in the history of the life sciences*, trans. A. Goldhammer. Cambridge, Mass.: MIT Press.

Canguilhem, G. 1989. *The normal and the pathological* (1944/1966), trans. C. Fawcett. New York: Zone Books.

Carrithers, M., S. Collins, S. Lukes (eds) 1985. *The category of the person: anthropology, philosophy, history*. Cambridge: Cambridge University Press.

Cassirer, E. 1951. *The philosophy of the enlightenment*, trans. F. Koelln & J. Pettegrove. New Jersey: Princeton University Press.

Castel, R. 1973. *Le psychanalysme*. Paris: Maspero.

Castel, R. 1985. Moral treatment: mental therapy and social control. In *Social control and the state*. P. Cohen & A. Scull (eds). Oxford: Blackwell.

Cavell, S. 1979. *The claim of reason: Wittgenstein, morality, and tragedy*. Oxford: Clarendon Press.

Clark, J.C.D. 1985. *English society, 1688–1832*. Cambridge: Cambridge University Press.

Collini, S. 1991. *Public moralists: political thought and intellectual life in Britain 1850–1930*. Cambridge: Cambridge University Press.

Collins, H.M. & S. Yearley 1992. Epistemological chicken. In *Science as practice and as culture*. A. Pickering (ed.). Chicago: University of Chicago Press.

Collins, R. 1979. *The credential society: an historical sociology of education and stratification*. New York: Academic Press.

Coser, L. 1965. *Men of ideas*. New York: Free Press.

Crawford, T. Hugh 1993. An interview with Bruno Latour. *Configurations* 1 (2), 247–68.

Danto, A.C. 1964. The artworld. *Journal of Philosophy*, **LXI** (17), 571–84.

Danziger, K. 1990. *Constructing the subject: historical origins of psychological research*. Cambridge: Cambridge University Press.

Darnton, R. 1987. The facts of literary life in eighteenth century France. In *The political culture of the old regime*. K.M. Baker (ed.). Oxford: Pergamon Press.

de Swaan, A. 1990. *The management of normality: critical essays in health and welfare*. London: Routledge.

Dean, M. 1994. *Critical and effective histories*. London: Routledge.

Debray, R. 1981. *Teachers, writers, celebrities: the intellectuals of modern France*, trans. D. Macey. London: Verso.

Deleuze, G. 1981. *Francis Bacon. Logique de la sensation.* Paris: editions de la différance.

Deleuze, G. 1988. *Foucault,* trans. S. Hand. Minnesota: University of Minnesota Press.

Deleuze, G. 1990. *Pourparlers.* Paris: Minuit.

Deleuze, G. 1992. Mediators. In *Incorporations.* J. Crary & S. Kwinter (eds). New York: Zone (see also Deleuze 1990).

Deleuze, G. & F. Guattari 1991. *What is philosophy?* trans. H. Tomlinson & G. Burchell. New York: Columbia University Press.

Deleuze, G. & C. Parnet 1987. *Dialogues.* trans. H. Tomlinson & B. Habberjam. London: Athlone Press.

Derrida, J. 1987. *The truth in painting,* trans. G. Bennington and I. McLeod. Chicago: Chicago University Press.

Dews, P. 1987. *Logics of disintegration: poststructuralist thought and the claims of critical theory.* London: Verso.

Douglas, M. & D. Hull (eds) 1992. *How classification works: Nelson Goodman among the social sciences.* Edinburgh: Edinburgh University Press.

Dreyfus, H. 1991. *Being-in-the-world.* Berkeley: University of California Press.

Durkheim, E. 1973 *Moral education: a study in the theory and application of the sociology of education* (1925), trans. E.K. Wilson & H. Schnurer. New York: Free Press.

Eagleton, T. 1990. *The ideology of the aesthetic.* Oxford: Blackwell.

Eagleton, T. 1995. *Heathcliffe and the great hunger.* London: Verso.

Eagleton, T. 1996. *The illusions of postmodernism.* Oxford: Blackwell.

Edelman, M. 1984. The political language of the helping professions. In *Language and politics.* M. J. Shapiro (ed.). New York: New York University Press.

Eley, G. & K. Nield 1995. Starting over: the present, the post-modern and the moment of social history. *Social History* **20**, 355–65.

Elias, N. 1978. *Involvement and detachment,* trans. E. Jephcott, Oxford: Blackwell.

Elias, N. 1983. *The court society,* trans. E. Jephcott, Oxford: Blackwell.

Elias, N. 1994. *Mozart: portrait of a genius,* trans. E. Jephcott. Cambridge: Polity Press.

Elliot, P. 1972. *The sociology of the professions.* London: Macmillan.

Elster, J. 1983. *Sour grapes.* Cambridge: Cambridge University Press.

Elster, J. 1993. *Political psychology.* Cambridge: Cambridge University Press.

Epictetus (ed.) 1928. *Discourses.* Book 2, trans. W.A. Oldfather. London: Heinemann.

Eyerman, R. 1994. *Between culture and politics: intellectuals in modern society.* Cambridge: Polity Press.

Farson, D. 1993. *The gilded gutter life of Francis Bacon.* London: Vintage.

Feyerabend, P. 1974. *Against method.* London: Verso.

Fleck, L. 1979. *The genesis and development of a scientific fact* (1935), trans. F. Bradley & T. J. Trenn. Chicago: University of Chicago Press.

Flynn, T. 1988. Foucault as parrhesiast: his last course at the Collège de France. In *The final Foucault.* J. Bernauer and D. Rasmussen (eds). Cambridge, Mass.: MIT Press.

Focillon, H. 1992. *The life of forms in art* (1934). New York: Zone.

Forester, T. 1985. *The information technology revolution.* Oxford: Blackwell.

Foucault, M. 1971. *Madness and civilisation* (1961). Harmondsworth: Penguin Books.

Foucault, M. 1976. *The history of sexuality, volume 1: an introduction,* trans. R. Hurley. Harmondsworth: Penguin Books.

Foucault, M. 1979. *Discipline and punish: the birth of the prison,* trans. A. Sheridan. Harmondsworth: Peregrine Books.

Foucault, M. 1984a. What is enlightenment? In *The Foucault reader*. P. Rabinow (ed.). Harmondsworth: Peregrine Books.

Foucault, M. 1984b. On the genealogy of ethics. In *The Foucault reader*. P. Rabinow (ed.). Harmondsworth: Peregrine Books.

Foucault, M. 1984c. What is an author? In *The Foucault reader*. P. Rabinow (ed.). Harmondsworth: Penguin Books.

Foucault, M. 1984d. À propos de la généalogie de l'éthique: un aperçu du travail en cours. See Foucault (1994), volume 4.

Foucault, M. 1986. *The use of pleasure*, trans. R. Hurley. Harmondsworth: Viking.

Foucault, M. 1988. The minimalist self. In *Michel Foucault: politics, philosophy, culture*. L. Kritzman (ed.). London: Routledge.

Foucault, M. 1989. An aesthetics of existence. In *Foucault live*. New York: Semiotext(e).

Foucault, M. 1991a. Governmentality. See G. Burchell, C. Gordon, P. Miller (1991).

Foucault, M. 1991b. Questions of method. See G. Burchell, C. Gordon, P. Miller 1991.

Foucault, M. 1994. *Dits et ecrits*. 4 volumes. Paris: Gallimard.

Foucault, M. 1996. What is critique? (1978), trans. K.P. Geiman. In *What is enlightenment? Eighteenth-century questions and twentieth-century answers*. J. Schmidt (ed.). Berkeley: University of California Press.

Freidson, E. 1970. *Professional dominance*. New York: Atherton Press.

Freidson, E. 1986. *Professional powers: a study of the institutionalization of professional knowledge*. New York: Dodd, Mead.

Frisby, D. 1985. *Fragments of modernity*. Cambridge: Polity Press.

Fukuyama, F. 1990. *The end of history and the last man*. Harmondsworth: Penguin Books.

Fukuyama, F. 1996 *Trust*. Harmondsworth: Penguin Books.

Fuller, S. 1992. Social epistemology and the research agenda of science studies. In *Science as practice and culture*. A. Pickering (ed.). Chicago: University of Chicago Press.

Gaukroger, S. 1995. *Descartes: an intellectual biography*. Oxford: Clarendon Press.

Gay, P. 1966. *The Enlightenment: an interpretation: vol. I*. New York: Vintage.

Gay, P. 1972. *The Enlightenment: an interpretation: vol. II: the science of freedom*. London: Wildwood.

Geertz, C. 1983. *Local knowledge*. New York: Basic Books.

Gella, A. (ed.) 1976. *The intelligentsia and the intellectuals: theory, method and case study*. London: Sage.

Gellner, E. 1974. *Legitimation of belief*. Cambridge: Cambridge University Press.

Gellner, E. 1985. *The psychoanalytic movement*. London: Paladin.

Gellner, E. 1988. *Plough, sword and book*. London: Collins.

Gellner, E. 1990. La trahison de la trahison des clercs. In *The political responsibility of intellectuals*. I. MacLean, A. Montefiore, P. Winch (eds). Cambridge: Cambridge University Press.

Gellner, E. 1992a. *Reason and culture: the historic role of rationality and rationalism*. Oxford: Blackwell.

Gellner, E. 1992b. *Postmodernism, reason and religion*. London: Routledge.

Giddens, A. 1991a. *The consequences of modernity*. Cambridge: Polity Press.

Giddens, A. 1991b. *Modernity and self-identity: self and society in the late modern age*. Cambridge: Polity Press.

Godelier, M. 1986. *The mental and the material: thought, economy, society*, trans. M. Thom. London: Verso.

Goldman, H. 1988. *Max Weber and Thomas Mann: calling and the shaping of the self*. Berkeley: University of California Press.

Goody, J. 1977. *The domestication of the savage mind*. Cambridge: Cambridge University Press.

Gordon, C. 1986a. Question, ethos, event: Foucault on Kant and enlightenment. *Economy and Society* **15** (1), 71–87.

Gordon, C. 1986b. Foucault en Angleterre. *Critique*, **471–2**, 826–40.

Gordon, C. 1987. The soul of the citizen: Max Weber and Michel Foucault on rationalities of government. In *Max Weber, rationality and modernity*. S. Lash & S. Whimster (eds). London: Allen & Unwin.

Gordon, C. 1991. Governmental rationality: an introduction. See G. Burchell, C. Gordon, P. Miller (eds) (1996).

Gouldner, A. 1979. *The future of intellectuals and the rise of the new class*. London: Macmillan.

Gramsci, A. 1971. *Selections from prison notebooks (1929–1935)*. London: Lawrence & Wishart.

Granet, M. 1975. *The religion of the Chinese people* (1922), trans. M. Freedman. Oxford: Blackwell.

Gray, J. 1995. *Enlightenment's WAKE: politics and culture at the close of the modern age*. London: Routledge.

Gray, J. 1997. *Endgames: questions in late modern political thought*. Cambridge: Polity Press.

Green, M. 1974. *The von Richtofen sisters: the triumphant and the tragic modes of love*. London: Weidenfeld.

Greenberg, C. 1965. Modernist painting. *Art and Literature*, **4**, 193–201.

Gross, P. & N. Levitt 1994. *Higher superstition: the academic left and its quarrels with science*. Baltimore: Johns Hopkins.

Guyau, J.-M. 1898. *A sketch of morality independent of obligation or sanction*, trans. G. Kapteyn. London: Watts.

Habermas, J. 1985. Modernity – an incomplete project. In *Postmodern culture*. H. Foster (ed.) London: Pluto.

Habermas, J. 1987a. *The philosophical discourse of modernity*, trans. T. McCarthy. Cambridge: Polity Press.

Habermas, J. 1987b. *The theory of communicative action: vol. 2. Lifeworld and system; a critique of functionalist reason*, trans. T. McCarthy. Boston: Beacon Press.

Hacking, I. 1982. Language, truth and reason. In *Rationality and relativism*. S. Lukes & M. Hollis (eds). Oxford: Blackwell.

Hacking, I 1983a. *Representing and intervening: introductory topics in the philosophy of natural science*. Cambridge: Cambridge University Press.

Hacking, I. 1983b The accumulation of styles of scientific reasoning. In *Kant oder Hegel? Uber formen der Begrundung in der Philosophie*. D. Henrich (ed.). Stuttgart: Klett-Cotta.

Hacking, I. 1986. Making up people. In *Reconstructing individualism*. T.C. Heller, M. Sosna, D. Wellsemy (eds). Stanford: Stanford University Press.

Hacking, I. 1988. The participant irrealist at large in the laboratory. *British Journal of the Philosophy of Science* **39**, 277–94.

Hacking, I. 1990. *The taming of chance*. Cambridge: Cambridge University Press.

Hacking, I. 1992a. The self-vindication of the laboratory sciences. In *Science as practice and culture*. A. Pickering (ed.). Chicago: University of Chicago Press.

Hacking, I. 1992b. Statistical language, statistical truth and statistical reason. In *The social dimensions of science*. E. McMullin (ed.). Indiana: University of Notre Dame Press.

Hacking, I. 1992c. World-making by kind-making: child abuse for example. In *How classification works: Nelson Goodman among the social sciences*. M. Douglas & D. Hull (eds). Edinburgh: Edinburgh University Press.

Hacking, I. 1995a. *Re-writing the soul*. Harvard: Harvard University Press.

Hacking, I. 1995b. The looping effects of human kinds. In *Causal cognition: a multidisciplinary debate*. D. Sperber, D. Premack, A. James Premack. Oxford: Clarendon Press.

Hadot, P. 1995. *Philosophy as a way of life, spiritual exercises from Socrates to Foucault*, trans. M. Chase. Oxford: Blackwell.

Hall, J.A. 1979. The curious case of the British intelligentsia. *British Journal of Sociology* **30** (3), 291–306.

Hall, J.A. 1985. The intellectuals as new class: reflections on Britain. *Culture, Education and Society* **39** (3), 206–20.

Halmos, P. 1979. *The faith of the counsellors*. London: Macmillan.

Halsey, A.H. 1965. Universities in advanced society. In *Readings in economic sociology*. N.J. Smelser (ed.). New Jersey: Prentice Hall.

Hamilton, P. 1996. The Enlightenment and the birth of social science. In *Modernity: an introduction to modern societies*. S. Hall, D. Held, D. Hubert, K. Thompson (eds). Oxford: Blackwell.

Hampson, N. 1968. *The Enlightenment*. Harmondsworth: Penguin Books.

Hankins, T. 1970. *Jean d'Alembert: science and the enlightenment*. Oxford: Clarendon Press.

Harré, R. 1983. *An introduction to the logic of the sciences*, 2nd edn. London: Macmillan.

Harris, N. 1994. Professional codes and Kantian duties. In *Ethics and the professions*. R. Chadwick (ed.). Aldershot: Avebury Press.

Harvie, C. 1976. *The lights of liberalism: university liberals and the challenge of democracy 1860–1886*. London: Allen Lane.

Havel, V. 1986. *Living in truth* (ed. J. Vladislaw). London: Faber.

Heidegger, M. 1966. *Discourse on thinking* (1959), trans. J.M. Anderson and E.H. Freund. New York: Harper & Row.

Heidegger, M. 1975. The origin of the work of art. In *Poetry, language, thought*, trans. A. Hofstadter. New York: Harper & Row.

Heidegger, M. 1977. The age of the world picture (1938). In *The question concerning technology and other essays*, trans. W. Lovitt. New York: Harper & Row.

Heidegger, M. 1981. *Nietzsche, volume one: the will to power as art*, trans. D. Farrell Krell. London: RKP.

Heilbron, J. 1995. *The rise of social theory*, trans. S. Gogol. Cambridge: Polity Press.

Hennis, W. 1988. *Max Weber: essays in reconstruction*, trans. K. Tribe. London: Allen & Unwin.

Hennis, W. 1991. The pitiless 'sobriety of judgement': Max Weber between Carl Menger and Gustav von Schmoller – the academic politics of value freedom. *History of the Human Sciences* **4** (1), 27–59.

Hennis, W. 1996. *Max Weber's Wissenschaft vom Menschen: neue studien zur biographie des werks*. Tubingen: Mohr.

Heyck, T.W. 1982. *The transformation of intellectual life in Victorian England*. London: Croom Helm.

Heyck, T.W. 1987. The idea of a university in Britain, 1870–1970. *History of European Ideas* **8** (2), 205–19.

Hindess, B. 1987. Rationality and the characterization of modern society. In *Max Weber, rationality and modernity*. S. Lash & S. Whimster (eds). London: Allen & Unwin.

Hirst, P. 1989. Endism. *London Review of Books* **23**, November 14.

Hirst, P. 1995. Is the university the enemy of ideas?, published as: Education and the production of new ideas. *AA Files* (annals of the Architectural Association of School of Architecture) **29**, 44–9.

Honigsheim, P. 1968. *On Max Weber*, trans. J. Rytina. New York: Free Press.

Honneth, A. & H. Joas 1988. *Social action and human nature*, trans. R. Meyer. Cambridge: Cambridge University Press.

Hookway, C. 1995. Fallibilism and objectivity: science and ethics. In *World, mind and ethics: essays on the ethical philosophy of Bernard Williams*. J.E.J. Altham & R. Harrison (eds). Cambridge: Cambridge University Press.

Hoy, D. & T. McCarthy 1994. *Critical theory*. Oxford: Blackwell.

Hulme, P. & L. Jordanova (eds) 1990. *The Enlightenment and its shadows*. London: Routledge.

Hunter, I. 1988. *Culture and government: the emergence of literary education*. London: Macmillan.

Hunter, I. 1990. Personality as a vocation: the political rationality of the humanities. *Economy and Society* **19** (4), 391–430.

Huxley, T.H. 1925. A liberal education and where to find it (1868). In *Science and education (collected essays, vol. III)*. London: Macmillan.

Illich, I. 1976. *Medical nemesis*. London: Calder & Boyers.

Inkster, I. 1991. *Science and technology in history: an approach to industrial development*. London: Macmillan Education.

Irwin, A. 1995. *Citizen science: a study of people, expertise and sustainable development*. London: Routledge.

Jacob, J. 1988. *Doctors and rules: a sociology of professional values*. London: Routledge.

Jamous, H. & B. Pelloile 1970. Professions or self-perpetuating systems? Changes in the French university-hospital system. In *Professions and professionalization*. J.A. Jackson (ed.). Cambridge: Cambridge University Press.

Johnson, R.V. 1969. *Aestheticism*. London: Methuen.

Johnson, T. 1972. *Professions and power*. London: Macmillan.

Kamper, D. 1973. *Geschichte und menschliche Natur: Die Tragweite gegenwärtiger Anthropologiekritik*. Munich: Hauser.

Kant, I. 1970. An answer to the question: 'What is enlightenment?' (1784). In *Political writings*, trans. H.B. Nisbet, H. Reiss (ed.). Cambridge: Cambridge University Press.

Kant, I. 1978. *Anthropology from a pragmatic point of view* (1798), trans. V.L. Dawdell. London: Feffer & Simons.

Kelly, M. (ed.) 1994. *Critique and power: re-casting the Foucault–Habermas debate*. Cambridge, Mass.: MIT Press.

Kendall, T. & N. Crossley, 1996. Governing love: on the tactical control of counter-transference in the psychoanalytic community. *Economy and Society* 25 (2), 178–94.

Khilnani, S. 1993. *Arguing revolution: the intellectual left in post-war France*. New Haven: Yale University Press.

Kirk, N. 1994. History, languages, ideas and post-modernism: a materialist view. *Social history* 19, 21–41.

Kneymeyer, F.-L. 1980. Polizei. *Economy and Society* 9 (2), 172–96.

Kuhn, T. 1979. *The essential tension*. Chicago: University of Chicago Press.

Kumar, K. 1979. *Prophecy and progress*: Harmondsworth: Pelican Books.

Kuspit, D. 1993. *The cult of the avant-garde artist*. Cambridge: Cambridge University Press.

Larson, M.G. 1984. The production of expertise and the constitution of expert power. In *The authority of experts: studies in history and theory*. T.L. Haskell (ed.). Bloomington: Indiana.

Larson, M.G. 1991. *The rise of professionalisation*. Cambridge: Cambridge University Press.

Lassman, P. & I. Velody 1989. Science, disenchantment and the search for meaning. In *Max Weber on 'science as a vocation'*. P. Lassman and I. Velody (eds). London: Unwin Hyman.

Latour, B. 1986.Visualisation and cognition: thinking with eyes and hands. In *Knowledge and society, vol. 6*. H. Kuchlick (ed.). Greenwich: JAI Press.

Latour, B. 1987. *Science in action*. Harvard: University of Harvard Press.

Latour, B. 1988a. *The pasteurization of France*, trans. A. Sheridan & J. Law. Cambridge, Mass.: Harvard University Press.

Latour, B. 1988b. The politics of explanation. In *Knowledge and reflexivity: new frontiers in the sociology of knowledge*. S. Woolgar (ed.). London: Sage.

Latour, B. 1992. One more turn after the social turn. In *The social dimensions of science*. E. McMullin (ed.). Notre Dame: University of Notre Dame Press.

Latour, B. 1993a. *We have never been modern*, trans. C. Porter. Hemel Hempstead: Harvester-Wheatsheaf.

Latour, B. 1993b. Pasteur on lactic acid yeast: a partial semiotic analysis. *Configurations* 1 (1), 129–46.

Latour, B. 1996. *Aramis, or the love of technology*. Cambridge, Mass.: Harvard University Press.

Latour, B. & S. Woolgar 1979. *Laboratory life: the construction of scientific facts*. Princeton, NJ: Princeton University Press.

Lawson, H. & L. Appignanesi (eds). 1989. *Dismantling truth*. New York: Weidenfeld & Nicholson.

Lipietz, A. 1987. *Mirages and miracles: the crisis of global fordism*, trans. D. Macey. London: Verso.

Lovibond, S. 1983. *Realism and imagination in ethics*. Oxford: Blackwell.

Lynch, M. 1984. *Art and artifact in laboratory science; a study of shop work and shop talk in a research laboratory*. London: Routledge RKP.

Lynch, M. & S. Woolgar (eds) 1988. *Representation in scientific practice*. Cambridge, Mass.: MIT Press.

Lyon, D. 1986. From postmodernism to the information society. *Sociology*. 20, 577–88.

Lyotard, J.-F. 1984a. *The postmodern condition: a report on knowledge*, trans. G. Bennington & B. Massumi. Manchester: Manchester University Press.

Lyotard, J.-F. 1984b. The sublime and the avant-garde. *Art forum.* **22**, 36–43.

Lyotard, J.-F. 1992. *The postmodern explained to children.* London: Turnaround.

Lyotard, J.-F. & J.-L. Thébaud 1985. *Just gaming.* Manchester: Manchester University Press.

McCormack, W. J. 1994. *From Burke to Beckett: ascendancy, tradition and betrayal in literary history.* Cork: Cork University Press.

Macey, D. 1995. Michel Foucault; *J'accuse. New Formations* **25**, 5–13.

Machlup, F. 1962. *The production and distribution of knowledge in the United States.* Princeton, NJ: Princeton University Press.

Machlup, F. 1981. *Knowledge and knowledge production.* Princeton, NJ: Princeton University Press.

Mackenzie, D. 1981. *Statistics in Britain, 1865–1930.* Edinburgh: Edinburgh University Press.

MacIntyre, A. 1981. *After virtue: a study in moral theory.* London: Duckworth.

MacIntyre, A. 1990. *Three rival versions of moral enquiry.* London: Duckworth.

Maffesoli, M. 1985. Le paradigme esthétique: la sociologie comme art. *Sociologie et sociétés* **XVII**, 33–9.

Malpas, J. 1996. Speaking the truth. *Economy and Society* **25** (2), 156–77.

Mannheim, K. 1936. *Ideology and utopia: an introduction to the sociology of knowledge*, trans. L. Wirth & E. Shils. New York: Harcourt & Brace.

Martin, L., H. Gutman, P. Hutton (eds) 1988. *Technologies of the self.* London: Tavistock.

Marx, K. & F. Engels 1976. *The German ideology* (1846), in *Collected works.* vol. 5. London: Lawrence & Wishart.

Merton, R.K. 1968. Science and democratic social structure (1942). In *Social theory and social structure.* New York: Free Press.

Mill, J.S. 1980. On genius (1832). In *The collected works of J.S. Mill*, volume one. J.M. Robson & J. Stichinger (eds). Toronto: Routledge & Kegan Paul.

Mill, J.S. 1992. *On liberty* (1859). London: Everyman.

Miller, P. & N. Rose 1988. The Tavistock programme: the government of subjectivity and social life. *Sociology* **22**, 171–92.

Miller, P. & N. Rose 1994. On therapeutic authority: psychoanalytic expertise under advanced liberalism. *History of the Human Sciences* **7** (3), 29–64.

Mills, C.W. 1963. Situated actions and vocabularies of motive (1940). In *Power, politics and people.* New York: Oxford University Press.

Mommsen, W. 1987. Personal conduct and social change. See S. Lash & S. Whimster (eds) *Max Weber, Rationality and Modernity.* London: Allen & Unwin.

Montefiore, A. 1990. The political responsibility of intellectuals. In *The political responsibility of intellectuals.* I. MacLean, A. Montefiore, P. Winch (eds). Cambridge: Cambridge University Press.

Munro, D. J. 1988. *Images of human nature: a Sung portrait.* Princeton: Princeton University Press.

Nietzsche, F. 1969. *Genealogy of morals* (1888), trans. W. Kaufmann. New York: Vintage.

Nietzsche, F. 1974. *The gay science* (1882/1887), trans. W. Kaufmann. New York: Vintage.

Nietzsche, F. 1983a. On the uses and disadvantages of history for life (1874). In

Untimely meditations, trans. R. J. Hollingdale. Cambridge: Cambridge University Press.

Nietzsche, F. 1983b. Schopenhauer as educator (1874). In *Untimely mediations*, trans. R. J. Holingdale. Cambridge: Cambridge University Press.

Norris, C. 1996. *Reclaiming truth: contribution to a critique of cultural relativism*. London: Lawrence & Wishart.

OECD 1989. *Science and technology indicators: report number 3*. Paris: OECD.

Oakeshott, M. 1989. *The voice of liberal learning*, T. Fuller (ed.). New Haven: Yale University Press.

Oestreich, W. 1982. *Neo-stoicism and the modern state*. Cambridge: Cambridge University Press.

Ong, W. J. 1982. *Orality and literacy: the technologizing of the word*. London: Methuen.

Outhwaite, W. 1987. *New philosophies of social science: realism, hermeneutics and critical theory*. London: Macmillan.

Owen, D. 1991. Autonomy and 'Inner Distance': a trace of Nietzsche in Weber. *History of the Human Sciences* 4 (1), 79–91.

Owen, D. 1994. *Maturity and modernity: Nietzsche, Weber, Foucault and the ambivalence of reason*. London: Routledge.

Owen, D. 1995. Genealogy as exemplary critique: reflections on Foucault and the imagination of the political. *Economy and Society* 24 (4), 489–506.

Owen, D. 1998. Nietzsche, Enlightenment and the problem of noble ethics. In *Nietzsche's futures*. J. Lippit (ed.). London: Macmillan.

Pasquino, P. 1986. Michel Foucault: the will to knowledge (1926–1984). *Economy and society* 15 (1), 97–109.

Peirce, C.S. 1992. *The essential Peirce: selected philosophical writings, volume one, 1867–1893*, N. Houser & C. Kloesel (eds). Indianapolis: Indiana University Press.

Peppiatt, M. 1996. *Francis Bacon: anatomy of an enigma*. London: Weidenfeld & Nicolson.

Perkin, H. 1989. *The rise of professional society: England since 1800*. London: Routledge.

Perkin, H. 1991. *Origins of modern English society* (1969). London: Routledge.

Phillipson, N. 1974. Culture and society in the eighteenth-century province: the case of Edinburgh and the Scottish Enlightenment. In *The University in society: volume II*, L. Stone (ed.). Princeton: Princeton University Press.

Phillipson, N. 1989. *Hume*. London: Weidenfeld & Nicolson.

Pocock, J.G.A. 1975. *The Machiavellian moment*. Princeton, NJ: Princeton University Press.

Pocock, J.G.A. 1980. Post-puritan England and the problem of enlightenment. In *Culture and politics from puritanism to the Enlightenment*. P. Zagorin (ed.). Berkeley: University of California Press.

Pocock, J.G.A. 1984. Verbalizing a political act: towards a politics of speech. In *Language and politics*, M. Shapiro (ed.). New York: New York University Press.

Podro, M. 1982. *The critical historians of art*. New Haven: Yale University Press.

Polanyi, M. 1946. *Science, faith and society*. London: Oxford University Press.

Porter, R. 1981. The Enlightenment in England. See Porter & Teich (1981).

Porter, T. & M. Teich (eds) 1981. *The Enlightenment in national context*. Cambridge, Cambridge University Press.

Poster, M. 1990. *The mode of information: post-structuralism and social context*. Cambridge: Polity Press.

Price, D. de Solla 1963. *Little science, big science.* New York: Columbia University Press.

Prigogine, I. & I. Stengers 1984. *Order out of chaos: man's new dialogue with nature.* London: Heinemann.

Rajchman, J. 1991. *Truth and eros.* London: Routledge.

Rieff. P. 1966. *The triumph of the therapeutic.* London: Chatto & Windus.

Rieff, P. 1983. The impossible culture. *Salmagundi* **58–9**, 406–26.

Rist, J.M. 1978. The Stoic concept of detachment. In *The Stoics.* J.M. Rist (ed.). Berkeley: University of California Press.

Rorty, R. 1989. *Contingency, irony and solidarity.* Cambridge: Cambridge University Press.

Rose, N. 1985. *The psychological complex: psychology, politics and society in England, 1869–1939.* London: RKP.

Rose, N. 1990. *Governing the soul: the shaping of the private self.* London: Routledge.

Rose, N. 1992a. *Towards a critical sociology of freedom.* London: Goldsmiths College.

Rose, N. 1992b. Governing the enterprising self. In *The values of the enterprise culture: the moral debate.* P. Heelas & P. Morris (eds). London: Routledge.

Rose, N. 1992c. Engineering the human soul: analyzing psychological expertise. *Science in Context* **5** (2), 351–69.

Rose, N. 1994. Expertise and the government of conduct. *Studies in Law, Politics and Society* **14**, 359–97.

Rose, N. 1996. *Inventing ourselves: psychology, power and personhood.* Cambridge: Cambridge University Press.

Rose, N. & P. Miller 1992. Political power beyond the state: problematics of government. *British Journal of Sociology* **43** (2), 172–205.

Ross, A. 1991. *Strange weather: culture, science and technology in the age of limits.* London: Verso.

Roth, G. 1978. Introduction. See Weber (1978).

Rothblatt, S. 1968. *The revolution of the dons: Cambridge and society in Victorian England.* London: Faber.

Ruas, C. 1986. An interview with Michel Foucault. In *Death and the labyrinth: the world of Raymond Roussel* (1963), trans. C. Ruas. New York: Doubleday.

Sartre, J.-P. 1948. *Existentialism and humanism* (1946), trans. P. Mairet. London: Methuen.

Sartre, J.-P. 1974. A plea for intellectuals. In *Between existentialism and Marxism*, trans. J. Matthews. London: New Left Books.

Scaff, L. 1989. *Fleeing the iron cage: culture, politics and modernity in the thought of Max Weber.* Berkeley: University of California Press.

Schaffer, S. 1988. Astronomers mark time: discipline and the personal equation. *Science in Context* **2** (1), 115–46.

Schalk, E. 1986. *From valour to pedigree: ideas of nobility in France in the sixteenth and seventeenth centuries.* Princeton: Princeton University Press.

Scheff, T. 1966. *Being mentally ill: a sociological theory.* London: Weidenfeld and Nicolson.

Schiller, F. 1967 *On the aesthetic education of man* (1795), trans. E. Wilkinson & L. A. Willoughby. Oxford: Clarendon Press.

Schluchter, W. 1979. The paradox of rationalization: on the relation of ethics and world. In *Max Weber's vision of history: ethics and methods*, G. Roth & W. Schluchter. Berkeley: University of California Press.

Schmitt, C. 1996. *The concept of the political* (1932), trans. J. Harvey Lomax. Chicago: University of Chicago Press.

Schroeder, R. 1991. 'Personality' and 'inner distance': the conception of the individual in Max Weber's sociology. *History of the Human Sciences* **4** (1), 61–78.

Schroeder, R. 1992. *Max Weber and the sociology of culture.* London: Sage.

Schroeder, R. 1995. Disenchantment and its discontents: Weberian perspectives on science and technology. *Sociological Review* **43** (2), 227–50.

Schucking, L.L. 1966. *The sociology of literary taste* (1931). London: Routledge & Kegan Paul.

Searle, J. 1995. *The construction of social reality.* Harmondsworth: Penguin Books.

Shapin, S. 1979. The politics of observation: cerebral anatomy and social interests in the Edinburgh phrenology disputes. In *On the margins of science: the social construction of rejected knowledge.* R. Wallis (ed.). London: Routledge.

Shapin, S. 1982. The history of science and its sociological reconstruction. *History of Science* **20**, 157–211.

Shapin, S. 1994. *The social history of truth: civility and science in seventeenth-century England.* Chicago: University of Chicago Press.

Shapin, S. & S. Schaffer 1985. *Leviathan and the air-pump: Hobbes, Boyle and the experimental life.* New Jersey: Princeton University Press.

Sinclair, A. 1993. *Francis Bacon: his life and violent times.* London: Sinclair-Stevenson.

Sloterdijk, P. 1987. *Critique of cynical reason*, trans. M. Eldred. Minneapolis: University of Minnesota Press.

Soffer, R. 1994. *Discipline and power: the university, history and the making of an English élite, 1870–1930.* Stanford: Stanford University Press.

Stedman Jones, G. 1972. History: the poverty of empiricism. In *Ideology in social science: readings in critical social theory,* R. Blackburn (ed.). London: Fontana.

Stehr, N. 1995. *Knowledge societies.* London: Sage.

Stubbs, W. 1887. *Seventeen lectures on the study of medieval and modern history and kindred subjects.* Oxford: Clarendon Press.

Sylvester, D. 1980. *Interviews with Francis Bacon, 1962–1979.* London: Thames & Hudson.

Taylor, C. 1985a. Introduction. In *Philosophy and the human sciences: philosophical papers,* vol. 2. Cambridge: Cambridge University Press.

Taylor, C. 1985b. Kant's theory of freedom. In *Philosophy and the human sciences: philosophical papers,* vol. 2. Cambridge: Cambridge University Press.

Taylor, C. 1989. *Sources of the self: the making of the modern identity.* Cambridge: Cambridge University Press.

Taylor, F.W. 1967. *The principles of scientific management* (1911). New York: Norton.

Tocqueville, A. 1969. *Democracy in America.* New York: Anchor.

Toulmin, S. 1990. *Cosmopolis: the hidden agenda of modernity.* Chicago: Chicago University Press.

Touraine, A. 1974. The post-industrial society, trans. L. Mayhew. London: Wildwood Press.

Turner, C. 1992. *Politics and modernity in the work of Max Weber.* London: Routledge.

Van Alphen, E. 1992. *Francis Bacon and the loss of self.* London: Reaktion.

Velody, I. 1981. Socialism as a sociological problem. In *Politics and social theory,* P. Lassman (ed.). London: Routledge.

Vernon, J. 1994. Who's afraid of the linguistic turn? The politics of social history and its discontents. *Social History* **19**, 81–97.

Veyne, P. 1976 *Le pain et le cirque*. Paris: Seuil. (Abridged (1990) as *Bread and circuses*. London: Allen Lane.)

Walzer, M. 1983. *Spheres of justice: a defense of pluralism and equality*. Oxford: Martin Robertson.

Watt, E.D. 1982. *Authority*. London: Croom Helm.

Weber, M. 1949. The meaning of 'ethical neutrality' (1917). In *The methodology of the social sciences*, E. Shils & H. Finch (eds and trans.). New York: Free Press.

Weber, M. 1962. *The religion of China; Confucianism and Taoism*, trans. H.H. Gerth. New York: Free Press.

Weber, M. 1973. The academic freedom of the universities (1909). In *Max Weber on universities: the power of the state and the dignity of the academic calling in Imperial Germany*, E. Shils (ed.). Chicago: University of Chicago Press.

Weber, M. 1978. *Economy and society* (1920), 2 vols. Berkeley: University of California Press.

Weber, M. 1991a. Science as a vocation (1919). In *From Max Weber*, H. Gerth & C.W. Mills (eds and trans.). London: Routledge

Weber, M. 1991b. Religious rejections of the world and their directions (1915). In *From Max Weber*, H. Gerth & C.W. Mills (eds and trans.). London: Routledge.

Weber, M. 1991c. National character and the Junkers (1921). In *From Max Weber*. London: Routledge.

Weber, M. 1992a. Introduction (1920). In *The Protestant ethic and the spirit of capitalism*, trans. T. Parsons. London: Allen & Unwin.

Weber, M. 1992b. *The Protestant ethic and the spirit of capitalism* (1905), trans. T. Parsons. London: Allen & Unwin.

Weber, M. 1994a. The nation state and economic policy (1895). In *Political writings*, trans. R. Spiers, P. Lassman (ed.). Cambridge: Cambridge University Press.

Weber, M. 1994b. The profession and vocation of politics (1919). In *Political writings*, trans. R. Spiers, P. Lassman (ed.). Cambridge: Cambridge University Press.

Weber, M. 1994c. On the situation of constitutional democracy in Russia (1906). In *Political writings*, trans. R. Spiers, P. Lassman (ed.). Cambridge: Cambridge University Press.

Webster, F. 1995. *Theories of the information society*. London: Routledge.

Weinberg, S. 1996. Sokal's Hoax. *The New York Review of Books*, 8 August, 11–14.

Williams, B. 1985. *Ethics and the limits of philosophy*. London: Fontana.

Williams, B. 1993. *Shame and necessity*. Berkeley, University of California Press.

Williams, B. 1995. Professional morality and its dispositions. In *Making sense of humanity*. Cambridge: Cambridge University Press.

Williams, R. 1980. The Bloomsbury fraction. In *Problems in materialism and culture*. London: Verso.

Wise, M. (ed.) 1995. *The values of precision*. Princeton: Princeton University Press.

Wittgenstein, L. 1969. *On certainty*, trans. D. Paul and G. Anscombe. Oxford: Blackwell.

Wittgenstein, L. 1994. 'The big typescript'. Excerpted in *The Wittgenstein reader*, A. Kenny (ed.). Oxford: Blackwell.

Wolff, J. 1981. *The social production of art*. London: Macmillan.

Wolpert, L. 1993. *The unnatural nature of science*. London: Faber.

Woodiwiss, A. 1997. Against modernity – a dissident rant. *Economy and Society* **26** (1), 1–21.

Wormald, B.H.G. 1993. *Francis Bacon: history, politics and science 1561–1626*. Cambridge: Cambridge University Press.

Wright, A. & A. Treacher (eds) 1982. *The social construction of medical knowledge*. Edinburgh: Edinburgh University Press.

Yeatman, A. 1994. *Postmodern revisionings of the political*. London: Routledge.

Index

Acton, J. 165
Adorno, T. 5, 109–10, 113
aesthetic enlightenment 10, 11, 13, 101–24
  aesthetic education 124, 125–6
  aestheticism 104–7
  aesthetic morality 102, 103–4
  aesthetic responsibility 119, 120, 121, 122–3
  aesthetic truth 110–12
  art 111
    and ethics of truth 109–10
    as ideology 107–9
  creativity and freedom 116, 117, 119, 122, 123
    teaching freedom 124
  ethic of the aesthetic 116–18, 119
  the "new" 113–15
  willing what cannot be willed 118–22
Althusser, L. 109, 187
altruism 163
Anderson, P. 161
Anscombe, G. 95
anthropology 35–6, 130
  negative 14–15, 130, 132
anti-clericalism 158, 160
anti-foundationalism
  and scientific enlightenment 57–65
  and truth 32–4
anti-simplicism 67–9
aristocracy 83–6
  of expertise 86–7
  of intellect 174
Aristotle 131

Arnold, M. 159
art *see* aesthetic enlightenment
artists, life of 105, 119, 120, 121
asceticism 36–40, 105, 129, 143, 165
authority 71, 72, 73
  of intellectuals 151
  and truth 27–9
  see also ethical subjection; expertise
autonomy
  in art 109, 110, 111, 112
  of intellectuals 151
  in social theory 178–81
avant-garde art 113–15

Bachelard, G. 48, 49, 52–3
Bacon, Sir F. 27–8, 115, 120–22
Baker, K. 42, 43–4, 46–7
Baudelaire, C. 106
Bauman, Z. 4, 90
  on intellectuals 150–51
  on modernity/postmodernity 5, 22–3, 30, 192
  on socialism 35
Baxandall, M. 111, 112, 115
beauty 124
Beckett, S. 159
Bell, D. 21
Benda, J. 33
Berger, J. 114
Berlin, I. 180
Bernard Shaw, G. 162
Bloomsbury 162
Blumenberg, H. 26–8
Born, M. 53, 68

Bourdieu, P. 89
    on aristocracies 84
    on art 107–8, 110, 111, 113–14, 115, 117
    on intellectuals 154, 160
Boyle, R. 50, 54
Burchell, G. 132
bureaucracy 83, 142
Bürger, P. 115
Butterfield, H. 167

Calvinism 142
Canguilhem, G. 53–6, 62, 90–1, 92
capitalism 21, 142, 143
Cassirer, E. 4
Catholicism 157–8
Cavell, S. 116
charisma 82
Chinese *literati* 81–2, 153
Clark, J.C.D. 85, 87
cognitive ethic 165, 166
Collini, S. 162–3, 165–6
communism 3–4
Comte, A. 2
concepts 184
conceptual art 115, 118–19, 123
Condorcet, Marquis de 42–4, 46
Confucianism 82
conscience 66
constructionism 24, 51, 60
contingency 15, 98, 181
conviction 141, 142, 143, 146
countervailing powers 39
creativity 62
    and freedom 116, 117, 119, 122, 123
        teaching freedom 124
    of intellectuals 152
critical sociology 189–90
cultural science 137, 144, 145, 146
culture 23
Cynicism 129

Danto, A.C. 111
Deism 160
Deleuze, G. 127
    on art 111–12, 115
Derrida, J. 32
Descartes, R. 26
diagnostics 9–10

Dicey, A.V. 165
disciplines 184, 187
disinterestedness 109, 110, 166
domination 81–3, 188–9
Dreyfusard intellectuals 157–8
Durkheim, E. 68
dynamic nominalism 94

economics 21, 188
education
    aesthetic 124, 125–6
    universities 171–5, 182–3
Einstein, A.t 53
Elias, N. 84
élitism 187
Elster, J. 85–6, 115, 117, 118
empiricism 164–6
endism 4
English intellectuals *see* intellectuals, English
enlightenment 1–16
    agents of 2
        see also intellectuals
    critical attitude to 5–6, 16, 26, 29
    ethics of 15–16, 191–3
    historical period of 2–3, 42–3
    negative 4–5, 16, 122–3, 124
    overview of aspects of 10–14
    politics of 2–4, 6
    questioning 125–47
    realism and 7–10
    and truth 24–7
epochal theories 17, 19, 23, 24
essentialism 84, 85
ethical conviction 128–9
ethical subjection 81–6
ethics 15–16, 25–7, 191–3
    of the aesthetic 116–18, 119
    and science 47–8, 65–7
    and truth 25–7
exemplarity 87–9
existentialism 155–6
experimentalism 49–50
expertise
    aristocracies of 86–7
    ethical and moral 73–6, 78–80, 88–90, 95

Fabians 162
fallibilism 51–6
fascism 5
feminism 10, 190
Feyerabend, P. 32, 62
fideism 33
Fleck, L. 60
Focillon, H. 114
Fordist organizations 21
Foucault, M. 12, 20, 22, 126–37
   and aesthetics of existence 13, 103–5,
      106, 107, 126, 127, 129–30
   asceticism and strategy 36, 39, 129
   and authority 80
   conception of ethics 127, 128, 129
   as critic of enlightenment 16, 145–7
   and freedom 127, 130–5
   and governmentality 29, 30, 131–5
   history of sexuality 78–9
   on intellectuals 156–7
   main principles 135–6
   and normalization 91
   on Raymond Roussel 120
   view of enlightenment 4, 8
foundationalism 9
France, intellectualism 156, 157–8, 160
freedom 2, 31, 130–5, 146
   aesthetic 116, 117, 119, 122, 123
   in science 67
   teaching 124
Freeman, E. 165
Freud, S. 78–9
Fukuyama, F. 4

Geertz, C. 32
Gellner, E. 18, 23, 34, 181
gender studies 10–11, 190
genius 119
George, S. 105
German intellectualism 158
Giacometti, A. 115
Giddens, A. 7, 71, 80, 97
Goody, J. 152
Gordon, C. 160
   on expertise 78
   on Foucault 4, 8, 29, 31, 146, 156
   on Weber 138
Gouldner, A. 150–1, 154

government 131–5
   and human plasticity 72–3
   of intentions 95–7
   and truth 29–32
Gramsci, A. 24, 152, 169
Gray, J. 3–4, 9, 180
Guyau, J-M. 83

Haacke, H. 108
Habermas, J. 4, 13, 77
Hacking, I.
   dynamic nominalism 94
   on intellectuals 95, 96, 97
   on normality 91
   on science 48, 49, 52, 54, 61, 66, 93
   truth games 25
Hadot, P. 36, 37–9
Hall, J.A. 161
Havel, V. 169–70
Heidegger, M. 25, 109, 110, 113
Hennis, W. 138, 139, 140, 143, 145
Hepworth, B. 117–18
Hirst, P.Q. 172, 174
historians/historiography 162–9
Hobbes, T. 50
humanism 43, 135
human nature 14–15, 35–6, 130, 132
Hume, D. 163–4
Hunter, I. 88–9, 125, 172
Huxley, T.H 67, 171

immaturity 6, 183
intellectuals 13–14, 149–75
   critical aspects 153–4
   definitions of 151–7
   English 159–62
      empiricism 164–6
      enlightenment 168–9
      historiography 162–9
      judgement 166–8
      moralists 162–4
   living in truth 169–71
   modernity 151–7
   truth and time 157–9
   vocation 149–51
intentions 95–7
Ireland, intellectualism 158–9
ironism 15

j'accuse model 157, 159, 160, 169
Jacob, J. 86
judgement 136, 166–8, 184

Kant, I. 1, 35–6, 144, 183, 184
knowledge, models of 24–5, 46
knowledge-society thesis 17, 20–24
Kuspit, D. 117

labelling theory 94
laboratory sciences 48–50, 59
Latour, B. 41, 42, 45, 50
    anti-foundationalism 32, 57–65
learning 20, 171–5, 182–3
liberalism 30, 132, 133, 134, 145
literati 81–2, 153
Lovibond, S. 191
Lyotard, J.-F. 6, 21, 53, 63, 102, 113, 114

MacIntyre, A. 16, 77, 173, 191, 192
Malpas, J. 26, 32, 185, 193
Mannheim, K. 24
Marx, K. 158, 164
Marxism 150, 152, 165
maturity 183, 185
medicine 90–1
memory and intentions 96, 97
Merton, R. 65
Mill, J.S. 25, 31, 33, 161, 171
Mills, C.W. 95
modern art 111–12, 114, 115, 116
modernity 6–7, 8–9, 73, 178, 179, 180, 183
    intellectual 151–7
    and knowledge 22–3
    and philosphical sociology 191–2
    and rationalization 18–20
    and reductionism 188
Mommsen, W. 139
Montefiore, A. 170
moral code 103, 127, 128
moralists 162–4
morality 103, 192
multiplicity 165

negative anthropology 14–15, 130, 132
negative enlightenment 4–5, 16, 122–3,
    124
Newton, Sir I. 42, 43
Nietzsche, F. 28–9, 72, 136, 147, 157, 168

normalization 75, 90–92, 93
Norris, C. 33

Oakeshott, M. 182, 183
objectivism 13
Oestreich, G. 73

Pasteur, L. 58
performativity 89–90
Perkin, H. 87
personality 65, 143, 144
Phillipson, N. 164
philosophical sociology 191–2
plasticity of humans 72–3
Plato 129
Pocock, J.G.A. 160
Polanyi, M. 66–7
politics 3–4, 141–2, 166, 183–5
    see also government
postmodern art 115
postmodernism 6–7, 8–9, 180, 183, 184,
    192–3
Price, D. de Solla 45
Prigogine, I. 53
professions, sociology of 76–8
projection 9, 47–8
psychoanalysis 78–9, 88
psychology 79–80, 92–5, 96, 98, 144
psychotherapy 96

rationalism 3, 12, 13, 46–7, 194
rationalization 17, 18–20, 144, 180
realism 7–10, 12–13
    in knowledge society 24
    and negative anthropology 13–14
    in science 60–61
reason 2, 3
    and rationalization 18–20
reductionism 187, 188–91
relativism 128, 182
    in science 62, 63, 64, 65
research 171, 182–3
responsibility towards truth 169–71
Rorty, R. 9, 15, 25–6, 98, 181–2
Rose, N.
    on expertise 73, 74, 75, 78, 79, 89, 90
    on psychologization 92, 93, 94
Roth, G. 82
Russell, B. 159

Sartre, J.-P. 151, 155–6, 157, 158
Scaff, L. 105, 143, 144
Schiller, F. 13, 124
Schmitt, C. 2
scientific enlightenment 10, 11, 12, 41–70
  and anti-science 42–4
  anti-simplicism 67–9
  and ethics 47–8, 65–7
  fallibilism and historicity 51–6
  freedom in 67
  and intervention 48
  laboratory sciences 48–50, 59
  Latourian anti-foundationalism 57–65
  projection and detachment 47–8
  social science 46–7, 54, 56, 57–65
  and society 44–6
scientists 26, 65–7
Scotland, intellectualism 158
Searle, J. 33
self and selfhood 71, 72, 97–8, 143
Sloterdijk, P. 5
socialism 35
social sciences 2, 46–7, 54, 56, 57–65
social theory 16, 34–5, 36–7, 178–81,
    193–4
  epochal 17, 19, 23, 24
  learning and politics 181–5
  see also modernity; postmodernism
sociology 2, 34–5, 185–8
  of creativity 117
  critical 189–90
  economic 21, 188
  of knowledge 24
  philosophical 191–2
  of professions 76–8
  of science see scientific enlightenment
Socrates 129
solidarity 189
Stengers, I. 53
Stoicism 37, 68, 81, 127
strategy and enlightenment 15, 39, 64,
    182
Stubbs, W. 166–7
subjectivism 13, 18, 19, 143
supplementary-dualist theories 19

Taylor, C. 27, 35
Taylor, F.W. 21

therapeutic enlightenment 10, 11, 12–13,
    71–99
  aristocracy 83–6, 86–7
  ethical subjection 81–6
  exemplarity 87–9
  expertise: ethical and moral 73–6, 78–
    80, 86–7, 88–90, 95
  governing intentions 95–7
  normalization 75, 90–92, 93
  performativity 89–90
  plasticity 72–3
  psychologization 79–80, 92–5, 96,
    144
  sociology of professions 76–8
  utopian ethics 97–9
Tocqueville, A. 85–6
Truscot, B. 171
truth
  and anti-foundationalism 32–4
  art and ethics of 109–10
  as authority 27–9, 80
  and enlightenment 24–7
  and government 29–32
  history 20
  and postmodernism 193
  responsibility towards 169–71
  scientific truth 48, 59–60
  fallibilism 51–6
Turner, C. 141

Universities 171–5, 182–3
utopianism 14, 34–6, 97–9, 130

vocation 76, 142, 144, 169
  enlightenment as 149–51

Weber, M. 72, 137–45
  and aestheticism 105, 106
  and asceticism 36–7
  on Chinese literati 81–2, 153
  and conviction 141, 142, 143, 146
  as critic of enlightenment 16, 145–7
  and domination/subjection 81–2, 83,
    188
  on intellectuals 155
  and personality 65, 143, 144
  and rationalization 18–19, 144
  and science 44, 48–9, 69

and universality of truth 28
on universities 173–4
and vocation 76–7, 142, 144
Whiggism 164, 167

Wilde, O. 106
Williams, B. 47–8, 128–9, 136
Williams, R. 162
Wittgenstein, L. 38, 50